International Dimensions of

MANAGEMENT

F O U R T H   E D I T I O N

ARVIND V. PHATAK
Temple University

SOUTH-WESTERN College Publishing

An International Thomson Publishing Company

Sponsoring Editor: Randy G. Haubner
Production Editor I: Crystal Chapin
Production House: DPS Associates, Inc.
Marketing Manager: Stephen E. Momper

GN69DA
Copyright © 1995
by South-Western College Publishing
Cincinnati, Ohio

ALL RIGHTS RESERVED

ISBN: 0-538-84485-X

1 2 3 4 5 6 7 MA 0 9 8 7 6 5 4

Printed in the United States of America

Library of Congress Cataloging-in-Publication Date

Phatak, Arvind V.
    International dimensions of management / Arvind V. Phatak.
—4th ed.
        p.   cm.
    Includes bebliographical references and index.
    ISBN 0-538-84485-X
    1. International business enterprises—Management. I. Title.
HD62.4.P52 1994
658'.049—dc20   94-21634
                                                            CIP

PREFACE

We now live in a world characterized by global interdependence among all countries on the earth. No longer can a country afford to be isolated from the global community of nations whose economies are closely intertwined with each other.

We are presently in the midst of a phenomenon of rapidly falling trade barriers between countries. Nations are joining together to form free-trade blocs because they realize that there is more to be gained by collaborating with each other than by remaining economically isolated. Regional trade blocs are forming at an astonishing pace. The twelve nations of the European Economic Community (EEC) have knit themselves into a unified common market by 1992 with a free flow of goods, services, capital, and people, as well as harmonious tax and regulatory policies. A free-trade agreement has been in place since January 1, 1989, between the United States and Canada. Its aim is to eliminate all tariffs on goods and services between the two countries by 1998. With the addition of Mexico, the North American Free-Trade Zone consisting of the United States, Canada, and Mexico has become the largest common market in the world, stretching from the Yukon to the Yucatan. With 364 million consumers and a total output of $6 trillion, it will be 25 percent larger than the European Economic Community. One could easily speculate that in the not too distant future a third free-trade bloc might be formed to include countries of the Pacific Basin such as Japan, South Korea, Taiwan, Singapore, Thailand, Indonesia, and Malaysia.

Multinational companies whose operations span the far-flung regions of the world, and who think of the entire world as their theater of operations and their marketplace, are playing a major role in the regional and global economic integration that the trade-bloc countries aspire to bring about. Their transnational business, such as the import and export of capital, raw materials, technology, intermediate and finished products, people and services—both within and outside of their own global network of subsidiaries—has a major impact on a country's trade, investments, and degree of economic integration with other countries.

Present-day graduates of business schools may establish their careers in global corporations, and those who do not will have to deal with such companies as buyers of products or services produced by global companies, as suppliers of such items to global companies, or as their competitors. Therefore, it is imperative that business school graduates have solid knowledge of how global companies operate and what might be the managerial tasks in such enterprises.

The basic premise of this book is that the management of a company having international operations differs in many important ways from that of a company whose business horizons are confined to just one country. The material in this book is focused on the managerial issues confronting senior executives as they attempt to plan, organize, staff, and control the worldwide operations of a global company. The spotlight is on management functions, as opposed to enterprise functions, such as finance, marketing, accounting, and production. While we are concerned with how these functions come into play from the managerial perspective of a global enterprise, our emphasis is on how management activities in a global enterprise differ from those in a purely domestic company.

In short, the purpose of this book is to provide the reader with an appreciation of the international dimensions of the management process. Many textbooks on management have responded to the demand to internationalize their content by either adding an "international" chapter or by giving some "international" examples in the text. However, this book offers an integrated and comprehensive discussion of management in global companies and in a transnational context. The book can be used in several ways. One approach is to use it as a text in conjunction with supplementary materials, such as articles and cases related to concepts in the book. Another approach is to use this book in conjunction with other South-Western International Series books for an international business course, or as a supplementary text in a general management or business policy course. In a business policy course, there has been a dramatic increase in the adoption of international cases. Some of the very popular cases from the Harvard Business School have a global context. As such, this book would serve the purpose of providing students with an understanding of how managerial decisions in a global company are affected by its being a player in a global industry and in a global environmental context. However it is used, the purpose of this book is to promote the internationalization of business management curricula.

I have inserted Practical Insights throughout the book which illustrate a particular concept. These practical insights come from business publications such as the *Wall Street Journal*, *Business Week*, the *Economist*, and *Fortune*. Moreover, all of them are current, and most of them illustrate events that occurred in 1990 to early 1993. Also included are numerous interesting and contemporary examples from the real world of global business. All statistics have been updated, and new materials have been added throughout the book.

I wish to thank the following reviewers of this edition: J. Stuart Devlin, New Mexico State University; Kenneth R. Tillery, Middle Tennessee State University; and Maureen J. Fleming, University of Montana, who reviewed the second edition.

I also wish to thank several people who assisted me during various phases of writing this book. At PWS-KENT, my thanks go to Assistant Editor Kathleen Tibbetts and Production Editors Sue Caffey and Patty Adams. At Temple University, Madan Annavarjula helped in proofreading the manuscript, obtaining permissions to use copyrighted materials, and performing many other tasks involved in preparing a manuscript. Sriram Beldona helped in obtaining materials that were very useful while I was writing the manuscript. I extend my gratitude to both for their assistance.

Arvind V. Phatak

Laura H. Cornell Professor
of General and Strategic Management
and International Business
Temple University

About the Author

Dr. Arvind V. Phatak is Laura H. Cornell Professor of General and Strategic Management and International Business at Temple University's School of Business and Management. He has served as Chairman of the General and Strategic Management Department from 1978-1981 and from 1987-1990. Dr. Phatak was the recipient of the Fulbright Summer Research Fellowship in 1986. He has also received several awards such as the Great Teacher Award of Temple University (Pioneer Recipient), the Distinguished Faculty Award, and the MBA Professor of the Year Award (Pioneer Recipient).

Dr. Phatak is the author of three books and coauthor of two books in the field of management and international management. He has also published several articles in reputable management journals. Dr. Phatak has lectured on various management topics before numerous professional groups and has presented several seminars in corporate settings in the United States and abroad. He has served as a consultant on Strategic Planning and Implementation problems to organizations such as John Hancock Company, Dominion Textile (Canada), CIGNA, and the Federal Reserve Bank of Philadelphia. Dr. Phatak has a Ph.D. in Management from U.C.L.A.

> To the everlasting memory of my dear brother, Anil V. Phatak (1939-1994).

CONTENTS

Chapter SIX

International Staffing   175

Chapter SEVEN

The Control Process in an International Context   223

Chapter O N E

An Introduction to International Management

The need for international management in a firm becomes critical when a company becomes involved in foreign direct investment. *Foreign direct investment* (FDI) is a long-term equity investment in a foreign firm; it gives the parent company (the investor), depending upon the percentage of ownership involved, varied degrees of managerial control over the foreign firm. The more FDI that a company makes in a foreign affiliate, the greater the managerial control that it has over that foreign affiliate. FDI involves the establishment of facilities, buildings, plant, and equipment for the production of goods and/or services in a foreign country. And FDI is accompanied by the need to manage, market, and finance the foreign production. Enterprise functions like marketing, production, and finance are managed by people. Managing the various enterprise functions abroad requires that managers in the parent company, as well as in every foreign affiliate, have the necessary skills and experience in international management. It therefore follows that the greater a company's FDI, the greater is its need for skilled international managers.

1

One can appreciate the importance of effective international management on a global scale by examining some FDI figures of U.S. companies and those of foreign companies in the U.S. Direct investments abroad by U.S. companies at the end of 1992, on a historical-cost basis, were in excess of $486 billion; and those by foreign companies in the United States, also on a historical-cost basis, amounted to more than $419 billion.[1] The magnitude of these investment outlays becomes apparent when one compares them with the gross national product figures of countries. For example, in 1989, the gross national product—which is the value of all final goods and services produced by a nation's economy—of every country of the world, excluding the ten wealthiest, was less than $371 billion; and that of every country, excluding the twenty-five wealthiest, was less than $89 billion.[2]

International management activities in a firm begin when the firm's managers either initiate the establishment of a foreign affiliate from scratch or buy an existing firm; and they continue as long as there are one or more functioning foreign affiliates owned by the parent company.

Throughout this book, when we consider the elements of international management, our subject will always be the so-called international, multinational, or global firm or company. Many scholars of international business make a distinction among an international, multinational, and global company; however, we shall be using the terms interchangeably. Also used synonymously are the terms affiliate and subsidiary; in addition, we make no distinction among these terms: company, corporation, enterprise, and firm.

WHAT IS INTERNATIONAL BUSINESS?

International companies are simultaneously involved in several international business activities such as export, import, counter-trade, licensing, and foreign direct investment. Therefore, we should at this juncture understand what is international business. There are many different definitions of international business. First, let us look at some of the definitions, and then we shall arrive at our own.

John D. Daniels and Lee H. Radebaugh define it as "all business transactions that involve two or more countries." The business relationships may be private or governmental. In the case of private firms, the transactions are for profit. Government-sponsored activities in international business may or may not have a profit orientation.[3] Donald A. Ball and Wendell H. McCullough, Jr., say that international business is "business whose activities involve the crossing of national boundaries."[4] To Betty Jane Punett and David A. Ricks, it is "any commercial, industrial or professional endeavor involving two or more nations."[5] There are many such definitions of international business. We shall define international business as those business activities of private or public enterprises that involve the movement across national boundaries of resources, goods, services, and skills. The resources that are involved in the transfer are raw materials, capital, people, and technology; goods transferred include semifinished and finished assemblies and products; services transferred include such things as accounting, legal counsel, and banking activities; and skills sent from one country to another include managerial and technical skills.

INTERNATIONAL MANAGEMENT DEFINED

In very general terms, international management is the management of a firm's activities on an international scale. Before we define international management, let us define the term management.

Management is the process aimed at accomplishing organizational objectives by (1) effectively coordinating the procurement, allocation, and utilization of the human and physical resources of the organization and (2) maintaining the organization in a state of dynamic equilibrium with the environment. There are two basic premises in this definition of management. First, management is needed to coordinate the human and physical resources—the raw materials, capital, technology, knowledge—and to integrate them into a unified whole. Without such coordination, the resources would remain unrelated and disorganized and, therefore, inefficiently used. The second premise in the definition is that an organization lives in a dynamic environment that constantly affects its operations. Thus, one managerial task is to forecast the environmental forces that are likely to have a significant impact on the firm in the immediate and distant future, and to determine the probable impact of these forces. Managers must design appropriate strategies to ensure the survival and growth of the organization as it interacts with its dynamic environment.

On the basis of the preceding definition of management, we can now define international management as a process of accomplishing the global objectives of an organization by (1) effectively coordinating the procurement, allocation, and utilization of the human and physical resources of the organization and (2) maintaining the organization in a state of dynamic equilibrium within the global environment.

INTERNATIONAL MANAGEMENT AND MULTINATIONAL COMPANIES

Any firm that has one or more foreign affiliates is involved in international management; it does not have to be a billion-dollar corporation. Even small and medium-sized firms can and do have international operations in several countries. Many multinationals do not qualify for the exclusive list of the Fortune 500 or the Forbes 1000 list of the largest U.S. and foreign multinationals. Even though they do not come close to Ford and General Motors in terms of total sales, gross profits, total assets, and other similar measures of company size, they are still multinational companies. Many firms in Europe and Japan have also developed a multinational structure; and in the last ten years or so, we have seen many government-owned enterprises that have become multinational. The 1960's laid the foundations for the massive growth abroad of U.S. multinational enterprises. The growth of that decade far exceeded any achieved earlier by the United States or the other industrialized countries of the world. Direct investments abroad by American business enterprises surged from $31.8 billion in 1960 to $78 billion in 1970, and they exceeded $486 billion in 1992. Those dollar values of foreign direct investments are the values carried on the books of U.S. parent companies. However, book value is the value of the investment at the time it was made, not adjusted to the changes in price due to inflation. Because inflation has been a global phenomenon since World War II, the book values of U.S. direct investments made ten or twenty years ago grossly understate their current replacement values. The current market price of U.S. direct investments abroad is much higher.

Of the $486.6 billion in foreign direct investments made by U.S. enterprises, 49 percent were made in Western Europe, 14 percent in Canada, 18 percent in Latin America and other Western Hemisphere countries, 16 percent in Asia and the Pacific, and the rest in Africa and the Middle East. Of the $419.5 billion in foreign direct investments made in the United States, Japan contributed almost $97 billion. Of the $248 billion invested by companies in Western Europe, the United Kingdom accounted for $94.7 billion, the Netherlands for $61 billion, and Germany for $29 billion.[6] As for yearly flows, U.S. direct investments abroad—equity capital outflows—in 1992 amounted to $8 billion and foreign direct investment equity capital inflows into the United States totaled $22.5 billion.[7]

The massive outflow of U.S. direct investments beginning in the 1960's represented the response by U.S. companies to business opportunities in foreign markets. The nature of the response had been dramatically different in the decades before the sixties. U.S. exports to foreign markets were replaced by direct production of the goods in company-owned plants located in the foreign markets themselves. The strategy of establishing production affiliates in foreign countries to serve one or more foreign markets was responsible for the growth and development of multinational enterprises—first in the United States and later in Western Europe and Japan. Today, the value of U.S. exports is dwarfed by the value of goods produced in U.S.-owned foreign affiliates. The sales figures of the foreign affiliates owned by U.S. companies ($1.5 trillion in 1991[8]) are about 3.75 times the value of U.S. exports ($ 416 billion in 1991[9]), and it is estimated that almost one half of the industrial output of the world today is produced by firms that have developed a multinational structure. U.S. multinationals are now playing the dominant role in the proliferation of U.S. business abroad and in the production and marketing of American products in foreign countries.

Although multinational enterprises are dissimilar in many respects—size of sales and profits, markets served, and location of affiliates abroad—they all do have some common features. To begin, a multinational company is an enterprise that has a network of wholly or partially owned producing and marketing affiliates located in a number of countries. The affiliates may be jointly owned with one or more foreign partners. The foreign affiliates are linked with the parent company and with each other by ties of common ownership and by a common global strategy to which each affiliate is responsive and committed. The parent company controls the foreign affiliates via resources which it allocates to each affiliate—capital, technology, trademarks, patents, and manpower—and through the right to approve each affiliate's long- and short-range plans and budgets.

As pointed out earlier, there are many small- and medium-sized multinational companies. However, generally we are talking about a large corporation whose revenues and assets typically run into hundreds of millions of dollars. For example, in 1992 the sales of General Motors, ranked number one in the world by *Fortune* magazine in terms of sales, were reported to be $132,774.5 billion. In that same year the profits of the Royal Dutch/Shell Group, the largest in the world in terms of profitability, were reported to be $ 5,408 billion[10]. Exhibit 1-1 classifies the ten largest industrial companies in the world in terms of sales, assets, profits, and employees.

Notice the dominance of American companies in almost every category, followed closely by Japanese and British companies. Of the 500 largest global companies in the Fortune magazine survey, 161 are American, 128 are Japanese, and 40 are British, followed by

EXHIBIT 1-1 The Biggest Companies in the World.

SALES

Rank	Company	Country	$ Million
1	General Motors	USA	132,775
2	Exxon	USA	103,547
3	Ford Motor	USA	100,786
4	Royal/Dutch Shell	Brit./Neth.	98,935
5	Toyota Motor	Japan	79,114
6	IRI	Italy	67,547
7	IBM	USA	65,096
8	Daimler-Benz	Germany	63,339
9	General Electric	USA	62,202
10	Hitachi	Japan	61,466

ASSETS

Rank	Company	Country	$ Million
1	General Electric	USA	192,876
2	General Motors	USA	191,013
3	Ford Motor	USA	180,545
4	Royal Dutch/Shell	Brit./Neth.	100,354
5	IBM	USA	86,705
6	Exxon	USA	85,030
7	Hitachi	Japan	76,668
8	Toyota Motor	Japan	76,132
9	Matshushita Elect.	Japan	75,645
10	Nissan Motor	Japan	62,978

PROFITS

Rank	Company	Country	$ Million
1	Royal Dutch/Shell	Brit./Neth.	5,408
2	Philip Morris	USA	4,939
3	Exxon	USA	4,770
4	General Electric	USA	4,725
5	Unilever	Brit./Neth.	2,279
6	Merck	USA	1,984
7	Hanson	Britain	1,976
8	Bristol-Myers Squibb	USA	1,962
9	Nestle	Switzerland	1,917
10	Procter and Gamble	USA	1,872

EMPLOYEES

Rank	Company	Country	Number
1	General Motors	USA	750,000
2	Siemens	Germany	413,000
3	IRI	Italy	400,000
4	Daimler-Benz	Germany	376,467
5	Pepsico	USA	371,000
6	Hitachi	Japan	331,505
7	Ford Motor	USA	325,333
8	IBM	USA	308,010
9	Fiat	Italy	285,482
10	Unilever	Brit./Neth.	283,000

Source: "The World's Largest Industrial Corporations," *Fortune*, July 26, 1993, 191-193.

Germany, France, and Sweden, which accounted for 32, 30, and 14 companies respectively.

In order to really appreciate the large size of global companies, take a look at Exhibit 1-2, which ranks countries and companies by gross national product and sales revenue respectively. Notice that in the 100 countries and companies on the list, there are 61 countries and 39 U.S. based companies. Notice also that General Motors is *"bigger"* than Austria and all countries below it in the list, and Ford Motor is *"bigger"* than Indonesia and South Africa and all countries listed below it.

EXHIBIT 1-2   Ranking of Countries and Companies

Country/Company	GNP/Sales	Country/Company	GNP/Sales
United States	5201.0	S. Africa	86.8
Japan	2820.0	Exxon	86.6
Soviet Union	2664.0	Iran	77.5
West Germany (FRG)	1207.0	Turkey	77.3
France	954.1	Egypt	69.8
Italy	860.0	Thailand	68.8
United Kingdom	834.4	Hungary	64.7
P.R. China	603.5	IBM	63.4
Canada	531.0	Yugoslavia	58.6
Brazil	462.3	General Electric	55.2
Spain	370.7	Argentina	54.1
India	267.4	Greece	52.9
Netherlands	222.5	Mobil	51.0
S. Korea	210.1	Bulgaria	49.6
Mexico	186.7	Algeria	45.3
Sweden	185.8	Portugal	44.6
Switzerland	184.3	Philippines	44.0
Poland	174.7	Venezuela	41.5
East Germany (GDR)	159.4	Peru	40.8
Belgium	154.6	Philip Morris	39.1
Taiwan	150.2	Colombia	36.9
General Motors	127.0	Pakistan	36.8
Austria	125.2	Chrysler	36.2
Czechoslovakia	123.2	Malaysia	36.0
Romania	113.4	E.I. DuPont	35.2
Ford Motors	96.9	Texaco	32.4
Indonesia	89.4	N. Korea	30.0

Country/Company	GNP/Sales	Country/Company	GNP/Sales
Chevron	29.4	Digital Equipment	12.9
Nigeria	27.5	Westinghouse	12.8
Amoco	24.2	Rockwell Intl.	12.6
Chile	23.3	Phillips Petroleum	12.5
Morocco	21.7	3M	12.0
Proctor & Gamble	21.7	Allied Signal	12.0
Shell Oil	21.7	Hewlett-Packard	11.9
Boeing	20.3	Sara Lee	11.7
Occidental Petroleum	20.1	Alcoa	11.2
Bangladesh	20.0	Caterpillar	11.1
United Tech	19.8	Goodyear	11.0
Syria	19.3	General Dynamics	10.1
Eastman Kodak	18.4	Unisys	10.1
USX	17.8	Zaire	9.2
Dow Chemical	17.7	Kenya	7.9
Xerox	17.6	Sri Lanka	6.9
Burma	16.3	Ethiopia	6.0
Atlantic Richfield	15.9	Ghana	5.1
Sudan	15.6	Uganda	4.0
Pepsico	15.4	Nepal	2.8
RJR Nabisco	15.2	Tanzania	2.6
McDonnell Douglas	14.9	Madagascar	2.3
Tenneco	14.4	Mozambique	1.1

Source: "The 500 Largest U.S. Industrial Corporations," *Fortune*, April 1989; *The National Data Book*, U.S Dept. of Commerce-Bureau of the Census, 112th Ed.

Another characteristic of multinational companies is that they own a large number of foreign affiliates. The largest 200 multinationals in the world have affiliates in twenty or more countries.

Multinational companies tend to gravitate toward certain types of business activities. Most multinational companies are engaged in the manufacturing sector, with petroleum running a distant second. Other industries in which multinationals are involved include banking, mining, agriculture, and public utilities.

A large proportion of the total business activities of multinational companies is located in the developed countries of Western Europe, Canada, and the United States. It is estimated that about two thirds of the world's direct investments are in the developed countries.

As for their operations in the manufacturing sector, multinational companies are particularly strong in certain kinds of industries, often holding a dominant position in drugs, chemicals, electronics, food processing, petroleum refining, synthetic fibers, and electrical equipment.

ENVIRONMENT OF INTERNATIONAL MANAGEMENT

A manager in an international company performs her or his managerial functions in an environment that is far more complex than that of her or his counterpart in a domestic company. The international environment is the total world environment. However, it is also the sum total of the environments of every nation in which the company has its foreign affiliates. The environment within each nation consists of four basic elements: legal, cultural, economic, and political. Exhibit 1-3 shows the variables typically found in each element of the environment.

An international manager—at least one who is responsible for managing the transfer of financial, material, managerial, technical, or human resources and goods or services across national boundaries— should be continuously monitoring the environmental variables of the countries involved, especially those that may have a significant positive or negative impact. For example, a manager of international finance should study and evaluate the inflation rates, currency stability, and corporate tax levels of various countries before deciding how to minimize the foreign exchange losses when the company transfers money from an affiliate in one country to that in another.

A close relationship exists between inflation rates in a country and the value of that country's currency in the foreign exchange market. If a country's economy is plagued with a chronic and very high inflation rate, then there is a very high probability that the currency of that country will be devalued vis-a-vis the currencies of other countries, as has happened in Argentina, Brazil, Mexico, and other countries that have had rapid price increases for several years in a row. For instance, the Mexican peso was worth 50 pesos to the dollar in the early eighties. In 1990, one could buy more than 3,000 pesos for a dollar. When the Soviet Union was still in existence, one could buy one ruble for two U.S. dollars. Now, with the disintegration of the Soviet Union and hyperinflation in what is now called Russia, one can buy 1200 rubles for one dollar. An American company that is generating cash in Russian rubles, either through sales of goods or services or by converting U.S. dollars into Russian rubles to finance its Russian operations, would stand to lose considerable sums of money in U.S. dollars while the Russian rubles were devaluating; the American

EXHIBIT 1-3   The International Environment

Legal Environment	*Cultural Environment*
Legal tradition	Customs, norms, values, beliefs
Effectiveness of legal system	Language
Treaties with foreign nations	Attitudes
Patent trademark laws	Motivations
Laws affecting business firms	Social institutions
	Status symbols
	Religious beliefs

Economic Environment	*Political System*
Level of economic development	Form of government
Population	Political ideology
Gross national product	Stability of government
Per capita income	Strength of opposition parties
Literacy level	and groups
Social infrastructure	Social unrest
Natural resources	Political strife and insurgency
Climate	Governmental attitude towards
Membership in regional economic	foreign firms
blocks (E.E.C.; L.A.F.TA.)	Foreign policy
Monetary and fiscal policies	
Nature of competition	
Currency convertability	
Inflation	
Taxation system	
Interest rates	
Wage and salary levels	

company would be able to get fewer U.S. dollars for the same number of Russian rubles.

A country that has historically had very high inflation rates and numerous devaluations of its currency is the South American country of Bolivia. The devastating impact of rampant inflation on Bolivia's economy and life-style is illustrated in Practical Insight 1-1. The Government of Bolivia has successfully introduced a severe austerity program for the government; the government does not spend a peso more than it collects from revenue. The program has resulted in a dramatic decline in inflation, which some economists forecast could now be as little as 6 percent. However, Practical Insight 1-1 illustrates the different types of problems that do occur in countries that have hyperinflationary economies and other conditions with which multi-national companies having operations in such countries have to deal.

PRACTICAL INSIGHT 1-1

When Inflation Rate Is 116,000%, Prices Change by the Hour

In Bolivia, the Pesos Paid Out Can Outweigh Purchases; No. 3 Import: More Pesos

LA PAZ, Bolivia—A courier stumbles into Banco Boliviano Americano, struggling under the weight of a huge bag of money he is carrying on his back. He announces that the sack contains 32 million pesos, and a teller slaps on a notation to that effect. The courier pitches the bag into a corner.

"We don't bother counting the money anymore," explains Max Loew Stahl, a loan officer standing nearby. "We take the client's word for what's in the bag." Pointing to the courier's load, he says, "That's a small deposit."

At that moment the 32 million pesos—enough bills to stuff a mail sack—were worth only $500. Today, less than two weeks later, they are worth at least $180 less. Life's like that with qua-druple digit inflation.

A 116,000 Percent Rate

Bolivia's inflation rate is the highest in the world. In 1984, prices zoomed 2,700 percent, compared with a mere 329 percent the year before. Experts are predicting the inflation rate could soar as high as 40,000 percent this year. Even those estimates could prove conservative. The central bank last week announced January inflation of 80 percent; if that pace continued all year, it would mean an annual rate of 116,000 percent.

Prices go up by the day, the hour, or the customer. Julia Blanco Sirba, a vendor on this capital city's main street, sells a bar of chocolate for 35,000 pesos. Five minutes later, the next bar goes for 50,000 pesos. The two-inch stack of money needed to buy it far outweighs the chocolate.

Changes in the dollar exchange rate—and thus in vendors' own prices—pass by word of mouth. One egg costs 10,000 pesos this week, up from 3,000 pesos last week.

Bolivians aren't yet lugging their money about in wheelbarrows, as the Germans did during the legendary hyperinflation of the Weimar Republic in the 1920's, when prices increased 10 billionfold. But Bolivia seems headed in that direction.

Tons of paper money are printed to keep the country of 5.9 million inhabitants going. Planeloads of money arrive twice a week from printers in West Germany and Britain. Purchases of money cost Bolivia more than $20 million last year, making it the third largest import, after wheat and mining equipment.

Weighing In

The 1,000-peso bill, the most commonly used, costs more to print than it purchases. It buys one bag of tea. To purchase an average-size television set with 1,000-peso bills, customers have to haul money weighing more than 68 pounds into the showroom. (The inflation makes use of credit cards impossible here, and merchants generally don't take checks, either.) To ease the strain, the government in November came out with a new 100,000-peso note, worth $1. But there aren't enough in circulation to satisfy demand.

"This isn't even good as toilet paper," says pharmacist Ruth Aranda, holding up a 100-peso bill. Indeed, she points out, admission to a public toilet costs 300 pesos.

Three years ago, she says, she bought a new luxury Toyota auto for what she now sells three boxes of aspirin.

"We're headed for the garbage can," says Jorge von Bergen, an executive of La Papelera S.A., a large paper-products company, who lugs his pocket-money around in a small suitcase. "When it comes to inflation, we're the international champs."

Mr. von Bergen says his wife has to take the maid along to the market to help carry the bales of cash needed for her shopping. But all that money buys so little that Mrs. von Bergen easily carries her purchases back on her own.

Food shortages abound, and fights break out as people try to squeeze into line to buy sugar at several times the official price. Some companies have resorted to barter.

The situation has upset all phases of life in Bolivia. Private banks were closed a few days ago because of worries about executive safety. Strikes frequently close the factories. Many shops have closed. Because pesos are practically worthless, dollars now are being demanded for big-ticket purchases. People get their dollars from the 800 or so street-side money vendors who line Avenida Camacho, along La Paz's Wall Street. Banking, in effect, has moved outside.

Wages have risen 1,500 percent since President Hernan Siles Zuazo took over from the military in 1982, but inflation has more than offset the gains, yielding a 25 percent decline in real terms. The result is that there were 540 strikes in Bolivia last year and 35 days of general strikes when virtually nothing functioned.

In one incident, state-hospital doctors struck, so state-hospital patients took to the streets on crutches, demanding medical care. The government caved in and gave the doctors a raise. In one recent week not much different from others, workers in 34 factories took 180 business executives hostage in wage disputes. Some weren't released for three days.

President Siles Zuazo's government, meanwhile, has gone through 74 ministers and six cabinets in its two years in office, but it still hasn't presented a comprehensive economic plan or budget. It has announced several devaluations and several austerity plans, without much effect. It is expected to announce more such actions soon.

Last fall, the 71-year old Mr. Siles Zuazo staged a four-day hunger strike to encourage a "climate of peace and reflection by all Bolivians." Four months earlier, he had been kidnapped from his bedroom for 10 hours in a coup attempt. Earlier still, workers seeking wage increases had cut off his telephone and water service. The current government is Bolivia's 189th in 159 years of independence, and most people seem to think the 190th will arrive prior to the elections scheduled for June, probably in a military coup.

The current crisis dates to the late 1970's, when large oil reserves the country thought it had didn't materialize and when large international loans began to come due. Meanwhile, the price of tin, the second-largest legal export, collapsed, and the market for the largest legal export, natural gas, turned sour because of the problems of its main customer, Argentina. (Bolivia's largest export is coca paste, used in making cocaine; but it's illegal and doesn't help the government's payments crunch.)

President Siles Zuazo was elected in 1980, but the military, which historically has played a dominant role here, wouldn't let him take office for nearly three more years. By the time he got in, the government was spending more than it was taking in. It began to print more and more money.

"Look at what democracy has brought us," says Severino Quispe Pari, who lives with his wife and two barefoot children in an adobe and mud hut in the small rural town of Yaurichambi. Mr. Pari says he used to trade the potatoes and yellow corn he grows on his half-acre plot for sugar, coffee, meat, and fish. Now he has been reduced to eating only yellow corn.

In the neighboring town of Batallas, some people think this is the apocalypse. Petronila Loguidis stands on a street corner with her six children clinging to her colorful Indian skirts. "They don't understand why there is no longer any bread," she says, pointing to the children. "The Bible says things would get very costly. You could no longer buy bread. There would be earthquakes and wars. I think this is coming."

Source: Sonia L. Nazario, *Wall Street Journal*, February 7, 1985, 1, 22. Reprinted by permission of *The Wall Street Journal*, © 1985 Dow Jones & Company, Inc. All Rights Reserved Worldwide.

The relative value of currencies also has a major impact on the trade balances of countries. When the U.S. dollar was selling for more than 250 Japanese yen, Japanese exports to the United States were cheaper and U.S. exports to Japan were more expensive than in October 1993, when the rate was 105 yen to the dollar. The cheaper yen helped Japanese companies in their export drive to the United States. However, in 1993, with the yen becoming stronger against the U.S. dollar, Japanese companies have been losing their competitive edge as their products are becoming more expensive in the U.S. market.

Currency values also affect the relative wage rates among nations. For instance, in 1985 the average hourly compensation in the United States exceeded the West German wage rate in dollar terms by 36 percent and the Japanese wage rate by 98 percent. Using 1991 compensation levels converted at the then prevailing average yearly exchange rate, German factory wages were 43 percent higher than U.S. wages, and Japanese production workers were receiving only 7 percent less than their American counterparts (see Figure 1-1).

The upshot is that the wage rates in the United States are on a competitive footing with those in Japan and are enjoying a significant advantage over West German wage rates. The recent surge of Japanese and German manufacturing investments in the United States is in large part due to the devaluation of the U.S. dollar.

Another factor that is important to the manager of a multinational company is the legal tradition and effectiveness of the legal environment in particular countries. The law frequently causes serious difficulties for globalized companies. For example, because of the labor laws in India, it is next to impossible to lay off workers, even when dire economic and financial circumstances dictate that the firm take such action. A very serious problem facing American industry and America itself is the theft of intellectual property—ideas, innovations protected by copyright, patents, and trademarks—due to the absence of effective domestic legislation for the protection of intellectual property.

The People's Republic of China is reported to be one of the most risky countries in the world regarding the safety of computer software, films, and books. U.S. publishers charge that the Chinese government itself is one of the biggest software thieves in China. The International Intellectual Property Alliance, a group of U.S. industry associations, estimates that the illegal copying of software in China cost American companies $400 million in 1990, a figure the U.S. Trade Representative's office says is fairly accurate.[11]

The U.S. International Trade Commission estimated in 1986 that American companies lose approximately $60 billion to piracy abroad each year. Companies that are hit the hardest are America's most innovative, fastest-growing companies in the computer software, pharmaceutical, and entertainment industries (see Exhibit 1-4). One can find pirated copies of the latest American movies, as well as audio cassettes and compact discs of the newest American vocalists, on the streets of any Asian or Latin American city. In 1985, fully 80 percent of the Japanese market of American films and videos seen there were pirated—usually by entrepreneurs associated with organized crime. Illegal copies of films are available in countries like Thailand less than two weeks after they are released in the United States. Film companies estimate their annual sales losses in Thailand at $20 million and album distributors put theirs at $50 million.

The pirating of patented drugs is costing pharmaceutical companies billions of dollars. It takes about twelve years and $299 million to

FIGURE 1-4   Hourly Compensation in Manufacturing: Japan, U.S., and Germany

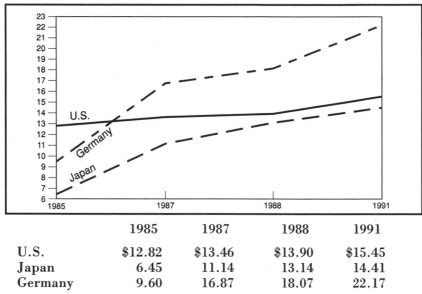

	1985	1987	1988	1991
U.S.	$12.82	$13.46	$13.90	$15.45
Japan	6.45	11.14	13.14	14.41
Germany	9.60	16.87	18.07	22.17

Source: U.S. Department of Labor, Bureau of Labor Statistics.

introduce a new medicine in the United States, according to the American Pharmaceutical Manufacturers Association. The introduction of new and more effective drugs is the basis for a competitive edge in the pharmaceutical industry, and pharmaceutical firms must market their products globally in order to obtain enough revenue to finance and support their innovative research. However, these efforts are drastically eroded by drug piracy by foreign companies in countries where no patent protection is available. Such piracy abroad is facilitated by U.S. regulations requiring that domestic companies applying for U.S. patents disclose their formulas in the process. This public disclosure makes copying the drugs and selling them abroad very easy and inexpensive. In many developing countries, where patent laws for drugs do not exist, imitations of patented drugs often beat the domestic company to the market in those countries. For example, Pfizer saw its products—Unasyn, an antibiotic, and Diflucan, an antifungal medicine—marketed in Brazil and Argentina before it could get there. Spain is one of the worst offenders in this regard. Unlike most Third-World countries, Spain has the technology to copy drugs developed abroad.

EXHIBIT 1-4   The High Cost of Piracy

Industry	Revenues Lost per Year* (in billions)	Hot Titles
PC software	$10 to $12	1-2-3, dBase, Word, Net Ware
Pharmaceuticals	$3 to $5	Zantac, Feldene, Lanoxin, Amoxil
Recording	$1.4	Hits by Michael Jackson, Madonna
Film	$1.2	*Ghost, Kindergarten Cop, L.A. Story*

*Industry Estimates

Source: Faye Rice, "How Copycats Steal Billions," *Fortune,* April 22, 1991, 158. © 1991 The Time Inc. Magazine Company. All rights reserved.

Moreover, Spanish counterfeiters are "protected" by the Spanish legal system, which takes up to ten years to settle a court case. The pirates are willing to risk paying a fine of a few million U.S. dollars because, while the case against them is in court, they stand to make many millions more than the anticipated fine, which may never be imposed at all.

Companies such as Pfizer spend millions of dollars yearly in battles to defend their patents abroad. Piracy of intellectual property severely hurts global companies not only from lost sales in the country making the pirated goods but also in lost revenues and market share positions in many other countries having no patent protection. This situation is especially prevalent in Africa and the Middle East, to which countries the pirates export their goods at substantially discounted prices. Exports of faked audio cassettes from Indonesia alone have been estimated at $13 million.[12]

The nature of the problems a company could face in working through the court system in a foreign country, and the difficulties and delays an American firm could encounter in collecting actual and punitive damages with the help of foreign courts, is clearly demonstrated in the plight of David L. Bryant.

In 1982, Mr. Bryant won a $1.6 million judgment against the Japanese firm Mansei Kogyo Co.—a big cigarette distributor based near Tokyo. The case began when Maruman Integrated Circuits, a subsidiary of Mansei, refused to honor an agreement between Maruman and Mr. Bryant. Maruman was to be the anchor tenant in a forty-acre development in Gresham, Oregon, spearheaded by Mr. Bryant.

Maruman claimed that the agreement was the result of a fraudulent scheme hatched between Maruman's former president, whom it fired, and Mr. Bryant. Both sides sued in the Santa Clara County (California) Superior Court. At the trial it was revealed that Mansei had been secretly negotiating to sell Maruman to Toshiba, a Japanese company, and that Toshiba wanted no part of a plant in Oregon. The jury sided with Mr. Bryant, awarding him $425,000 in actual damages and $1.1 million in punitive damages. Toshiba was cleared of any wrongdoing, but Mansei left the United States. The verdict was upheld on appeal and the award now totals $2.9 million, including interest.

In 1988, Mr. Bryant hired a lawyer in Japan and filed suit in a Tokyo district court to force Mansei to honor the American court's verdict. According to the lawyer for Mansei, the case was proceeding "according to international law." However, he noted that the concept of "punitive damages" is not found in Japanese law, implying that a concept that does not exist in Japanese jurisprudence would be difficult to implement in the Japanese legal system.

Mr. Bryant's experience illustrates some differences between American and Japanese ideas about justice. It is also an example of the problems that a global company could encounter because of differences in the laws of various countries.[13]

A decision to establish a manufacturing plant abroad will also require a study of those environmental variables that would have a major impact on the operation and long-term survival of the plant in the foreign country—political stability, governmental attitude towards foreign firms, wage and salary levels, social infrastructure (roads, electricity, water, transportation), and per-capita income. In addition, the decision to transfer a managerial technique from the parent company or foreign affiliate to another affiliate located in a different country must be preceded by an evaluation of the relevant environmental factors. A transfer of a leadership technique from one country to another must take into account the values, beliefs, attitudes, and motives of the people in the recipient country. For example, a participative leadership style may be effective in the U.S. culture whose values and beliefs are democratically oriented, but it may be wholly unworkable in a culture that respects authority and paternal influence, as is the situation in Mexico.

Not only must the international manager monitor the environment of countries in which the company currently has operations, he or she must also make a continuous surveillance of other nations' environments. Both opportunities and threats can arise anywhere in the world, so it is important for management to stay on top of developments occurring in many different parts of the world.

One can say that the international environment of a firm is the world at large. However, on a smaller, "firm-specific" level, a multinational company's environment is that of the countries to which it transfers its resources, goods, or services.

DIFFERENT TYPES OF INTERNATIONAL BUSINESS

An international company can achieve its international business aims via different forms of activities, ranging from the import and export of resources, goods, and services to the production and marketing of products in foreign markets. Let us briefly examine these international business activities.

Direct Import and Export

In direct import and export, a firm directly imports goods from abroad and exports its goods to foreign buyers without the help of a middle person or agency in the home country.

Countertrade

It is estimated that between 25 and 40 percent of the world's total exports are generated via countertrade, which is big business. Of the many varieties of countertrade, we will discuss the five principal ones: pure barter, clearing arrangement, switch trading, counterpurchase, and buy-back.

Pure Barter. In *pure barter*, both sides in the business arrangement agree to accept each other's goods as payment for the transaction. For example, in an agreement with the Soviet Union, PepsiCo trades its syrup for cases of Stolichnaya vodka. The Soviet Union markets Pepsi domestically under a franchising arrangement with PepsiCo, which receives an equivalent value of Stolichnaya vodka in return for the franchise rights and syrup that it sells to the Soviets. PepsiCo in turn markets the Russian vodka in the United States.

In Mexico, PepsiCo adopted a creative barter arrangement that helped the company to grow in a country where price controls and a big drop in the local currency against the U.S. dollar would have resulted in lower U.S. dollar profits.

During Mexico's economic collapse in 1982, the Mexican government imposed price controls and devalued the peso several times. Seeing their profits in United States dollars dropping precipitously, many U.S.-based companies like Anderson Clayton and Nabisco sharply cut back their Mexican operations. Not so for PepsiCo, which elected to build instead. It is now cashing in on one of the world's most promising economies.   How did PepsiCo do it? PepsiCo's ingenious strategy was to use the Mexican pesos earned from local sales to buy from local producers wheat, frozen juices, and pineapples—hardly considered PepsiCo's core businesses—for export to the United States, where they were sold to third parties. In 1991, this business was worth $30 million.

Rather than run away from a problem currency and difficult economic conditions, PepsiCo chose to stick around and, by using a creative barter arrangement, was able to convert the profits generated in Mexico into U.S. dollars without suffering the losses incurred in currency conversions from pesos to dollars. In 1991, PepsiCo was Mexico's largest consumer products company, with an estimated $1.2 billion in sales—larger than Procter & Gamble or Colgate-Palmolive.

It is alleged that American companies have a much shorter perspective than Japanese companies. The former are supposedly much more concerned about quarterly profits, whereas the latter are known to stress long-term growth and market share, hoping that profits will eventually come to those who wait patiently. But perseverance and creative strategies are what it takes to penetrate foreign markets. Fortunately, PepsiCo had both in its approach to Mexico, as this example illustrates.[14]

In another interesting deal in the Ukraine, PepsiCo has agreed to sell Ukranian built commercial ships in the world market in exchange for the opportunity to market Pepsi and open several Pizza Hut restaurants (which PepsiCo owns) in the Ukraine. This arrangement between PepsiCo and the Ukrainian Government, and another between McDonald Douglas and the Ugandan Government in which McDonnell Douglas and the Ugandan Government will exchange helicopters and fruit concentrate, is presented in Practical Insight 1-2.

PRACTICAL INSIGHT 1-2

Pepsi and McDonnell Douglas Sell Ships and Passion Fruit; Countertrade Deals Make Life Interesting for Global Firms

Pepsi for Commercial Ships
For more than 20 years, PepsiCo Inc. has been engaged in countertrade with the former Soviet Union. Under the agreement with

PepsiCo, the Soviet Union obtained the right to market Pepsi in the Soviet Union and PepsiCo, in exchange, received Stolichnaya vodka, which it marketed in the U.S.A.. A much more unique version of countertrade was a deal signed by PepsiCo with the Soviet Union in the early 1990's. Under this agreement, PepsiCo agreed to accept not only Russian vodka but also ships built in the Ukraine as a way to conduct commerce in Russia, which lacked convertible currency. Pepsico sells the vodka and the commercial ships in the world market. Now, in an effort to further boost its sales in the former Soviet Union, PepsiCo has entered a joint venture with Ukraine worth $1 billion to market in the world market commercial ships built in the Ukraine. Under the agreement, Pepsi will cooperate with three Ukrainian companies to market the ships. Some of the proceeds from the ship sales will be reinvested in the shipbuilding venture, and some will be used to build five Pepsi bottling plants and to buy soft-drink equipment. The balance will be used to finance the opening of 100 Pizza Hut restaurants in the Ukraine. Pepsi also owns the Pizza Hut chain. Since the Ukraine does not have the hard currency, this type of arrangement will be very beneficial to both PepsiCo and the Ukraine.

Helicopters for Passion Fruit

Uganda wanted to buy 18 helicopters to help eradicate elephant and rhino poaching but didn't have the $ 25 million to pay for them. Enter McDonnell Douglas Helicopter. McDonnell Douglas set up several projects in Uganda to generate the hard currency required. It set up a plant to catch and process Nile perch and a factory which produced pineapple and passion fruit concentrate, for which McDonnell Douglas found buyers in Europe. Uganda received the badly needed 18 helicopters and McDonnell Douglas got paid in the convertible currency.

Sources: Adapted from "Why Countertrade Is getting Hot," *Fortune*, June 29, 1992, 25; and Michael J. McCarthy, "Pepsi Seeking To Boost Sales To Ukrainians," *The Wall Street Journal*, October 23, 1992, A9.

Clearing Arrangements. Under a *clearing arrangement* two countries agree to exchange products by signing a "purchase and payment agreement." This agreement specifies the goods to be traded, their monetary value, and the settlement date. Any deficit on either side at the end of the contract is "cleared" either by accepting unwanted goods or by paying the balance in a specified currency such as U.S. dollars or West German marks.

Switch Trading.   *Switch trading* is trade involving three or more countries. For instance, England agrees to trade computers worth $500,000 to Brazil in exchange for coffee that has an equivalent market value of $500,000. The English may not want the coffee and so, with the help of a switch specialist, they sell the coffee to an Italian company for $450,000. England gets the cash for the sale minus the 5 to 10 percent that may be paid to the switch trader. Because the English side knows in advance that the coffee will be sold elsewhere at a discount, it will have hiked the price of the computers upward to compensate for the discount and the commission paid to the switch trader.

Counterpurchase.   In a *counterpurchase* deal, Country A exports to Country B, and in return promises to spend some or all of the receipts on importing from B. The details of those imports need not be specified, but they must be bought within a particular period—usually three years.

Buy-Back.   *Buy-back* involves licensing of patents or trademarks, selling production know-how, lending capital, or building a plant in another country and agreeing to buy part or all of its output as payment. In one case of buy-back, the General Electric Company provided Poland with the technology and equipment to manufacture electrocardiogram meters, which, in turn, Poland shipped back to General Electric. In another famous deal, Fiat built an automobile factory in Russia, and the Russians paid Fiat for the factory partly in Russian-made Fiats.

Portfolio Investment

As an international business activity, *portfolio investment* refers to the transfer of funds across national boundaries by an international company or person for the purpose of buying the stocks, bonds, or notes issued by a foreign company, or the treasury notes or bills sold by a foreign government agency. The person or company making such investments is primarily interested in dividends and capital appreciation.

Contract Manufacturing

A contractual agreement between a company and a foreign producer under which the foreign producer manufactures the company's product is called *contract manufacturing*. Under this agreement the company retains responsibility for the promotion and distribution of its product. For example, an American pharmaceutical company may contract a company in India to manufacture its cough syrup. The Indian company manufactures it and does all the packaging of the product as per the requirements of the American company. Then the American company takes the packaged product and markets it in India or even globally.

Licensing

In a foreign *licensing* agreement the international company, or licensor, agrees to make available to another company abroad, the licensee, use of its patents and trademarks, its manufacturing processes and know-how, its trade secrets, and its managerial and technical services. In exchange, the foreign company agrees to pay the licensor a royalty or other form of payment according to a schedule agreed upon by the two parties. The licensing agreement could be between the parent company of the international enterprise and one or more of its foreign affiliates, or it could be between the international enterprise and an independent foreign, private, or government enterprise. For example, Firestone has given a license to the Mody Group in India to manufacture and market tires in the Indian domestic market. Similarly, General Foods has licensed the Kothari Group in India to market Tang, the soft drink mix.

Turnkey Projects

When an international company engages in setting up a *turnkey* operation abroad, it assumes responsibility for the design and construction of the entire operation, and, upon completion of the project, it hands over the total management to local personnel whom it has trained. In return for the completion of the project, the international company receives a fee, which can be quite substantial. International companies become involved in the construction of dams, electric power stations, roads, and factory complexes such as steel mills, refineries, chemical plants, and automobile plants.

Examples of American and foreign companies that have completed turnkey projects abroad include Bechtel and Fluor, two American companies that have constructed many foreign plants and projects. Also, Rust Engineering Company, another American company, has built chemical plants abroad, many of them in Eastern Europe; and an entire automobile plant has been constructed in the Soviet Union by Fiat, the famous Italian company.

Foreign Manufacturing

By establishing a manufacturing subsidiary, or by acquiring an existing manufacturing plant in a foreign country, an international company engages in foreign manufacturing. Such a subsidiary may be wholly owned by the international company, or it may be a joint venture between it and one or more foreign business enterprises. In a joint venture, the foreign business partner may be a private company or the host government. Several U.S., European, and Japanese companies have joint ventures with government-owned firms in the developing countries. The output of the foreign subsidiary may be geared to meet the domestic demand in the foreign country, or it may be designated in part or in total for export to markets in still other countries. For example, several Japanese multinational automobile companies such as Nissan, Honda, Toyota, Subaru, and Mazda have set up manufacturing plants in the United States which have the latest manufacturing technology and management techniques. Their purpose is to give the Japanese companies the greatest competitive edge in serving the domestic U.S. market as well as a base for sales to Europe, which tightly limits imports from Japan but not from the United States.[15]

Typically, an international company engages in all of the preceding international business activities simultaneously in different areas of the world. The parent company of the international enterprise decides which foreign affiliate will be responsible for each international activity; this decision is made as a company gradually evolves into a global company. Next, we shall see how this evolution of a global enterprise takes place.

EVOLUTION OF A GLOBAL ENTERPRISE

As a uninational (domestic) company evolves into a full-fledged global enterprise, it goes through several distinct but overlapping evolutionary stages. Some companies go through these stages rapidly—in a few years—whereas others may take many years to evolve into truly global firms. And all companies do not systematically proceed from one evolutionary stage to another; some in fact skip one or several of the stages.

Stage I   Foreign Inquiry

Stage one begins when a company receives an inquiry about one of its products directly from a foreign businessperson or from an independent domestic exporter and importer. The company may ignore the inquiry, in which case there is no further evolutionary development. However, if the company responds positively and has its product sold in the foreign market at a profit, then the stage is set for more sales of its products abroad; and the company executives probably become favorably disposed toward the export of their products. Other inquiries from the foreign buyers are received more enthusiastically, and the company sells its products abroad through a domestic export middleperson. The middleperson could be an export merchant, an export commission house, a resident buyer (a buyer who is domiciled in the exporting company's home market and represents all types of private or governmental foreign buyers), a broker, a combination export manager (an exporter who serves as the exclusive export department of several noncompeting manufacturers), or a manufacturer's agent. (Unlike the combination export managers, who make sales in the name of each company they represent, the manufacturer's agents retain their identifies by operating in their own names.)

Stage 2   Export Manager

As the company's exports continue to expand and the executives decide that the time is ripe to take the export management into their own hands and not to rely any more on unsolicited inquiries from abroad, a decision is made to assume a proactive rather than a reactive posture towards exports. Hence, an export manager with a small staff is appointed to actively search for foreign markets for the company's products.

Stage 3   Export Department and Direct Sales

As export sales continue their upward surge, the company has difficulty operating with only an export manager and his or her little staff. A full-fledged export department or division is established at the same level as the domestic sales department. The company then drops the domestic export middleperson and starts to sell directly to importers or buyers located in foreign markets.

Stage 4   Sales Branches and Subsidiaries

Further growth of export sales requires the establishment of sales branches abroad to handle sales and promotional work. A sales branch manager is directly responsible to the home office, and the branch sells directly to middlepersons in the foreign markets. A sales branch gradually evolves into a sales subsidiary, which is incorporated and domiciled in the foreign country and which enjoys greater autonomy than it had as a sales branch.

Stage 5   Assembly Abroad

Assembly abroad occurs for three major reasons: cheaper costs for shipping unassembled products, lower tariffs, and cheaper labor. The company may begin assembly operation in one or more of the foreign markets if it is more profitable to export the unassembled product abroad rather than the whole (assembled) product. Often, tariffs and transportation costs are lower on unassembled parts and components than on the assembled, finished product. For example, the parts of an unassembled TV set can be packed in a smaller box than can a fully assembled set. Because surface freight is charged on volume, unassembled parts in a smaller box are cheaper to ship than a fully assembled set in a much larger box. Also, tariffs in the form of customs duties on imports are often less on the unassembled product (because of the smaller amount of value-added in an unassembled product) than on the finished product. A large number of Japanese TV sets are assembled in India for these reasons.

Companies often establish assembly operations abroad for a third reason—to take advantage of the foreign country's pool of cheap labor. For this purpose, many American, European, and Japanese companies have established assembly operations in Mexico, Singapore, India, Sri Lanka, Mauritius, and the Dominican Republic. Products assembled in these countries are primarily meant to serve the American and third-country markets of Europe and Japan. For example, Westinghouse Electric Corporation has built four plants in the Dominican Republic to assemble a wide variety of electromechanical and electronic products which are then shipped to its plants in Puerto Rico or the United States for finishing and testing. Carter-Galvis, a Greensboro, North Carolina apparel firm, also has a plant in the Dominican Republic where shirts, pants, and jeans are sewn from fabric cut in the United States. Factory wages in the Dominican Republic average about 60 cents an hour, including fringe benefits. Even at higher skill levels, wages are much lower than those in the United States, with experienced mechanics and electricians earning approximately $310 a month.

Stage 6   Production Abroad

After the previous stages have been accomplished, the next step is the establishment of production abroad. At this time, the company has a well-developed export program supported by country market studies, by promotion and distribution programs tailored to the needs of each country market, and by research into the identification of new foreign markets. The company's executives may now begin to experience difficulties in increasing the total sales volume and profit in foreign markets in which they currently have a foothold; or they may find it impossible to enter other potentially lucrative markets via exports. These difficulties often occur when the local governments impose high tariffs or quotas on the import of certain products, or when they ban their import totally if the products are being produced locally by a domestic company. In such cases the company executives decide to penetrate the foreign market by producing the product right in the foreign market itself.

Three methods are generally available for commencing foreign production: (1) contract manufacturing, (2) licensing, and (3) direct investment in manufacturing facilities. Each of these methods has advantages and disadvantages; therefore, the appropriate strategy or method will depend on the special circumstances of the company concerned.

Contract Manufacturing

As explained earlier in this chapter, under a contractual agreement, the foreign producer makes and sells the company's product in the foreign market, but the company continues to promote and distribute its product. By and large, U.S. companies have avoided contract manufacturing and have started with licensing and gradually moved toward direct investment in production facilities.

Licensing

In a licensing agreement, the foreign company pays a royalty to the international company for its patents, trademarks, and trade secrets. If the international company adopts this route to foreign manufacturing, more often than not it finds licensing to be a less than satisfactory approach to penetrating the foreign market. The dissatisfaction of the international company with licensing may come from the company executives' belief that the foreign licensee is not doing enough to promote sales of the licensed product or that the licensee is not maintaining product quality (thus damaging the reputation and trademark of the company). There are many other reasons that could cause dissatisfaction with the licensee's performance and with the total licensing arrangement.[16] Even when the licensee performs well, the company may feel that it can do better financially and operationally without the licensee.

For the licensor company, then, establishing a manufacturing facility via direct investment becomes an increasingly attractive method for tapping foreign markets.

Investment in Manufacturing

After establishing a manufacturing facility in a foreign market, the company now manages its total business in a foreign country. It must, therefore, perform the many business functions abroad—purchasing, finance, human resource planning and management, manufacturing, marketing, and so on. The company is also obligated to make significant commitments of technical, management, and financial resources to the new foreign entity.

The company learns from its experience with the first foreign manufacturing venture, and this knowledge paves the way for the establishment of other foreign manufacturing plants abroad. At the same time, the company continues to export its products and to license its technology to foreign businesses and, increasingly, to its own foreign affiliates.

In maturing as an international exporter, licensor, and producer of products, the company meets the global demand for its products with exports from several of its foreign-production affiliates, as well as with exports from the parent company and with the products of the foreign licensing arrangements. As the complexity of managing the geographically far-flung operations in several countries increases, the parent company managers recognize the benefits of integrating and tightening up the company's global operations and of managing the entire company as one global organizational system. The motivation to use the so-called systems approach in managing the company as one unit, with each foreign and domestic affiliate functioning as a subunit of the whole company, arises when several questions emerge to confront the company:

1. Which of the several foreign affiliates should export to a third-country market?
2. Different affiliates operate in countries with differing inflation rates and corporate tax structures. How should the financial resources of each affiliate be managed with the objective of maximizing the total global earnings of the entire company?
3. Can promotional expenditures be lowered by standardizing advertising internationally?

Questions such as these make the parent company management

perceive the company as one global enterprise system and not merely as an aggregation of several autonomous domestic and foreign affiliates. When the parent company's management begins to see the advantages of making strategic decisions—in various functional areas such as purchasing, finance, production, marketing, personnel, and research and development—from the perspective of the company as one integrated system, the stage is set for the company's evolution to a multinational enterprise.

Stage 7   Integration of Foreign Affiliates

As the parent company managers decide to integrate the various foreign affiliates into one multinational enterprise system, the affiliates lose considerable autonomy as strategic decisions are now made by top management at the company headquarters. The company's management begins to view the entire world as its theater of operations; it plans, organizes, staffs, and controls its international operations from a global perspective. Strategic decisions are made after a careful analysis of their worldwide implications: In what country should we build our next production facility? Throughout the world, where are our markets, and from which production center should they be served? From which sources in the world should we borrow capital to finance our current and future operations? Where should our research and development laboratories be located? From which countries should we recruit people? When the management of the company starts thinking and operating in global terms, then it has evolved into a true global enterprise (see Figure 1-2).

Not all companies go through each of the seven stages described in the preceding sections. Some companies stop short of complete integration of their domestic and foreign operations, preferring instead to manage their domestic and foreign operations in a decentralized manner, without an overall global strategy. Others may choose to coordinate the operations of affiliates in a certain region of the world, such as Europe, and keep the affiliates in other regions unattached and semiautonomous. Still other companies may decide to think globally with respect to only a few, but not all, of the enterprise functions. For instance, managers may think in worldwide terms where financial and production issues are concerned but not for marketing, personnel, purchasing, and research and development. Thus there are different degrees of globalization of operations. Some firms may progress further along the multinational path and become true global enterprises, whereas others may choose to end their journey along the path at various milestones.

FIGURE 1-2 The Evolution of a MultiNational Enterprise

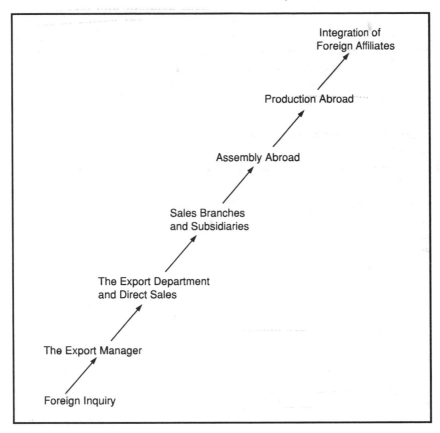

Many changes in management practices and organizational structure occur as a firm evolves into a multinational company. Some of these changes involve a radical reorientation in the attitudes and values of the managers with respect to both the role of the company in the world economy and the allegiance of the company to the home country. Another significant arena for change is the managers' perceptions of people of different nationalities, cultures, and races.

GLOBAL COMPANIES :   OBJECTIVES AND SOURCES OF COMPETITIVE ADVANTAGE

Sumantra Ghoshal, in his seminal article "Global Strategy: An Organizing Framework,"[17] has offered an excellent framework that explains the broad categories of objectives of a global firm and the sources for developing a global firm's competitive advantage. The framework is presented in Exhibit 1-5.

As shown in Exhibit 1-5, there are three categories of objectives pursued by a global firm: (1) achieving efficiency, (2) managing risks, and (3) innovating, learning, and adapting. The key is to create a firm's competitive advantage by developing and implementing strategies that optimize the firm's achievement of these three categories of objectives. This may require trade-offs to be made between the objectives because on occasion they may conflict with each other. For example, the objective of achieving efficiency through economies of scale in production may conflict with the objective of minimizing risks emanating from economic or political conditions in a country where the plant may be located. Ghoshal identifies three sources through which a global firm may derive its competitive advantage: (1) national differences, (2) scale economies, and (3) scope economies. According to Ghoshal, "The strategic task of managing globally is to use all three sources of competitive advantage to optimize efficiency, risk, and learning simultaneously in a worldwide business. The key to a successful global strategy is to manage the interactions between these different goals and means."[18]

Achieving Efficiency. If a firm is viewed as an input-output system, its overall efficiency is defined as a ratio of the value of all its outputs to the costs of all its inputs. A firm obtains the surplus resources needed to grow and prosper by maximizing this ratio. It may enhance the value of its products or services (outputs) by making them of higher quality than those of its competitors, and at the same time may lower the costs of inputs by obtaining low cost factors of production, such as labor and raw materials. Different business functions, such as production, research and development, marketing, etc., have different factor intensities. A firm could exploit national differences by locating a function in that country which has a comparative advantage in providing the factors required to perform it. As such, a firm could exploit country differences in wage rates by locating labor intensive production in low-wage countries like Malaysia or Mexico, and locating R & D activities in countries that have capable scientists who can do the work but who do not have to be paid high salaries. As an example, many American companies like Hewlett-Packard and Digital have transferred their software development work to India, where qualified personnel to write innovative software are plentiful and can be employed for as low as $300 a month.

A firm could enjoy the benefits of scale economies like lower costs and higher quality resulting from specialization by designating one plant

EXHIBIT 1-5   Global Strategy: An Organizing Framework

Strategic Objectives	Sources of competitive advantage		
	National Differences	Scale Economies	Scope Economies
Achieving efficiency in current operations.	Benefitting from differences in factor costs—wages and cost of capital.	Expanding and exploiting potential scale economies in each activity.	Sharing investments and costs across products, markets, and businesses.
Managing Risks.	Managing different kinds of risks arising from market or policy-induced changes in comparative advantages of diff. countries.	Balancing scale with strategic and operational flexibility.	Portfolio diversification of risks and creation of options and side-bets.
Innovating, learning, and adapting.	Learning from societal differences in organizational and managerial processes and systems.	Benefitting from experience—cost reduction and innovation.	Sharing learning across organizational components in diff. products, markets, or businesses.

Source: Sumantra Ghoshal, "Global Strategy: An Organizing Framework," *Strategic Management Journal*, Vol. 8, 1987, 428.

to serve as the sole producer of a component for use in the final assembly of a product. For example, a plant in the Philippines may make transmissions, another in Malaysia the steering mechanisms, and one in Thailand the engines. Each country would then do the final assembly. Toyota motor company is rapidly moving in this direction.

The concept of scope economies is based upon the notion that savings and cost reductions will accrue when two or more products can share the same asset, such as a production plant, distribution channel, brand name, or staff services such as legal, public relations, etc. A global company like Coca-Cola enjoys a competitive advantage because it is in a position to produce two or more products in one plant rather than two separate plants, market its products through common distribution channels, and share its world-famous brand name across a wide range of products.

Managing Risks. A global company faces a number of different types of risks—economic, political, legal, competitive. The nature and severity of such risks are not the same for all countries. A global company is in a position to manage such risks effectively by planning and implementing effective strategies aimed at diffusing risk. For example, in a country that has high levels of unemployment, a global company could deflect restrictive and unfriendly governmental policies by sourcing products for world markets in that country, thus increasing much needed employment opportunities for the local populace. An example of such a strategy is the transfer of significant amounts of car production to the U.S.A. by Japanese automakers like Toyota, Honda, and Nissan. One of the principal motivations behind this strategy was to minimize the growing anti-Japanese sentiment in the U.S.A. due to the alleged job losses caused by Japanese imports.

The benefits of scale economies must be weighed against the risks of economies of scale. A plant located in a country because of its low wages could lose its locational advantage if the wage rates in the country rise significantly because of economic development or appreciation of the country's currency. Global companies manage such risks by distributing production in more than one country even at the expense of benefits due to lower scale economies. Japanese car companies have managed currency and wage-rate risks, caused by rising wage rates in Japan and the much stronger Japanese yen vis-a-vis the U.S. dollar, by exporting cars made in U.S. based plants back to Japan. The flexibility afforded to Japanese car companies by plants both in the U.S.A. and Japan was responsible for their effective management of risk.

Innovation and Learning. A global company has a distinct advantage over its purely domestic competitor because of the diversity of environments in which the global company operates. A company that has operations in many countries is exposed to a diversity of experiences and stimuli. Being in many countries allows it to develop a variety of capabilities. It provides a global company with opportunities to learn skills and acquire knowledge of a country which can be transferred and applied in many other countries where it has operations. For example, a company that has operations in Japan can learn about the very best aspects of the Japanese management system and adapt and use those that are most useful in its American operations. General Electric is marketing in India an ultrasound unit designed by Indian engineers, the technology of which was developed in GE's Japanese operations.

Hewlett-Packard has continued pouring resources in the Asian region, opening a laboratory in Japan and new manufacturing facilities in Japan and Malaysia, and simultaneously beefing up its engineering, project management, and design capacity in Singapore. Such investments provide not only increased sales in the region but also skills and expertise in how to improve the production process, something that it lacks in the United States. According to a Hewlett-Packard spokesman, "In the U.S., all great engineers want to work on product innovation; in Asia, the best guys want to work on improving the production process." Hewlett-Packard can learn process improvement techniques from its Asian operations and transfer the knowledge not only to its U.S. operations but to operations worldwide.[19]

Ford, Toyota, and Honda have embarked upon the ambitious project of building a "world car." Practical Insight 1-2 shows how the companies are taking advantage of national differences, economies of scale, and economies of scope, with the intent of achieving greater efficiency, spreading risk, and learning from worldwide operations.

PRACTICAL INSIGHT 1-3

Want To Be More Efficient, Spread Risk, and Learn and Innovate at the Same Time? —Try Building a "World Car."

A Ford Motor spokesperson announced that the Company will start exporting from its U.S. plants automatic transmissions, steering components, and engines to Europe for a new model that will replace the Tempo/Topaz models in the U.S. and Canada and the Sierra in Europe. The new compact car was mostly engineered by Ford Europe but will be manufactured and marketed on both continents. The hope is that this "world car" will reduce the

Company's engineering expenditures. Ford tried once before to build a "world car" with its Escort model but ended up with two different versions of the same car that looked similar but had few common component parts. Ford hopes to succeed this time with the new "world car."

Ford Europe will also export some components to the U.S. operations, such as manual transmissions, to be used in the "world car."

Along the same lines as Ford, Japanese car companies like Toyota and the Honda Motor Company are pioneering the auto industry's truly global manufacturing system. The companies' aim is to perfect a car's design and production in one place and then churn out thousands of "world" cars each year that can be made in one place and sold worldwide. In an industry where the cost of tailoring car models to different markets can run into billions of dollars, the "world car" approach of Toyota and Honda—and which Ford is hoping to emulate—is targeted at sharply curtailing development costs, maximizing the use of assembly plants, and preserving the assembly line efficiencies that are a hallmark of the Japanese "lean" production system.

As for Honda, the goal is to create a "global base of complementary supply," says Roger Lambert, Honda's manager of corporate communications. "Japan can supply North America and Europe, North America can supply Japan and Europe, and Europe can supply Japan and the United States. So far, the first two are true. This means that you can more profitably utilize your production bases and talents."

The strategy of shipping components and fully assembled products from the U.S. to Europe and Japan couldn't have come at a more opportune time for the Japanese car companies, especially when political pressures are intense to reduce the Japanese trade surplus with the United States. The task was made easier due to the strength of the Japanese yen, which has risen about 50 percent against the U.S. dollar. That has made production of cars in the United States cheaper, by some estimates, by $2,500 to $3000 per car. That saving more than compensates for the transportation costs for a car overseas.

For the first time, Toyota is creating a system that will give it the capability to manage the car production levels in Japan and the United States. It is moving towards a global manufacturing system that will enable it to enhance manufacturing efficiency by fine-tuning global production levels on a quarterly basis in response to economic conditions in different markets.

Source: Adapted from Paul Ingrassia, "Ford to Export Parts to Europe For a New Car," *The Wall Street Journal*, September, 29, 1992, A5.; Jane Perlez, "Toyota and Honda Create Global Production System," *The New York Times*, March 26, 1993, A1 and D2.

WHY INTERNATIONAL COMPANIES ENGAGE IN FOREIGN PRODUCTION

An international company may have several motivations for establishing foreign production facilities. Some of them have been alluded to in the preceding paragraphs on the evolution of multinational enterprises. Let us examine some of the other motivations for foreign production.

To protect and maintain a market position abroad, many companies have been forced to establish production facilities in foreign markets that once were served through exports because the foreign governments later threatened to impose high tariffs or quotas. The so-called voluntary restrictions of 1980 of exports to the United States of Japanese automobiles prompted Japanese auto companies like Toyota and Nissan to build car manufacturing plants in the United States. Similarly, many U.S. companies have established plants in the European Economic Community—commonly known as the European Common Market—to jump over the common tariff and non-tariff barriers raised by the member countries against imports from non-EEC countries.

The expectation of immense business opportunities in an integrated and unified market of 320 million people in the twelve European countries including Great Britain, Ireland, France, Germany, the Netherlands, Belgium, Luxembourg, Italy, Greece, Spain, Denmark, and Portugal has brought an upsurge of Japanese direct investment in Europe. Japanese banks and companies in the manufacturing sector have been investing, buying European companies, setting up manufacturing subsidiaries, and boosting sales forces all over Europe. They are investing now, believing that Europe will be a good market. Also, they fear that, unlike the United States, Europe will resist mass imports of Japanese goods when most internal European trade barriers fall, as expected, by the year 2000.

Japan's business activities in Europe intensified in 1990 when Japanese companies decided Europe was serious about market unification after 1992. Now Japanese companies want a foothold in

Europe before protectionism keeps them out. The existence of huge European trade imbalances with Japan has prompted a number of European countries to adopt measures such as import quotas and antidumping tariffs. Japanese companies have responded by building new manufacturing plants and buying existing manufacturing capacity inside what could become a European fortress.

Another reason companies set up foreign plants is to eliminate or reduce high transportation costs, particularly if the ratio of the per-unit transportation expenditures to the per-unit selling price of the product is very high. For instance, if the product costs $10 to ship but can be marketed for no more than $25 in the foreign market, all other things being nearly equal, the company may decide to produce it in the market in order to improve its profit margin.

Cheap labor is often the strongest incentive for companies to establish foreign operations. For example, over the past two decades more than 2,000 maquiladoras plants have sprung up near the United States-Mexico border. These plants take advantage of cheap labor to assemble American-made components for reexport to the United States. Farther inside Mexico, in Mexico City, Chrysler assembles the Ram Charger for shipment to the U.S. market.[20] The economics of assembly in Mexico are favorable because jobs that fetch $12 an hour, fully "burdened" with benefits, Social Security, and so on, can be had in Mexico for between $1.50 and $2 an hour.[21] In the 1950's and 1960's, many American companies had established not just assembly plants but fully integrated manufacturing plants in countries of Southeast Asia such as Taiwan, Singapore, and Hong Kong. As wages in these countries have risen, companies are now shifting their investment sights and moving to Malaysia and Thailand.

Rapid expansion of a foreign market for the company's product, along with the desire to obtain a large market share in it before a major competitor can get in, are other strong driving forces for companies to engage in foreign production. There are many distinct advantages that a firm can enjoy by producing a product in a foreign market, even if there are no import barriers. For example, the firm achieves the ability to meet the demand for the product quickly, builds good public relations with customers and the host government, and improves service. Moreover, local production often allows the company to take advantage of incentives that the host government may be offering to foreign companies that make direct investments in the country, such as reduced taxes for several years, free land, low-interest loans, and a guarantee of no labor strife.

The need for vertical integration is another reason often responsible for the multinationalization of operations. Companies are pushed into making direct investment abroad so that they can capture a source of supply or new markets for their products. For example, a company in the oil exploration and drilling business may integrate "downstream" by acquiring or building an oil refinery in a foreign country that has a market for its refined products. Conversely, a company that has strong distribution channels (gas stations) in a country but needs a steady source of supply of gasoline at predictable prices may integrate "upstream" and acquire an oil producer and refiner in another country.

Yet another reason for establishing foreign operations is to follow the company's major customers abroad. When the Japanese automakers—Honda, Toyota, Nissan, Mazda, Subaru, and Isuzu—established car manufacturing plants in the United States, their Japanese suppliers followed and set up their own plants in the United States. There are today approximately 270 Japanese-owned parts suppliers in the United States representing an investment of $5.5 billion and employing more than 30,000 workers. Most of these supplier-firms provide glass, brake systems, seats, air conditioners, heaters, filters, fuel pumps, and other components directly to the production plants.[22] AT&T has made a big push overseas, mainly to satisfy the telecommunications needs of its large global customers who had themselves made their own push into overseas markets. Fearing that its major customers—the global companies—would turn to rival companies such as IBM and Japan's NEC if it did not operate advanced voice and data networks around the world, the company formed several joint ventures and strategic alliances around the globe. Employment abroad for AT&T has jumped from a mere fifty people in 1983 to 21,000 in more than forty countries.[23] Like AT&T, Federal Express, too, followed the lead of its customers who increasingly wanted packages sent to Asia and Europe. Accordingly, with the aim of "keeping it purple"—the color of Federal's planes and vans—the company set out to duplicate its business abroad.[24]

The small size of the domestic market is the reason given by European companies that have developed multinational structures. Companies such as Hoffman La-Roche, Sandoz, and Ciba-Geigy, based in Switzerland—a nation whose population is only about six million—could not have survived in their industry had they limited their business horizons to only the Swiss market. These companies, and others like them, were forced to seek markets abroad, which eventually led to the creation of foreign manufacturing facilities in their major markets.

Companies in pharmaceutical and high-technology industries that must spend large sums of money on research and development for new products and processes are compelled to look for ways to improve their sales volume in order to support their laboratories. If the domestic sales volume and exports do not raise the necessary cash flow, then strategically located manufacturing and sales affiliates are established abroad with the objective of attaining higher levels of sales volume and cash flow.

A large number of companies have established production facilities abroad to exploit the strong brand names of their products. Realizing that they could not fully exploit their advantage by way of exports, they have set up plants in their major foreign markets. Examples of companies that have used this strategy are Coca-Cola, Heinz, Corn Products, and Del Monte.

A global company may decide to locate its manufacturing plant in a country that is of strategic importance for the company's exports to a third country. For instance, Japanese companies have strictly observed the Arab boycott of Israel and therefore cannot export to Israel directly from Japan. However, Japanese plants in the United States can export their U.S.-made products to Israel, and this is exactly what the Japanese auto company, Honda Motor Company, is doing. It is exporting Honda Civic sedans to Israel from its plant in Ohio. In the same vein, Northern Telecom Ltd., the Canadian telecommunications giant, has moved many of its manufacturing operations to the United States in order to gain the competitive edge that an American company can obtain in securing Japanese contracts. Northern Telecom made this strategic move to the United States knowing that the Japanese would favor U.S. companies because of Japan's huge trade surplus with the United States.[25]

Firms have been known to move their operations to ecologically and environmentally friendly countries. It has been alleged that companies have moved their environmentally harmful operations to countries in Africa, Asia, and Latin America, which do not have strict laws for environmental protection as in the United States. Companies do not necessarily have to migrate to developing countries to avoid environmental risks. A case in point is Germany's BASF, which moved its biotechnology research laboratory focusing on cancer and immune-system research from Germany—where it faced legal and political challenges from the environmentally conscious Green movement—to Cambridge, Massachusetts which, according to BASF's director of biotechnology research, had more or less settled any controversies involving safety, animal rights, and the environment.[26]

Recognizing that scientific talent and brain power are not the monopoly of any one country or group of countries, global companies are establishing technological research and development centers around the world. Companies like IBM have established such centers in Japan to tap into the Japanese "innovation culture." Several global companies in a variety of knowledge-based industries such as biotechnology, pharmaceutical, and electronics have set up such centers in the countries of the so-called Triad comprising Europe, the Pacific Basin (including Japan), and the United States. This strategy has paid rich dividends for Xerox, which has introduced eighty different office-copier models in the United States that were engineered and built by its Japanese joint venture, Fuji-Xerox Company.

Earlier in this chapter we referred to the impact of currency values on comparative wage rates among countries. A factor that companies take into account in locating production plants is the comparative production costs in their major country markets. For example, a company that has major market positions in Japan, Germany, and the United States would be concerned about how costs are affected by the cross-exchange rates between the Japanese yen, the German mark, and the U.S. dollar. If the yen were to rise significantly in value against the U.S. dollar and the German mark, then exports to the United States and Germany of the company's Japanese-produced products could become relatively noncompetitive because of the rise of the yen denominated Japanese wage rates and exports, especially if labor costs added significantly to the total product value. In such an event, the economics of production and distribution permitting, the company would gain if it could shift its production to either the United States or Germany. In fact, in 1990 and 1991 when the yen appreciated against the U.S. dollar, Japanese auto companies used their U.S. plants to ship cars to Europe, and even back to Japan! In 1993, BMW and Mercedes, two of the major luxury car-makers of Germany, have decided to commence manufacturing of some models in the U.S. because of the highly noncompetitive labor rates in Germany due largely to the high value of the German mark. Global companies invest in favor of operational flexibility and in the ability to shift the sourcing of products and components from country to country. Global companies are therefore motivated to make major investments in production and supply sites in their major country markets.

SUMMARY

The purpose of this chapter was to provide an introduction to international management and to the world of the so-called multinational or global companies. The nature of international business was explained first, and we saw that the need for international management and managers arises when companies begin to export goods or services.

Although there are scores of small multinational companies, generally when one speaks of multinational companies the reference is to the large multinationals. Increasingly, people are referring to these giant companies, with operations throughout the world, not as international but as global companies. International management and global companies are more or less like Siamese twins or two sides of a coin. The growth of global companies has resulted from the astute management of these enterprises by international managers. And the management of multinational corporations epitomizes what international management is all about.

We saw something of the dimensions and dramatic growth of multinational companies during the 1960's, which was followed by a description of the nature of the international environment in which international management activities occur. Next we looked at the different international business activities of multinational companies; then we examined the typical stages in the evolution of multinational companies. After this we studied how global companies exploit economies of scale, economies of scope, and national differences to achieve their three generic objectives: (1) efficiency in current operations, (2) managing risks, and (3) innovation, learning, and adaptation. This was followed by an overview of the different reasons for international production by multinational companies.

QUESTIONS

1. What is international business? How does it differ from international management?
2. Discuss the characteristics of multinational companies. What forces have contributed to their development and growth?
3. How does a domestic company typically evolve into one that is multinational? How and why does change occur in the relationship between the parent company and foreign affiliates as the company becomes multinational?
4. Identify and explain the three categories of broad objectives of global companies. What strategic actions can a global company take in order to develop competitive advantage against its competitors?
5. Discuss the key differences between economies of scale and economies of scope.
6. Discuss how national differences can serve as a source of competitive advantage for a global company.

FURTHER READING

Bible, Geoffrey C. "Global Competition: Getting Ahead, Staying Ahead. *Executive Speeches*. Vol. 7, no. 2 (October/November 1992): 1-6.

Daniels, John D., and Radebaugh, Lee H. *International Business: Environments and Operations*. 5th ed. Reading, Mass.: Addison-Wesley, 1989.

Farmer, Richard N., and Richman, Barry B. *International Business: An Operational Theory*. Homewood, Ill.: Richard D. Irwin, 1966.

Lei, David and Slocum, John W., Jr. "Global Strategy, Competence-Building and Strategic Alliances." *California Management Review*. Vol. 35, (1) (Fall 1992): 81-97.

Phatak, Arvind V. *Evolution of World Enterprises*. New York: American Management Association, 1971.

Phatak, Arvind. *Managing Multinational Corporations*. New York: Praeger Publishers, 1974.

Vernon, Raymond, and Louis T. Wells, Jr. *Manager in the International Economy*. 4th ed. Englewood Cliffs, N.J.: Prentice-Hall, 1981.

Walle, A. H. "International Business and Raging Tigers: Operationalizing the Global Paradigm." *Management Decision*. Vol. 30, no. 2 (1992): 35-39.

Weigand, Robert E. "International Trade Without Money." *Harvard Business Review* (November-December 1977).

NOTES

[1] U.S. Department of Commerce, *Survey of Current Business*, July1993, 67 and 100.

[2] U.S. Department of Commerce, *The National Data Book*, Bureau of Census, 112th ed.

[3] John D. Daniels and Lee H. Radebaugh, *International Business: Environment and Operations*, 6th ed. (Reading, Mass.: Addison-Wesley, 1992), 8.

[4] Donald A. Ball and Wendell H. McCullough, Jr., *International Business: Introduction and Essentials*, 4th ed. (Homewood, Illinois: BPI/Irwin, 1990), 17.

[5] Betty Jane Punett and David A. Ricks, *International Business* (Boston: PWS/Kent Publsihing Company, 1992), 7.

[6] U.S. Department of Commerce, *Survey of Current Business*, op. cit., 67 and 100.

[7] U. S. Department of Commerce, *Survey of Current Business*, op. cit., 73 and 108.

[8] U. S. Department of Commerce, *Survey of Current Business*, op. cit., 42.

[9] U. S. Department of Commerce, *Survey of Current Business*, September 1992, 58.

[10] "The World's Largest Industrial Corporations," *Fortune*, July 26, 1993, 191.

[11] "Beijing's 'Blatant Piracy' Could Slash Its U.S. Trade," *Business Week*, April 22, 1991, 46.

[12] Faye Rice, "How Copycats Steal Billions," *Fortune*, April 22, 1991, 157-164.

[13] Richard D. Schmitt, "Claimant Against Japanese Learns the Word for Delay," *Wall Street Journal*, December 14, 1990, B1-B2.

[14] Claire Poole, "Pepsico's Newest Generation," Forbes, February 18, 1991, 88.

[15] *Business Week*, March 7, 1988, 55.

[16] For a detailed account of licensing and its advantages and disadvantages, see Arvind V. Phatak, *Managing Multinational Corporations.* (New York: Praeger Publishers, 1974), 276-288.

[17] Sumantra Ghoshal, "Global Strategy: An Organizing Framework," *Strategic Management Journal*, Vol. 8 (1987): 425-440.

[18] Ibid., 427.

[19] Paul Blustein, "Hewlett-Packard's Role in Asia marks growth area for U.S.," *Philadelphia Inquirer*, November 26, 1993, C4.

[20] Paul Magnusson, Stephen Baker, David Beach, Gail DeGeorge, and William C. Symonda, "The Mexico Pact: Worth the Price?" *Business Week*, May 27, 1991, 33-34.

[21] Kevin McDermot, "Border Crossing Ahead," *D & B Reports* (January-February 1991): 24.

[22] Martin Kenney and Richard Florida, "How the Japanese Industry Is Rebuilding the Rust Belt," *Technology Review* (February-March 1991): 28.

[23] Dinah Lee, Jonathan Levine, and Peter Coy, "ATT Slowly Gets Its Global Wires Uncrossed," *Business Week*, February 11, 1991, 82.

[24] Daniel Pearl, "Federal Express Finds Its Pioneering Formula Fall Flat Overseas," *Wall Street Journal*, April 15, 1991, A8.

[25] William J. Holstein, Stanley Reed, Jonathan Kapstein Todd Vogel, and Joseph Weber, "The Stateless Corporation," *Business Week*, May 14, 1990, 99.

Chapter T W O

The Cultural Environment of International Management

The multinational operations of companies have brought executives in face-to-face contact with the cultures of different nations and regions, many of which seem very strange. The importance of understanding the cultures of countries in which a company operates—as well as the similarities and differences between those cultures—becomes clear when one looks at the multitude of blunders international executives have made because of insensitivity to cultural differences.[1] Investigators who have studied the performance and problems of corporations and individuals abroad have concluded that it is usually the human problems associated with working in a different culture that are likely to be critical to the success or failure of their endeavors.[2] Analyses of problems and failures abroad have shown that the techniques, practices, and methods that have proved effective in one country may not work as well in other countries. One dominant, interfering factor is culture.

The following old oriental story vividly dramatizes the consequences of ignorance, and it is an appropriate metaphor for the kinds of problems that can arise when people of diverse cultures come into contact without preparation.

> Once upon a time there was a great flood; and involved in this flood were two creatures, a monkey and a fish. The monkey, being agile and experienced, was lucky enough to scramble up a tree and escape the raging waters. As he looked down from his safe perch, he saw the poor fish struggling against the swift current. With the very best of intentions, he reached down and lifted the fish from the water. The result was inevitable.[3]

Just as the monkey in the story assumed that the fish's environment was similar to his and behaved accordingly, so do many international executives unconsciously assume that all people think and feel the way they do. Management practices that are suited to their own cultural environment may bring about undesirable, perhaps terrible, consequences in another culture. In international business dealings, then, ignorance of cultural differences is not just unfortunate; it is bad business.

To avoid such problems, the international manager must understand his or her own culture first. A person's behavior is based on a commonly shared cultural system of values, beliefs, and attitudes of the society. When the international manager fully comprehends her or his own culture, as well as that of the country into which the business plans to expand, the manager can be certain of not unconsciously expecting the foreign nationals to behave like the "normal" people of her or his own culture. The manager must recognize the cultural imperatives abroad, making appropriate changes in her or his own interpersonal behavior and managerial practices.

In this chapter, we shall examine the concept of culture and the value orientations that are typical of American and most Western societies. We shall study how these value orientations differ from those of nonWestern societies and how problems occur when the diverse Western and nonWestern value orientations interact with each other as people from these cultures come face to face.

A manager living abroad needs a framework in which to analyze and understand the differences between her or his own culture and that of the host society. We shall look at one such scheme for evaluating cultural differences. Before we go on with our study of culture in international management, let us first take a test. Look at Practical Insight 2-1 and answer the questions that test your understanding of cultural differences.

PRACTICAL INSIGHT 2-1   Are You World Wise?

GOING GLOBAL? BEFORE YOU BUY YOUR PLANE TICKETS, test your business etiquette knowledge (some questions have more than one answer):

1. DURING BUSINESS MEETINGS, USE FIRST NAMES IN:
a) Great Britain, because everyone is oh so chummy.
b) Australia, because informality is the rule.
c) China, because the first name is the surname.
d) Japan, because the last names are easy to mispronounce.

2. IN CHINA, OFFER EXPENSIVE GIFTS TO YOUR HOSTS:
a) Every time they ask for one.
b) When you need help getting out of the country.
c) Never—if they can't reciprocate, they'll lose face.

3. IN WHICH COUNTRY IS A BUSINESS CARD AN OBJECT OF RESPECT?
a) Japan: An executive's identity depends on his employer.
b) Taiwan: It explains a person's rank and status.
c) France: Especially cards describing a man's mistress.

4. WHEN DOING BUSINESS IN JAPAN, NEVER:
a) Touch someone.
b) Leave your chopsticks in the rice.
c) Take people to pricier restaurants than they took you.
d) All of the above.

5. POWER BREAKFASTS ARE INAPPROPRIATE IN ALL BUT:
a) Italy: They like to bring the family along.
b) Mexico: They don't bother to get to work till 10 a.m. anyway.
c) United States: We invented them.
d) France: They're at their most argumentative in the morning.

6. IN SOME COUNTRIES, COLORS ARE KEY. WHICH IS TRUE?
a) For Koreans, writing a person's name in red signifies death.
b) In China and Japan, gifts wrapped in white or black should only be presented at funerals.
c) Purple suits in Great Britain represent lack of taste.

7. WHICH OF THESE CHOICES ARE OBSCENE GESTURES?
a) The okay sign in Brazil.
b) A hearty slap on the back in Switzerland.
c) Doing anything with the left hand in Saudi Arabia.
d) Thumb between second and third finger in Japan.

Source: Business World, May 1990, 27.

ANSWERS: 1-b,c; 2-c; 3-a,b; 4-d; 5-c; 6-a,b; 7-a,c,d

THE MEANING OF CULTURE

There are as many definitions of culture as there are books in anthropology. Culture is the way of life of a group of people. It is "that complex whole which includes knowledge, belief, art, morals, customs, and any other capabilities and habits acquired by man as a member of society."[4] In other words, it is the distinctive way of life of a group of people; their complete design for living.[5] A person is not born with a given culture; rather, she or he acquires it through the socialization process that begins at birth. An American is not born with a liking for hot dogs, or a German with a natural preference for beer; these behavioral attributes are culturally transmitted.

Dressler and Carns list the following characteristics of culture:

1. Culture exists in the minds of individual human beings who have learned it in their past associations with other human beings and who use it to guide their own continuing interaction with others.
2. Human cultures vary considerably, one from another.
3. But although different in some respects, cultures resemble one another to a considerable extent.
4. Once a culture has been learned and accepted, it tends to persist.
5. All cultures are gradually and continuously being changed, even though human beings tend to resist these changes.
6. Different individuals of the same society may behave differently in response to a given situation, even though all have internalized certain elements of the same culture.
7. No person can escape entirely from his culture.[6]

Dressler and Carns offer the following as functions of culture:

1. Culture enables us to communicate with others through a language that we have learned and that we share in common.
2. Culture makes it possible to anticipate how others in our society are likely to respond to our actions.
3. Culture gives standards for distinguishing between what is considered right and wrong, beautiful and ugly, reasonable and unreasonable, tragic and humorous, safe and dangerous.
4. Culture provides the knowledge and skill necessary for meeting sustenance needs.
5. Culture enables us to identify with others; that is, include ourselves in the same category with other people of similar background.[7]

CRITICAL CULTURAL VALUE DIFFERENCES

The nature of most of the problems encountered by international managers abroad may be perceived as this: a conflict exists between the basic values held by two or more groups of people. The problems and misunderstandings occur because of the ethnocentric attitudes of members of each group, who take for granted that their values, especially those that tend to be acted on unconsciously, are correct and indeed best. In the following section, we shall identify and discuss some specific values held by Americans which frequently are at odds with those of people of other cultures. These values may not be characteristic of all Americans—after all, America is considered the melting pot of many different cultures and nationalities—but they do represent values common to many Americans and tend to distinguish the United States culture from other contemporary cultures.

Individualism

Individualism describes the attitude of independence of a person who feels a large degree of freedom in the conduct of his or her personal life. In American culture, this individualism may motivate personal accomplishment, and self-expression is considered to be of the greatest worth. By contrast, individualism is not considered important in other cultures. In the Chinese and Japanese cultures, the group is preeminent in social life; so conformity and cooperation are values that rank higher than individualism. Individual successes or failures are shared by the family, clan, or community.

No country in the world exemplifies the characteristics of "groupism" better than Japan. We can speak of Japan as a country whose society could be organized into several concentric circles. The outer circle consists of Japanese society at large with its long history and the feudal traditions of the Shogun Dynasty. Historically, Japan has been an isolated country. Until the fifteenth century, Japan was insulated from foreign influence by the natural barrier of its surrounding seas. In spite of the dramatic changes in the rest of the world brought about by the maritime power of Western countries, the political policies of the Tokugawa Shogunate kept foreigners out of the country. Until the mid-nineteenth century, Japan was the country least influenced by Western European culture. Its maritime barriers not only kept foreigners out, they also prevented people from leaving the country. The mountains in Japan made travel difficult within the country, which in turn led to the further isolation of social groups.

Because of the mountains, only 10 percent of the land can be cultivated. So, if one uses people per square mile of arable land as a measure, Japan is the most densely populated country in the world. Thus, isolation from the outside world and crowding inside the country have contributed to making the Japanese into a tightly knit, organized society that places a high value on obedience, cooperation, and interpersonal and group harmony, and which abhors the independence, equality, and individuality that are so characteristic of American society.[8]

Within the outer circle—consisting of the Japanese social structure—lies an inner concentric circle consisting of the various social groups and institutions in Japanese society. These groups include the family and other organized groups such as business groups, labor unions, governmental agencies, political parties, consumer groups, and so on. The societal values that put a high premium on cooperation and collaboration encourage the social groups in the inner circle to work together in a collaborative mode for the good of Japanese society at large. It is precisely because of the high premium placed on collective behavior that one sees such a high degree of collaboration between the government, business firms, labor unions, and financial institutions in Japan. The objective of this collaboration is to fight against a common "enemy" of Japan, which in contemporary terms means the other nations of the world with whom Japan competes for world dominance.

One also sees this collaboration principle in almost all companies and in all industries in Japan. For example, the labor unions in Japan are not adversarial in nature as they are in the United States. Trade unions in the United States cut across company boundaries, while in Japan labor unions are predominantly company unions, with each company having its own separate labor union. In such a labor union, the loyalty of the members is to the company to which they belong and not to a union that transcends company boundaries. The objective of union leadership in Japan is to promote harmony in labor-management relations and to work things out amicably. Consequently, in Japan the number of man-days lost to strikes or labor unrest are minuscule compared to the number lost in the United States, which amount to thousands of man-days per year. The loyalty of the Japanese worker is to her or his group, and it also extends to the company, which is the larger group to which she or he belongs. In return, the company shows loyalty to its employees by treating them as members of a family, providing them with long-term and often life-long employment.

An enlightening example of the groupism concept is presented in Practical Insight 2-2. It refers to the tradition of enshrining deceased employees in a company memorial, a practice that is unheard of in the United States.

PRACTICAL INSIGHT 2-2

Japanese Companies Keep Employees Together—Even the Dearly Departed

OSAKA, Japan—One gray December day, the president of Asahi Breweries Co. secretly gave hundreds of employees the low-down on the firm's results. But none of them rushed to call their brokers. Where they are, they don't need brokers. Like tens of thousands of other loyal—and deceased—workers in Japan, the names of 673 Asahi employees have been enshrined at a company memorial after their deaths. On the rice-paper pages of a barley-color book, their names, job titles, tenures, and dates of death are meticulously kept by the company. Twice a year or so, Asahi's top executives show up at the two-year-old, 500 million yen ($3.6 million), winged black-marble shrine to install new names and appease their late colleagues' souls with detailed reports on the company's progress.

Common Consciousness

"Workers spend more than half their lives at the company, and we should return their commitment," says Asahi spokesman Naoki Izumiya. "One of the unique Japanese characteristics is a common consciousness. We want to preserve it."

And so, as if the exercising together each morning, laboring and drinking together into the night, and playing golf together on weekends weren't enough, more and more Japanese companies now offer their employees eternal corporate togetherness. In most cases, that means having your name included on a permanent record attached to a stone monument.

"It may look unusual to Americans that people belonging to different religions and backgrounds are enshrined in the same monument," says a spokesman for candy company Ezaki Glico Co., which has memorialized 88 employees. "But to be enshrined gives a feeling of relief to Japanese workers. Their spirits can be together always."

Employees seem to like the idea. A survey of a few dozen workers at Asahi's main brewery found that five out of six want to spend forever with their coworkers. "I want to leave a footnote showing that I existed in this company," says 28-year-old Kimito Kawamura.

Management experts say shrines foster loyalty. Malcolm Salter, a professor at Harvard University's graduate business school, visited Asahi's shrine and declares the sentiments it fosters "not phony at all." The practice of "honoring and remembering employees is part of the ongoing renewal of the company."

Companies don't expect employees' attitudes to change just because of a shrine. "We aren't expecting employees to appreciate the company for this," says Eiro Hamada, a personnel manager at Kubota Corp., an industrial group that has kept a shrine since 1952. "Our way of thinking is simply to tie what employees of the past have done to what employees today are doing. It is very Japanese."

Actually, it is very Kansai, the region around Osaka. Companies in Tokyo and elsewhere in Japan sometimes help employees' families arrange burial plots. But few have company shrines. The Kansai companies that do pay up to $5 million for them, and memorial services cost as much as $100,000 each year. That may be one reason it's mainly companies with strong earnings, such as Asahi, who keep the shrines. Unlike Asahi, most Japanese companies in this area keep their memorials in Koyasan, a 1,000-year-old Buddhist mission in the lush, steep mountains outside Osaka.

A stroll among the graceful stone memorials is like a walk through an industrial park. There, under the towering Japanese cedars, Matsushita Electric Industrial Co. remembers thousands of its late employees in a rough-hewn granite temple. Embossed on a polished, black-marble slab is a testament to hundreds of Sharp Corp.'s workers. A bronze statue of two uniformed workers marks Nissan Motor Co.'s memorial. Komatsu Ltd., the heavy-equipment maker, is just up the path from a temple to the World War II infantrymen who died in Japan's North Borneo campaign.

Lavish Designs

What sets the corporate memorials apart from the more traditional temples are their expansive, sometimes lavish, designs. Kirin Brewery Co. boldly displays its trademark mascot, a stylized, mythical animal. And one small technology company's shrine boasts a space rocket. Most peculiarly Japanese of all are the squat stone or wood boxes at the shrine entrances. They are for depositing business cards, meishi in Japanese. "Companies with business relationships will put their meishi in to show that they are thinking of their old business connections," says Taiei Gotoh, a dark-robed, 31-year-old Buddhist priest.

As the local authority on company shrines, Mr. Gotoh also is knowledgeable on recent Japanese corporate history. He remembers, for example, that Matsushita bought a rival refrigerator maker in 1973, because that's when Matsushita took over the smaller company's shrine. He knows how companies are doing because he sits in on the sort of corporate updates that Asahi's president delivers.

Source: Marcus W. Brauchli, *Wall Street Journal,* July 10, 1989, A6. Reprinted by permission of The Wall Street Journal, 1989, Dow Jones & Company, Inc. All Rights Reserved Worldwide.

Informality

The American culture is not one that attaches a great deal of importance to tradition, ceremony, and social rules. This informality has caused serious problems for businesses operating in other cultures. Latin American countries, for example, are extreme cases of a formal society. The Latin American likes pomp and circumstance and is quite at ease with it. He or she likes lavish public receptions and processions and would expect that an outsider would carefully observe all the amenities of personal etiquette and hospitality. An American, when immersed in a culture like this, is likely to feel ill at ease; she or he must take special precautions to avoid appearing blatantly casual and informal in words and deeds in order not to offend the Latin hosts.

Another value related to informality is the American inclination not to "beat around the bush"; to get to the point of the matter in business meetings and conversations. In Saudi Arabia or Latin American countries, however, it is customary to converse first about unrelated matters before embarking on the business discussions for which the meeting was arranged. An American should realize that people of other cultures often feel it is important to get to know one another and develop mutual trust before getting down to business negotiations or problems. Barging straight into the business issue, without the informal small talk at the beginning, may make a Saudi Arabian or Latin American so uncomfortable that the American who insists on such an approach may very well not get what he or she came for.

Materialism

The United States has been blessed with abundant natural resources, a fact which seems to have made Americans, in the eyes of foreigners, wasteful in their consumption of both resources and material goods. Visiting foreigners are often astonished to see cars less than 10 years old heaped in junkyards. These cars would probably still be on the road in most countries because other cultures seem more inclined to foster an awareness of the need for conserving resources and preserving material goods. The more wasteful American attitude has been said to arise from the American Frontier philosophy that humans are the masters of nature and should therefore conquer, change, and control nature for the benefit of humankind. This philosophy is at total variance with the philosophies of the people of India, Korea, and Egypt. In India and Korea, worship of nature is part of the religious dogma. And even for persons for whom religion is not the significant determinant of behavior, the river Ganges in India and the Nile in Egypt are revered for their power over the economic and physical well-being of the people. An American must strive to be aware of the differences between her or his own attitude toward nature and those of other cultures. All of us should be careful not to judge other cultures on the basis of the quality or quantity of physical goods present in daily life.

There is also a tendency in Western cultures to attach status to certain physical objects, such as a suit made by a famous clothing manufacturer or a recent-model car. Many nonWestern cultures foster no interest in acquiring such symbols; rather, the emphasis is on finding and enjoying aesthetic and spiritual values. An understanding of these differences in values is important for the international manager, because behavior that may seem strange to an American may be the necessary expression of fundamental values held by a person from a different culture.

Change

Societies differ in their attitudes toward change and progress. Although change is inevitable, nonWestern people look upon change as a phenomenon that occurs naturally and as part of the overall evolution of humans and their universe. Change in such societies is accepted, but passively, without any deliberate effort to bring it about. The people in Western societies, however, feel that the future is not predestined and that humans, by actions and deeds, are capable of manipulating the environment in which they shall live in the future and of changing it to their liking.

These differences in attitudes toward change may account for the often fatalistic attitude of nonWestern people, and their passivity may be partially responsible for the difficulties encountered by Western managers and technicians when introducing innovations into nonWestern societies.

Time Orientation

Time can be considered a communication system, as are words or languages. Like different spoken languages, the languages of time are also different. These so-called unspoken languages "are informal, yet the rules governing their interpretation are surprisingly ironbound."[9] Western cultures, and particularly the American, perceive time as a resource—and an extremely scarce one that is continuously depleting. Americans, therefore, emphasize the efficient use of time. Phrases such as *time is money*, *time never comes back*, and *time is the enemy* are often used to promote the effective use of time. This orientation is due to the Western belief that there is a limited amount of total time available to a person—that which he or she has from birth to death—and, therefore, one should make the most of it. This perception of time has made Americans conscious of the need for establishing deadlines for work to be done and to stick to them. It also accounts for Americans being very fastidious about making and keeping appointments.

In contrast, Eastern cultures view time as an unlimited and unending resource. For a Hindu, time does not begin at birth or end at death. Belief in reincarnation gives life a nontemporal dimension. Time is perceived to be an inexhaustible resource. This attitude towards time makes people in Eastern cultures quite casual about keeping appointments and deadlines, an indifference which makes Americans dealing with them very anxious and frustrated.

The rather cavalier Eastern attitude toward time is illustrated in the following incident:

> In comparing the United States with Iran and Afghanistan, very great differences in the handling of time appear. The American attitude toward appointments is an example. Once while in Teheran I had an opportunity to observe some young Iranians making plans for a party. After plans were made to pick up everyone at appointed times and places, everything began to fall apart. People would leave messages that they were unable to take so-and-so or were going somewhere else, knowing full well that the person who had been given the message couldn't possibly deliver it. One girl

was left stranded on a street corner, and no one seemed to be concerned about it. One of my informants explained that he himself had many similar experiences. Once he had made eleven appointments to see a friend. Each time one of them failed to show up. The twelfth time they swore they would both be there; that nothing would interfere. The friend failed to arrive. After waiting forty-five minutes, my informant phoned his friend and found him still at home. The following conversation is an approximation of what took place: "Is that you, Abdul?" "Yes." "Why aren't you here? I thought we were to meet for sure." "Oh, but it was raining," said Abdul with a sort of whining intonation.[10]

In the United States, the time spent waiting outside a person's office beyond the appointed time is seen as a measure of the importance of the person kept waiting. Americans therefore get very upset if they are kept waiting for thirty minutes or more and consider this to be a personal affront. In the Middle East there is no such interpretation; a businessperson may keep a visitor waiting for a long time, but once the businessperson does see the visitor, the interview will last as long as may be necessary to complete the business at hand. But this approach means that the businessperson is likely to keep the next visitor waiting for hours, too.

There are many more value orientations in which the American and Western cultures differ from nonWestern cultures. The scope of this chapter does not permit the discussion of every one of them. However, the purpose of the preceding discussion of value orientations was to point out that differences in behavior are due to differences in the value orientations of societies.

PROBLEMS CAUSED BY CULTURAL DIFFERENCES

We have seen that the international manager can face, or cause, many problems in a foreign host country because of cultural differences. This section gives a few examples of problems created by cultural insensitivity. One such example follows:

Some years ago, in 1946, an agricultural extension worker introduced a new type of hybrid maize into a community of Spanish American farmers in New Mexico. He was already well known and liked. He was able to demonstrate that the new seed yielded three times as much as the seed the farmers normally planted, and he was certain that he was doing right in persuading them to grow it. They followed his advice, but within three years they had nearly all gone back to growing their old low-yielding variety.

This sounds almost incredible, but it can be explained quite simply. The farmers ate the maize they grew. They ground it into flour and with the flour their wives made tortillas, the flat round cakes that formed the staple of their diet. But the new type of maize gave a flavor to the cakes the people did not like. The people valued the high yield but did not like the price they had to pay in taste, and the innovation failed because the agency had overlooked the need to test for taste as well as yield before the seed was given to the farmers.[11]

The preceding example shows the influence of cultural preferences and the difficulties we can encounter if we assume that others have the same tastes as we do or the same priorities.

The following incident shows the impact of the differences in time orientation. In Western societies, one can suffer severe penalties for not completing work on time and enjoy significant rewards for meeting work schedules and deadlines. The Western worker feels that he or she is duty bound to keep promises and believes that her or his reputation will be tarnished for failure to deliver on time. When two persons involved in a business transaction have two totally opposite orientations toward time schedules, a lot of difficulty will result; the following is an example:

> The Middle Eastern peoples are a case in point. Not only is our idea of time schedules no part of Arab life but the mere mention of a deadline to an Arab is like waving a red flag in front of a bull. In his culture, your emphasis on a deadline has the emotional effect on him that his backing you into a corner and threatening you with a club would have on you.

One effect of this conflict of unconscious habit patterns is that hundreds of American-owned radio sets are lying on the shelves of Arab radio repair shops, untouched. The Americans made the serious cross-cultural error of asking to have the repair completed by a certain time.

How do you cope with this? How does the Arab get another Arab to do anything? Every culture has its own ways of bringing pressure to get results. The usual Arab way is one which Americans avoid as "bad manners." It is needling.

An Arab businessman whose car broke down explained it this way:

> First, I go to the garage and tell the mechanic what is wrong with my car. I wouldn't want to give him the idea that I didn't know. After that, I leave the car and walk around the block. When I come back to the garage, I ask him if he has started to work yet. On my way home for lunch I stop in and ask him how things are

going. When I go back to the office I stop by again. In the evening, I return and peer over his shoulder for awhile. If I didn't keep this up, he'd be off working on someone else's car. If you haven't been needled by an Arab, you just haven't been needled.[12]

Language can also pose a problem for international managers. And the problem with language is not just with having to learn a new vocabulary. Many international managers have learned from experience that one word or idiom may have a different meaning and implication in another culture that uses the same language. For instance, in England the word *homely* means friendly, warm, and comfortable; in the United States it means plain, or even ugly. Similarly, the phrase *come any time* can have different interpretations:

Visiting time involves the question of who sets the time for a visit. George Coelho, a social psychologist from India, gives an illustrative case. A U.S. businessman received this invitation from an Indian businessman: "Won't you and your family come and see us? Come any time." Several weeks later, the Indian repeated the invitation in the same words. Each time the American replied that he would certainly like to drop in, but he never did. The reason is obvious in terms of our culture. Here, *come any time* is just an expression of friendliness. You are not really expected to show up unless your host proposes a specific time. In India, on the contrary, the words are meant literally that the host is putting himself at the disposal of his guest and really expects him to come. It is the essence of politeness to leave it to the guest to set a time at his convenience. If the guest never comes, the Indian naturally assumes that he does not want to come. Such a misunderstanding can lead to a serious rift between people who are trying to do business with each other.[13]

American brand names can also take on strange meanings when translated into a foreign language. American Motors' Matador became *killer* in Spanish. Ford's problems with the Spanish language are also well known. Its low-cost truck Fiera, when translated into the Spanish language, meant *ugly old woman*. Similarly, Fresca soft drinks in Mexico did not do too well; there the word is slang for *lesbian*. And the famous Pepsi-Cola slogan *Come alive with Pepsi* was translated in Germany as *Come out of the grave* and in Taiwan as *Bring your ancestors back from the dead*. More recently, Goodyear expanded its Servitekar tire specialty stores from Indonesia and Malaysia into Japan, and found customers snickering. It seems that the word means *rusty car* when pronounced in Japanese.[14]

The experience of Federal Express when it first entered the European market illustrates the problems that ethnocentric attitudes can create for global companies. Federal encountered serious problems breaking into the European market partly because it had not done its homework regarding how people there live and work. For instance, all company brochures, promotional material, and shipping bills were in English. And to keep arrival times constant, package pickup deadlines were set for 5:00 p.m. even though the Spanish, for example, work as late as 8:00 p.m. Federal had assumed that life-styles and work schedules were the same in Europe as in the United States, and that was a big mistake.[15]

Cross-national joint ventures, mergers, and acquisitions are being forged with increasing frequency in today's global economy. One sees such "marriages" between companies from diverse cultures when, for example, a Japanese company forms an alliance with an American company. Sometimes such alliances between companies having quite different cultures can cause problems when executives from the companies involved begin to work in teams. A good illustration of this point is the acquisition of the American company, Firestone Tire & Rubber Company, by the Japanese tire giant, Bridgestone Corporation. Cultural differences between the Japanese and American managers, especially regarding language and the difficulties in adjusting to two different styles of work, caused major problems. The Japanese, who are used to working until 9:00 p.m., could not understand why the Americans would not stay that late, and the Americans could not get used to Japanese arrangements, such as open offices and desks facing each other.[16] In the American culture, it is generally expected that when a manager asks her or his subordinate if a task could be completed by a certain date, the latter will say yes or no and give the reasons why if the answer is no. But once the subordinate has agreed to complete the task on time, she or he is expected to abide by the promise. Western society emphasizes the value of truthfulness in interpersonal behavior.

However, in Japan or India a person is likely to make a promise to do something while knowing quite well that it cannot be kept. The reluctance to say no to a request is due to the person's reluctance to displease someone with a negative answer, and also to save the embarrassment of having to admit that one is incapable of doing what he or she has been asked to do. The following incident illustrates this phenomenon and the problems that it can create for a Western businessperson:

> An American businessman would be most unlikely to question another businessman's word if he were technically qualified and said that his plant could produce 1000 gross of widgets a

month. We are "taught" that it is none of our business to inquire too deeply into the details of his production system. This would be prying and might be considered an attempt to steal his operational plans.

Yet this cultural pattern has trapped many an American into believing that when a Japanese manufacturer answered a direct question with the reply that he could produce 1000 gross of widgets, he meant what he said. If the American had been escorted through the factory and saw quite clearly that its capacity was, at the most, perhaps 500 gross of widgets per month, he would be likely to say to himself, "Well, this fellow probably has a brother-in-law. Besides, what business is it of mine, so long as he meets the schedule?"

The cables begin to burn after the American returns home and only 500 gross of widgets arrive each month. What the American did not know was that in Japanese culture one avoids the direct question unless the questioner is absolutely certain that the answer will not embarrass the Japanese businessman in any way whatsoever. In Japan, for one to admit being unable to perform a given operation or measure up to a given standard means a bitter loss of face. Given a foreigner who is so stupid, ignorant, or insensitive as to ask an embarrassing question, the Japanese is likely to choose what appears to him the lesser of two evils. Americans caught in this cross-cultural communications trap are apt to feel doubly deceived because the Japanese manufacturer may well be an established and respected member of the business community. [17]

The war against Iraq in 1991 involved many American soldiers in the Allied effort to drive Saddam Hussein out of Kuwait. Most foreign troops in the Allied effort were stationed in Saudi Arabia. Saudi Arabia is a very conservative Islamic country. Some of the holiest places of Islam are in Saudi Arabia. In fact, the Koran is the constitution of Saudi Arabia. It is as if the Bible were the Constitution of the United States. Many forms of behavior which would be considered quite normal in Western cultures are totally unacceptable in Saudi Arabia, such as the displaying of affection between the sexes in public, displaying the sole of one's shoe while crossing one's legs, dancing in public, driving by women in public, and the exposing by women of their legs, neck, and arms. Consequently, American soldiers in Saudi Arabia were given a crash course in the etiquette and social customs of that country. An illustration of the cultural background training which was given to American soldiers is illustrated in Practical Insight 2-3.

PRACTICAL INSIGHT 2-3

In Preparation for Joint Saudi-U.S. Exercises, Marines Get the Word on Kisses and Crucifixes

NORTHERN SAUDI ARABIA—Silver crucifixes gleaming on the collar of his camouflage fatigues, Chaplain Stan Scott paces the sand before a group of U.S. Marines. The men, squatting in the sun with their M-16's beside them, listen raptly as the chaplain gives what he calls "a down and dirty on 2,000 years of history." In just over an hour, his talk sweeps from the caravans of ancient Arabia to the contemporary mores of Saudi society. Topics include table manners ("If you've had enough coffee, wiggle your cup. Don't put your hand over it or he'll just keep pouring and you'll end up with a burned hand"), women's veils ("You may see it as a bummer but for them there's prestige that goes with it"), and dissatisfaction with colonially drawn borders ("The Arabs do have some gripes out here").

Too Close for Comfort

To show how Arab men traditionally greet their friends, he hauls a burly Marine out of the front row, kisses him three times on the cheek and locks him in a tight embrace. "You feeling comfortable now?" he asks. The Marine's eyes roll in embarrassment. "We have a bubble of privacy," he says. "The Saudis don't have that. Male embracing and hand-holding don't have sexual overtones. Don't impose on this culture your indicators of homosexuality."

Chaplain Scott is giving this talk because these troops, the weapons company of the First Battalion, Third Marine Regiment, are about to move north for five days of combined training with Saudi forces. Three months into the Gulf crisis, such exercises are still extremely rare among ground forces. Most U.S. troops have yet to meet a Saudi. With Arab forces—mostly Saudis, with some Egyptians, Kuwaitis, Moroccans and Syrians—stationed close to the northern border, chances are that in an initial battle some would have to pass through U.S. lines. Confusion, as U.S. troops tried to tell Arab allies from enemies, could cost lives. "So far, U.S. Marines have had some limited training with Saudi marines and national guardsmen," says Brig. Gen. Thomas Draude, assistant division commander. "But combined training has taken a back seat so far in the rush to get U.S. troops deployed."

"The Saudis are very patient about organizing combined exercises," says Capt. Michael Callaghan, whose troops are taking part in this week's training. "We don't want to rush into anything overambitious and offend their sensibilities."

Mistaken Intentions

The few U.S. troops who have so far met Saudis have found that that's quite easy to do. One Marine private recently shared guard duty with a Saudi soldier. Touched by the Saudi's generosity in sharing his food and water, the Marine tried to reciprocate by showing him a magazine with a picture of a woman in a bathing suit. "He said 'no, no' and looked real embarrassed," the Marine recalls.

The chaplain's briefing is meant to head off such misunderstandings. To explain the Saudis' approach to women, the chaplain tells an anecdote from his earlier tour of duty in the country between 1979 and 1982. His wife, he said, would get offended when the landlord would come with workmen to fix something in the apartment and pass by her at the door without speaking.

"She'd tell me when I got home, 'That son of a gun can't even be polite enough to say good morning.'" In fact, Chaplain Scott explains to the troops, the landlord was being very polite by not presuming to invade her privacy by speaking to her without her husband present. "He was honoring her the best way he knew how."

As a further gesture to Saudi sensitivities, the company has checked its prepacked meal rations to be sure that no pork or ham entrees are included in supplies being taken north.

But a few Marines think all this sensitivity is too much. Michael Austin, a 25-year-old corporal from Elgin, Ill., asks why Marines were told not to wear crucifixes. "I don't see how any man should be asked to hide his faith," he says.

Chaplain Scott explains that Marines can wear their crosses so long as they wear them under their T-shirts. He adds that Saudis adhere to an especially strict branch of Islam and feel special responsibilities as custodians of Islam's two holiest mosques in Mecca and Medina.

"The concessions that this country has made to allow me to be here are phenomenal," says the chaplain, who wasn't permitted to wear his crosses on his uniform nor to openly identify himself as a clergyman on previous visits to Saudi Arabia. "You might not see it," he tells the troops, "but I see it as a tremendous step forward in religious dialogue."

Source: Geraldine Brooks, *Wall Street Journal,* October 10, 1990, A16. Reprinted by permission of The Wall Street Journal, 1990, Dow Jones & Company, Inc. All Rights Reserved Worldwide.

ANALYZING CULTURAL DIFFERENCES

An international manager needs a conceptual scheme to analyze cultural differences between his native culture and the foreign culture.

An approach that may be useful in identifying the various dimensions along which cultural differences could be measured is one developed by Geert Hofstede,[18] who undertook an enormous questionnaire survey of 117,000 IBM employees in 88 countries. His study found that national cultures can be differentiated along four major dimensions:

1. Individualism/Collectivism
2. Masculinity/Femininity
3. Power Distance
4. Uncertainty Avoidance

A fifth dimension, called "Confucian Dynamism," was identified by Michael H. Bond.

Individualism/Collectivism

Individualism exists when people look at themselves primarily as individuals and secondarily as members of groups. Self-interest motivates behavior, and everyone is expected to look after themselves and their immediate families. *Collectivism* is the opposite of individualism. In collectivist societies, people see themselves primarily as members of groups and secondarily as individuals. The group (family, clan, tribe, organization, social club) is the main determinant of individual beliefs and values. The United States is supposed to have an individualistic culture, whereas Japan is said to have a collectivist culture.

Masculinity/Femininity

Masculine cultures emphasize assertiveness and the acquisition of money and things as opposed to a concern for people. *Feminine* cultures have dominant values that emphasize concern for others and relationships with people. Masculine cultures, like macho men, are supposed to be tough and assertive. Feminine cultures, like tender females, are supposed to be gentle and caring of the feelings of others and with the quality of life. Masculine societies define gender roles more rigidly than do feminine societies; e.g., feminine societies would be far more accepting than masculine societies of women driving trucks and of men as nurses or ballet dancers. Japan, Mexico, and Italy scored high on the masculinity scale in Hofstede's study, with Japan scoring the highest points. Norway, Finland, Sweden, and Denmark scored high on the femininity scale.

Power Distance

Power distance is a measure of the extent to which those who have less power in society accept that power is distributed unequally among members of the society, and therefore some members of the society have the "right" to have more power than others. For example, in high power distance countries like India, Mexico, and Brazil, employees accept the concept that the boss must be obeyed because he/she is the boss with the right to issue orders. In contrast, in low power distance countries like the United States, Australia, and Denmark, employees would tend to obey the boss only if they believe that he/she has the competence to make the right decisions, or that the boss' way is the right way to get things done.

Uncertainty Avoidance

Uncertainty avoidance measures the extent to which a culture programs its members to feel either uncomfortable or comfortable in unstructured situations. People in high uncertainty avoidance cultures feel threatened by risky, uncertain, or unknown situations. Uncertainty-avoiding cultures try to minimize the possibility of such situations by establishing strict laws and rules, high degrees of formalization, and intolerance of behaviors and opinions that differ from their own. Countries like Japan, Argentina, Italy, and Israel scored high on the uncertainty avoidance scale in Hofstede's study. Countries scoring low on this dimension included the United States, Great Britain, Sweden, and Denmark.

Confucian Dynamism

Michael Bond, of the Chinese University of Hong Kong, has identified a new, fifth cultural dimension which he calls Confucian dynamism, which was not identified by Hofstede in his IBM study. Bond identified this cultural dimension in his Chinese Value Survey that was administered to 50 male and 50 female students in a variety of disciplines in each of 22 countries selected from all five continents.[19]

"*Confucian dynamism* is an acceptance of the legitimacy of hierarchy the valuing of perseverance and thrift, all without undue emphasis on tradition and social obligations which could impede business initiative."[20] The study showed that four of the Five Dragons—Hong Kong, Taiwan, Japan, and South Korea—scored the top positions on the Confucian dynamism scale. Brazil, India, Thailand, and Singapore got the next highest scores. The Netherlands, Sweden and West Germany took the middle positions. The English-speaking countries of Australia, New Zealand, the United States, Britain, and Canada scored on the lower end, as did Zimbabwe, Nigeria, the Philippines, and Pakistan scored on the lower end.[21]

A very intriguing finding of the study was the relationship between the prevalence of Confucian dynamism in the culture of a country and its economic growth. Employing two samples of 18 and 20 countries and economic growth data for the periods 1965-80 and 1980-87, the results of the study showed that Confucian dynamism was the most consistent explanatory power for most of the differences in national economic growth rates. Confucian dynamism appears to explain the relative success of the East Asian economies like Hong Kong, Taiwan, Japan, and South Korea.

Managerial Implications of Cultural Dimensions

One would expect many consequences for management practices resulting from cultural differences along Hofstede's four dimensions discussed above. For instance, in high power distance countries a leader characterized as a benevolent autocrat would be most effective, whereas in low power distance countries a leader who is people-oriented and participative in his leadership style would be most effective.

In countries that are high on individualism, the most appropriate reward system would reward individuals for their own performance (as opposed to group performance). Competition between individuals for monetary and nonmonetary rewards such as status and promotions would be encouraged. In collectivist societies, rewards to individuals based upon the performance of their group would be most appropriate. Yearly bonuses based upon the profitability of the whole company, or divisional profits, are illustrative of group performance-based rewards.

Countries characterized by masculine cultures expect women to play certain roles, such as staying home and taking care of the children, or working as nurses or secretaries. Japan, which has a masculine culture, has the reputation for a very low "glass ceiling" for women. It is not uncommon in Japan to see women get fired because of marriage. And women in Japan are not expected to assume responsible managerial positions at any time. Similar conditions exist in Italy and Mexico, both of which are known for their "macho" men. In feminine cultures like Sweden, Finland, Norway, and Denmark, women have equal status with men. This is reflected in the societal expectation that women should work, and businesses are required to make this easier for women by providing both men and women with paid paternity or maternity leave to take care of newborn children.

In high uncertainty avoidance cultures, one finds organizations that have clearly formulated rules and procedures which reduce uncertainty with regard to what should be done in certain circumstances or what is acceptable or unacceptable behavior, and so on. People in such cultures appreciate stability and the certainty that accompanies it. Hence, one finds that in such cultures people do not change jobs readily, but prefer to stay with a company for their entire careers. This is typical of Japan and Italy, which are high uncertainty avoidance countries. Low uncertainty avoidance countries, such as the United States and Great Britain, favor organizations that provide managers with freedom to take prudent risks. These countries are also known for very high rates of job mobility.

Another approach to understand cultural differences is that which has been developed by Herskovits.[23] He lists five dimensions of culture:

1. Material Culture
2. Social Institutions
3. Man and the Universe
4. Aesthetics
5. Language

Material Culture

Material culture affects the level of demand for goods and the quality and types of products demanded. It is composed of two aspects:

technology and economics. Technology refers to the techniques used to produce material goods, as well as the technical know-how of a country. Economics can be described as the manner in which a culture makes use of its capabilities, and the resulting benefits. A multinational company involved in selling electrical appliances, for example, should analyze the material culture of the proposed foreign market. For instance, a firm may be able to sell microwave ovens in England and France but will find few buyers in New Guinea. It would be good to be able to anticipate that outcome by understanding the material cultures of the three nations.

Social Institutions

Social institutions—whether they be of a business, political, family, or social-class nature—influence the behavior of individuals. An American in Japan, for example, must recognize that in Japan social institutions favor a paternalistic leadership style and decision making that is by nature participative and consensus oriented. In India, a fair amount of nepotism is a feature of the joint-family system.

Man and the Universe

This dimension is composed of the elements of religion and superstitions, both of which have a profound impact on the value and belief systems of individuals. Making light of superstitions when doing business with other cultures may prove to be an expensive mistake. In parts of Asia, for example, ghosts, fortune telling, palmistry and soothsayers are all integral parts of the culture and must be understood as being influential in people's lives and in business dealings as well.

In the United States and many Western countries, the owl is a symbol of wisdom. Temple University in Philadelphia has an owl as its mascot. Temple University has several campuses abroad in places like Tokyo, London, and Rome. Should Temple decide to open yet another campus in Bombay, India, it may well have to change its mascot, at least for its India campus, and in all of its advertisements and publications sent to India. In many parts of India the owl is looked upon as a symbol of death. Superstitions are quite pervasive in the Chinese culture as well. As you will see in Practical Insight 2-4, numbers have a very special meaning—good or bad—depending upon the particular number or combination of numbers being considered.

Aesthetics

This category includes the art, folklore, music, and drama of a culture. The aesthetics of a particular culture can be important in the interpretation of symbolic meanings of various artistic expressions. Failure to correctly interpret symbolic values can be problematic for multinational companies. For instance, folklore has established the owl as a symbol of bad luck in India, so clearly the owl should not be used in advertising.

Language

Of all the cultural elements that an international manager must study, language is probably the most difficult. One needs more than the ability to speak a language; one also needs the competency to recognize idiomatic interpretations that are quite different from those found in the dictionary. Thus, the international manager cannot take for granted that he or she is always communicating effectively in another language. Small nuances of the local tongue may elude a foreigner who has not been immersed in the foreign culture for a long time.

PRACTICAL INSIGHT 2-4

By the Numbers
Superstition Is Bottom Line for Some Chinese

Emblazoned in three-foot-high characters on the side of a medical office building in Monterey Park are the numbers 941-943. The numbers are merely the building's address, but when the numerals 9, 4, 1, 3 are pronounced in Mandarin or Cantonese dialects, they sound like a common Chinese saying: "Nine die; one lives." "It means the possibility of surviving is almost zero," said one real estate agent, shaking his head in disbelief. "Imagine a medical building with that number? I won't even mention the property to a client."

Now consider the BMW 528e, that trendy symbol of the American yuppie. In Cantonese, the model number is easily recognizable as the phrase: "Not easy to prosper." The first two digits of the Volvo 240 have the even more horrifying pronunciation: "Easy to die." "They're not popular cars" among Chinese, said Gregory Tse, owner of Wing On Realty in Monterey Park, the only city in the nation with a majority Asian population.

Such is the world of Chinese numerology, an amalgam of linguistic coincidences and age-old superstitions from the Far East that is exerting a quirky effect on American life in places where Asians have settled. The superstition has influenced choices on buying cars, selecting telephone numbers, picking lucky Lotto combinations, and even determining wedding dates.

But nowhere has it had a more far-reaching effect than in the world of commercial and residential real estate, especially in the San Gabriel Valley with its burgeoning Chinese population. Real estate agents say fear of the number four, which, when translated, sounds like the word "death," and the popularity of the number eight, which sounds like "prosperity," have become factors in the marketplace. Some deals have dangled in escrow waiting for a lucky date to close, prices have been determined by the number of eights in the final figure, and even hardened investors have become squeamish when a property has the number four in its address.

While many Chinese speakers are aware of the superstition, only some actually believe it.

Double Meaning Recognized

For example, in the Monterey Park building on 941-943 South Atlantic Boulevard, two of the eight offices are rented to Chinese. Yu Dafang, an acupuncturist who has an office in the building, said he recognized the double meaning of the address the minute he saw it, but decided it was unimportant. "At first, people said things, but not anymore," he said. "It's not polite."

Nonetheless, awareness about the effect of the superstition has spread to the point where even non-Chinese are now watching their numbers.

Last year, Toni Foster-Quiroz, president of Cosmic Escrow Corp., in Monterey Park, opened a new office on Garvey Avenue. One of the first things she did was pay the city $500 to change the building's address from 114 to 116 to remove the number four. "I don't believe it, but if it makes my clients feel better about coming here, it's OK with me," she said: "It gives us a little edge."

The key to the superstition lies in the tonal nature of Chinese in which one pronunciation can have many meanings depending on which tone is used. Mandarin, the dialect spoken by those from

Taiwan and parts of mainland China, has four tones. Cantonese, the dialect of Hong Kong and Guangdong province, has nine.

The Cantonese, by most accounts, are the main followers of the superstitions. In that dialect, every digit except seven and zero has a clear dual meaning. The number one is the same as "certainly," two is "easy," three is "life, birth or to do business," four is "death," five is "no or not," six is "happiness, wealth or continuous," eight is "prosperity," and nine is "long lasting."

The fascination with numbers is more extensive in Hong Kong, Taiwan, Singapore and other parts of Asia. In Singapore, properties are sometimes offered at a discount because of unlucky addresses and in Hong Kong, vehicle license plates with lucky numbers, which are competitively bid, can cost thousands of dollars to obtain.

The most notorious of the numbers is four, and some buildings such as the Bank of Trade building in Chinatown, have no fourth floor just because of the connotation of death. Woe be to the person with the address of 14, which sounds like the phrase: "certain death." The number 24 is a slight improvement, "easy to die." Watch out for 424, which in Mandarin is pronounced in the same way as "die and die again."

Just having four anywhere in an address can be unsettling. Three years ago, architect C. K. Moh bought a rental house in Monterey Park with the address 434. Moh said he was not worried about the address when he bought the property but later paid the city $500 to have it changed to 438 after he became involved in a lawsuit related to the property. "I don't really believe in it, but, well, I'm trying to avoid bad luck," he said. "I'm playing it safe."

City officials in Monterey Park report they receive two or three requests a month for address changes. The vast majority of applicants, who pay $500 for the service, are Chinese.

Arcadia gets about 40 requests a month, all of which are futile because the City Council about two years ago banned address changes, said Joseph Lopez, director of public works. "There was such a large volume of requests," Lopez said."If we made a change for every request, it would really create an intolerable work load."

Four can be lucky in certain combinations, such as the number 154, which sounds like the phrase: "No way to die." Likewise, the pronunciation of the number 148 closely resembles: "A lifetime of prosperity."

Eight is by far the most sought-after number, and the arrival of Aug. 8 last year—8/8/88—sparked a flurry of weddings, banquets and Lotto purchases in areas with large Chinese populations, such as San Francisco and Los Angeles.

The reputation of the number is such that some sales people have latched onto it as a gimmick to attract Chinese buyers. Georgene Neely, a San Marino real estate agent, said she has noticed in recent years that more home sellers are using the number in asking prices, such as a house that was recently on the market for $988,000. "It's an obvious ploy to appeal to the foreign buyer," she said, adding that she views the practice as unprofessional. Neely said buyers also have asked to add the number eight to real estate prices for good luck, such as a recent lease agreement involving several thousand dollars in which the tenant added $1.88 to the final figure.

But these digits are the easy cases. The meanings of other combinations can be open to a wide range of interpretation. Numbers that sound one way in one dialect also can sound entirely different in another.

Take the number 169. Mandarin speakers would shrug their shoulders, but to a Cantonese, "It's one of the worst numbers you can have," said Valiant Chiu, the head of Garfield Realty in Monterey Park. The number is pronounced like an obscene slang term.

How much effect all this really has on business is uncertain. Richard Brooks, spokesman for BMW of North America Inc., said he was unaware of the meaning of the BMW 528e, which coincidentally was discontinued last year. But George Sarrade, sales manager of Century Motor Sales, a major BMW dealership in Alhambra, said he has noticed that the dealership has sold few 528e models to Chinese. "Son of a gun," he said. "It might have something to do with that."

Most real estate agents say superstition's power to affect the market has been blown way out of proportion. Jimmy Shen, manager of Huntington Realty in San Marino, said a good house at a good price will always sell no matter how bad the number. Shen, for example, lives in a house with the street number 404. "It's been a lucky number for me," he said. "I don't even care. This is America."

Tse of Wing On Realty agreed that the superstition plays only a small role in business. "It's minor," he said. To prove his point,

Tse mentions the recent sale of a house with the street number 664—a terribly inauspicious number that sounds like the phrase: "continuous death." "We just cleared escrow on the house," he said. Only later does he explain that the sale to a Chinese family was contingent on changing the address from 664 to 662, which means "always easy."

Number Superstitions

In various Chinese dialects, some numbers sound like threatening phrases. Houses with such numbers may be considered unlucky, cars with such numbers may be shunned. On the other hand, the number 8 sounds lucky. Here are a few numbers and their "translations" in Chinese Superstitions.

In English	In a Chinese Dialect
9,4,1,3	"nine die; one lives"
(BMW)528	"not easy to prosper"
4	"death"
8	"prosperity"
14	"certain death"
424	"die and die again"
154	"no way to die"
148	"a lifetime of prosperity"
664	"continuous death"

Source:　Ashley Dunn, *Los Angeles Times*, May 28, 1989, 12,19.

Religion

To the list compiled by Herskovits we could add one more category—religion. We saw that religion can reasonably be considered a part of the man-and-the-universe dimension, but it could well be a dimension by itself, especially in cultures in which religion is a central, organizational feature. Religion in such societies has a profound effect on how business is conducted.

For example, international hotel chains in Israel must make sure their business practices conform with the Jewish religious beliefs. Not doing so means risking the loss of rabbinical sanction and, eventually, customers. Hence, on the Jewish Sabbath they program elevators to stop automatically at designated floors so that guests do not have to violate religious prescriptions against pressing the buttons themselves. Rabbinical supervisors inspect their kitchens. And their room service staff will refuse to deliver milk and meat on the same plate or on the same order, even if they are for different guests, because Jewish religious laws prohibit the mixing of dairy products and meat.[24]

Consumption of pork is forbidden by law in Islam and Judaism. Therefore, companies are not able to market hot dogs and sausages containing pork as one of the ingredients in countries where those religions are practiced. Instead, all-beef hot dogs and sausages, and beef bacon already marketed in the United States and Europe to serve the needs of Jewish customers, would have to be introduced in Islamic countries of the Middle East, such as Saudi Arabia, Iraq, and Iran, and in the Southeast Asian countries of Indonesia and Malaysia.

Practical Insight 2-5 discusses problems that fast-food chains like McDonald's have encountered in Israel and India due to religion-based dietary restrictions.

PRACTICAL INSIGHT 2-5

Are You ready For Kosher Hamburgers, Or Burgers Without Beef?

Omri Padan owned a successful chain of clothing stores. But he has given that up just so that he could start a chain of McDonald's hamburger restaurants in his native land. After all, who does not like McDonald's hamburgers. Mr. Padan owns the McDonald's franchise in Israel and he wants to make the "golden arches" a mammoth success in the holy land.

But there looms on the horizon what could be a potentially big problem—should McDonald's sell kosher or non-kosher hamburgers in the Jewish State? "And what exactly does kosher mean?" is a quandary for Mr. Padan. Because of the sensitivity of the issue, McDonald's executives in Oak Park, Illinois would rather not talk about it, which will not help Mr. Padan. Mr. Padan is aware that even large segments of the Israeli population who are not Orthodox believers prefer that their food be prepared according to Jewish dietary laws. Of course he knows that Jewish dietary laws do not allow mixing meat and dairy products like milk and cheese, but the term "kosher" has many different interpretations amongst the Israelis. He will therefore conduct surveys to learn how, exactly, Israel's 4.1 million Jews define "kosher."

Mr. Padan knows that his McDonald's restaurants are not obligated to serve kosher fare. There are many nonkosher restaurants across Israel. He has watched Wendy's and Wimpy's chains enter Israel and serve kosher food, and neither has proven to be a huge success. But Mr. Padan is a pragmatic businessman who wants to succeed. He wants his cheeseburgers and milk shakes to be the fast-food of choice of all Israelis. And so ultimately his decision will be a business decision. However, Israeli consumers and potential competitors are watching how he and McDonald's, with its dominant global profile in the fast-foods business, balance the perhaps conflicting demands of religious precepts and business imperatives.

McDonald's In India

The problem for McDonald's in India, as in Israel, is the dietary imperatives imposed by religious beliefs. The Indian Government has given McDonald's permission to open 20 restaurants throughout the country. McDonald's is eager to do well in a country of 850 million people and a middle class population that is larger than that of the United States. However, there is a problem that McDonald's must face head-on. Four out of five Indians are Hindu and eat no beef. Can McDonald's make a beefless hamburger and still call it a Big Mac? It could look at the success of local competitors like Nirula's, which has 18 restaurants in New Delhi and three in Nepal. Nirula's is "India's McDonald's" says one customer who frequently patronizes the restaurant in busy Connaught Circus in the heart of New Delhi. "Look at their menu," he says. "They serve hamburgers, milk shakes, and cola, just like McDonald's in America." However, the hamburgers at Nirula's are made from ground mutton, not beef. And they are a lot more spicy than the bland version handed out in the typical McDonald's. "Indians like their food a bit more spicy than most Westerners," he says. And they like their hamburgers made of mutton, not beef, thank you!!!

Source: Adapted from Clyde Haberman, " Jerusalem Journal: Dishing Up Lunch for a Land That Isn't All Kosher," *New York Times*, April 16, 1993, A4, and personal observations and experiences of the author in India.

In Christian societies, Sunday is the day of rest, whereas in Islamic countries it is Friday, and in Israel it is Saturday. American executives working in Islamic countries experience a mild culture shock when they are forced to get dressed and go to work on Sunday. This was reported to have happened to many American expatriates who, while working on construction projects in Saudi Arabia, had to get used to violating their own religious precepts of not working on Sundays in order to abide by the religious norms of the host nation.

Islam forbids "excessive" profit, which is considered to be a form of exploitation. Islam preaches moderation and the sharing of wealth with others less fortunate, so individuals are held accountable for the well-being of the community. The concept of sharing wealth is manifested in one form called *zakat*, which is an annual tax of 2.5 percent collected from individuals and used for the benefit of the community. Islam also forbids usury; hence, banks in fundamentalist Islamic nations take equity in financing ventures, sharing profits as well as losses in the joint ventures. The prohibition of usury means that using credit as a marketing tool is not acceptable if the interest charged is deemed to be "excessive" by local standards. Companies operating in such cultures would have to create other forms of selling inducements for the customer, such as discounts for cash transactions and raising prices on products purchased on an installment basis. One would therefore suspect that credit-card companies like MasterCard and VISA, which charge high interest on unpaid balances, would have a difficult time in very orthodox Islamic countries.

Muslims are expected to pray facing the holy city of Mecca five times every day. Western companies in Islamic countries must be aware of this religious ritual and make the necessary adjustments that would allow employees to stop working during prayer time. It is not considered unusual in Saudi Arabia and in contemporary Iran for managers and workers to put a carpet on the floor and kneel to pray several times during a typical work day. Therefore work schedules, meeting times, and sales calls must be planned accordingly. The impact of fundamentalist Islamic concepts and culture on marketing in Islamic countries is so significant that it is worthwhile to look at it in greater detail. Exhibit 2-1 shows how some elements of the institutionalized Islam religion affect international marketing.

SUMMARY

In this chapter we focused on the cultural environment of international management. Culture was defined as "that complex whole which includes knowledge, belief, art, morals, customs, and any other capabilities and habits acquired by man as a member of society." It has been emphasized throughout the chapter that most problems facing managers who live abroad are those arising from conflicts between the value orientations of different cultures.

Some specific values held by Americans which frequently conflict with those of peoples of other cultures were discussed: Individualism, informality, materialism, attitude toward change, and orientation toward the concept of time.   Next, we looked at several illustrations of problems caused by cultural differences.   Finally, we considered Hofstede's, and Herskovits' frameworks for analyzing cultural differences.

EXHIBIT 2-1 Marketing in an Islamic Culture

Elements	Implications for Marketing
Fundamental Islamic Concepts	
Unity. (Concept of centrality, oneness of God, harmony in life.)	Product standardization; mass techniques; central balance; unity in advertising copy and layout; strong brand loyalties; a smaller evoked size set; loyalty to company; opportunities for brand-extension strategies.
Legitimacy. (Fair dealings, reasonable level of profits.)	Less need for formal product warranties, greater need for institutional advertising and advocacy advertising, especially by foreign firms; a switch from profit maximizing to a profit satisfying strategy.
Zakaat. (2.5 percent per annum compulsory tax binding on all classified as "not poor.")	Use of "excessive" profits, if any, for charitable acts; corporate donations for charity; institutional advertising.
Usury. (Cannot charge interest on loans. A general interpretation of this law defines "excessive interest" charged on loans as not permissible.)	Avoid direct use of credit as a marketing tool; establish a consumer policy of paying cash for low-value products; for high-value products offer discounts for cash payments and raise prices of products on an installment basis; sometimes possible to conduct interest transactions between local/foreign firm in other non-Islamic countries; banks in some Islamic countries take equity in financing ventures, sharing resultant profits (and losses).
Supremacy of human life. (Compared to other forms of life and to objects, human life is of supreme importance.)	Pet food and products are less important; avoid use of statues and busts, which are interpreted as objects of idolatry; symbols in advertising and promotion should reflect high human values; use floral designs and artwork and advertising as a representation of aesthetic values.
Community. (All Muslims should strive to achieve universal brotherhood—with allegiance to the "one God." One way of expressing community is the required (if at all possible) pilgrimmage	Development of an "Islamic consumer," who is served with Islam-oriented products and services—for example, "kosher" meat packages, gifts exchanged at Muslim festivals, and so forth; development of community services; train persons in marketing or nonprofit organizations and skills.

(continued)

EXHIBIT 2-1   Continued

Elements	Implications for Marketing
Fundamental Islamic Concepts	
to Mecca for all Muslims, at least once in their lifetime.)	
Equality of peoples.	A participative communication system exists in Islam, especially with regard to abstinence: roles and authority structures may be rigidly defined but accessibility at any level is relatively easy. Market possibilities: products that are nutritious, cool, and digested easily can be formulated for Sehr and Iftar (beginning and end of the fast).
Abstinence. (During the month of Ramadan, Muslims are required to fast without food or drink from the first streak of dawn to sunset—as a reminder to those who are most fortunate to be kind to the less fortunate and as an exercise in self-control.)	
Consumption of alcohol and pork is forbidden, as is gambling.	Opportunities for developing nonalcoholic items and beverages (for example, soft drinks, ice cream, milk shakes, fruit juices) and nonchance social games, such as Scrabble; food products should use vegetable or beef shortening.
Environmentalism. (The universe created by God was pure. Consequently, the land, air, and water should be held as sacred elements.)	Anticipate environmental, antipollution laws; opportunities for companies involved in maintaining a clean environment; easier acceptance of pollution-control devices in the community (for example, recent efforts in Turkey have been well received by the local communities).
Worship. (Five times a day; timing of prayer varies.)	Need to take into account the variability and shift in prayer timings in planning sales calls, work schedules, business hours, customer traffic, and so forth.
Elements of Islamic Culture	

(continued)

78

Obligation to family and tribal traditions.	Importance of respected members in the family or tribe as opinion leaders; word-of-mouth communication, as well as customer referrals, may be critical; social or clan allegiances, affiliations, and associations may be possible surrogates for reference groups; advertising home-oriented products stressing family roles may be highly effective—for example, electronic games.
Obligation to parents is sacred.	Enhance the image of functional products with advertisements that stress parental advice or approval; even with children's products, there should be less emphasis on children as decision makers.
Obligation to extend hospitality to both insiders and outsiders.	Product designs that are symbols of hospitality, outwardly open in expression; rate of new product acceptance may be accelerated and eased by appeals based on community.
Obligations to conform to codes of sexual conduct and social interaction. These may include the following: 1. Modest dress for women in public.	More colorful clothing and accessories are worn by women at home, so promotion of products for use in private homes could be more intimate—such audiences could be reached effectively through women's magazines; avoid use of immodest exposure and sexual implications in public settings.
2. Separation of male and female audiences (in some cases).	Access to female consumers can often be gained only through women as selling agents, salespersons, catalogs, home demonstrations, and women's specialty shops.
Obligations to observe religious occasions. (For example, there are two major religious observances that are celebrated: Eid-ul-Fitr, Eid-ul-Adha.)	Purchase likely for these occasions—new shoes, clothing, sweets, and preparation of food items for family reunions, Muslim gatherings; there has been practice of giving money in place of gifts; increasingly, however, a shift is taking place to more gift giving; owing to use of lunar calendars, dates are not fixed.

Source: Adapted from Mushtaq Luqmani, Zahir A. Quraeshi, and Linda Delene, "Marketing in Islamic Countries: A Viewpoint," *MSU Business Topics,* Summer 1980, pp. 20-21.

QUESTIONS

1. Why should an international executive understand cultural differences?

2. Even though the United States has been described as a "melting pot," are there any significant differences in the observed behavior of ethnic groups (Italian, Irish, Asian, Polish, German) that can be attributed to cultural differences?

3. Discuss the differences between the following cultural dimensions identified by Hofstede: (a) Individualism and Collectivism, and (b) Masculinity and Femininity.

4. Discuss the following concepts: (a) Power Distance, (b) Uncertainty Avoidance, (c) Confucian Dynamism.

5. Where does the Unites States rank in comparison with some other countries on each of Hofstede's cultural dimensions?

6. Explain the role of religion in international management.

FURTHER READING

Adams, Dan. "The Monkey and the Fish: Cultural Pitfalls of an Educational Advisor." *International Development Review*, No. 2 (1969).

Arensberg, Conrad M., and Arthur H. Neihoff. *Introducing Social Change: A Manual for Americans Overseas*. Chicago: Aldine Publishing Co., 1964.

Batten, Thomas R. *Communities and Their Development*. New York: Oxford University Press, 1957.

Cleveland, Harlan, Gerard J. Mangone, and John C. Adams. *The Overseas Americans*. New York: McGraw-Hill, 1960.

Dressler, David, and Donald Carns. *Sociology, the Study of Human Interactions*. New York: Alfred A. Knopf, 1969.

Fayerweather, John.   *The Executive Overseas*.   Syracuse: Syracuse University Press, 1959.

Foster, George M. *Traditional Cultures: And the Impact of Technological Change*. New York: Harper & Brothers, 1962.

Francis, June N.P. "When in Rome? The Effects of Cultural Adaptation on Intercultural Business Negotiations." *Journal of International Business Studies*, Vol. 22, no. 3, Third Quarter 1991, 403-428.

Glover, M. Katherine. "Do's & Taboos: Cultural Aspects of International Business." *Business America*, Vol. 111, no. 15, Aug. 13 1990, 2-6.

Hall, Edward T. "The Silent Language in Overseas Business." *Harvard Business Review* (May-June 1960).

Hall, Edward T. *The Silent Language*. Garden City, N.Y.:   Anchor Press Doubleday, Anchor Books Edition, 1973.

Hall, Edward T., and William F. Whyte. "Intercultural Communication: A Guide to Men of Action." *Human Organization*, 19, no. I (Spring 1960).

Harris, Philip R., and Robert T. Moran. *Managing Cultural Differences*.

2nd ed. Houston, Texas: Gulf Publishing Company, 1987.

Herskovits, Melville J. *Man and his Works*. New York: Alfred A. Knopf, 1954.

Lerner, Daniel, and Harold D. Lasswell, eds. *The Policy Sciences*. Stanford: Stanford University Press, 1951.

Luqmani, Mushtaq, Zahir A. Quraeshi, and Linda Delene. "Marketing in Islamic Countries: A Viewpoint." *MSU Business Topics* (Summer 1980).

Montgomery, John D. "Crossing the Culture Bars: An Approach to the Training of American Technicians for Overseas Assignments." *World Politics*, 13, no. 4 (July 1961).

Ricks, David, Marilyn Y. C. Fu, and Jeffrey S. Arpan. *International Business Blunders*. Columbus, Ohio: Grid, Inc., 1974.

Terpstra, Vern. *The Cultural Environment of International Business*. Cincinnati: South-Western Publishing Company, 1978.

Townsend, Anthony N, Scott K. Dow, and Steven E. Markham. "An Examination of Country and Culture-Based Differences in Compensation Practice." *Journal of International Business Studies*. Vol. 21, no. 4, Fourth Quarter, 1990, 667-678.

Ueno, Susumu and Sekaran Uma. "The Influence of Culture on Budget Control Practices in the U.S.A and Japan: An Empirical Study." *Journal of International Business Studies*. Vol. 23, no. 4, Fourth Quarter 1992, 659-674.

NOTES

[1] For an excellent documentation of incidents illustrating such blunders, see David Ricks, Marilyn C. Fu, and Jeffrey S. Arpan, I*nternational Business Blunders* (Columbus, Ohio: Grid, Inc., 1974).

[2] See, for example, Harlan Cleveland, Gerard J. Mangone and John Clarke Adams, *The Overseas Americans* (New York: McGraw-Hill Book Co., 1960); John D. Montgomery, "Crossing the Culture Bars: An Approach to the Training of American Technicians for Overseas Assignments," *World Politics 13*, no. 4 (July 1961): 544-560; George M. Foster, *Traditional Cultures: And the Impact of Technological Change* (New York: Harper and Brothers, 1962); John Fayerweather, *The Executive Overseas* (Syracuse: Syracuse University Press, 1959); and Conrad M. Arensberg and Anther H. Niehoff, *Introducing Social Change: A Manual for Americans Overseas* (Chicago: Aldine Publishing Co., 1964).

[3] Don Adams, "The Monkey and the Fish; Cultural Pitfalls of an Educational Advisor," *International Development Review* 2, no. 2 (1969), 22.

[4] Melville J. Herskovits, *Man and His Works* (New York: Alfred A. Knopf, 1952), 17

[5] Clyde Kluckhohn, "The Study of Culture," in *The Policy Sciences*, ed. Daniel Lerner and Harold Laswell (Stanford: Stanford University Press, 1951), 86.

[6] David Dressler and Donald Carns, *Sociology, The Study of Human Interaction* (New York: Alfred A. Knopf, 1969), 56-59.

[7] Ibid., 60.

[8] John L. Graham and Yoshihiro Sano, *Smart Bargaining: Doing Business with the Japanese* (Cambridge, Mass.:   Ballinger Publishing Co., 1989), 18.

[9] Edward T. Hall, "The Silent Language in Overseas Business," *Harvard Business Review* (May-June 1960), 138.

[10] Edward T. Hall, *The Silent Language* (Garden City, N.Y.: Anchor Press, Doubleday, Anchor Books ed. 1973), 18. Copyright 1959 by Edward T. Hall. Reprinted by permission of Doubleday & Co. Inc.

[11] Thomas R. Batten, *Communities and Their Development* (New York: Oxford University Press, 1957), 10-11. Reprinted by permission.

[12] Edward T. Hall and William Foote Whyte, "Intercultural Communication: A Guide to Men of Action," *Human Organization* 19, no. 1 (Spring 1960), 9. Reproduced from *Human Organization* by permission of the Society for Applied Anthropology.

[13] Ibid., 8-9.

[14] *Business Week* Mar 7, 1988, 28.

[15] Daniel Pearl, "Federal Express Finds Its Pioneering Formula Falls Flat Overseas," *Wall Street Journal*, April 15, 1991, A8.

[16] Thomas F. O'Boyle, "Bridgestone Discovers Purchase of U.S. Firms Creates Big Problems," *Wall Street Journal*, April 1, 1991, A1.

[17] Hall and Whyte, "Intercultural Communications: A Guide to Men of Action," 6-7.

[18] Geert Hofstede, *Culture's Consequences: International Differences in Work Related Values* (Beverly Hills: Sage publications, 1980). *Also* Geert Hofstede, "Motivation, Leadership, and Organizations: Do American Theories Apply Abroad?" *Organizational Dynamics* (Summer 1980), 42-63.

[19] Geert Hofstede and Michael Harris Bond, "The Confucius Connection: From Cultural Roots to Economic Growth," *Organizational Dynamics*, Vol. 16, no.4 (Spring 1988), 4-21.

[20] Richard H. Franke, Geert Hofstede, and Michael H. Bond, "Cultural Roots of Economic Performance," *Strategic Management Journal*, Vol. 12 (1991), 167.

[21] Hofstede and Bond, "The Confucius Connection: From Cultural Roots to Economic Growth," 16-17.

[22] Franke, Hofstede, and Bond, "Cultural Roots of Economic Performance," 165-173.

[23] Herskovits, *Man and His Works*, 17.

[24] Clyde Haberman, "Jerusalem Journal, Dishing Up Lunch for A Land That Isn't All Kosher," *The New York Times*, April 16, 1992, A4.

Chapter T H R E E

Planning in a Global Setting

This chapter is about the planning function in a global setting. The international setting is complex; hence the problems and issues confronting global planning are equally complex. Lack of planning almost certainly results in the misallocation of resources and a disappointing performance by a company's global operations. But a well-designed global corporate strategy allows a company to set realistic objectives and to deploy and use its resources efficiently on a global scale.

The focus of this chapter is on planning at the parent company level of an international company. At the core of this presentation are the issues with which top management at headquarters have to come to grips in developing strategies for the company's international involvement.

WHAT IS PLANNING?

Planning is one of the basic functions in the management process. Every manager must have plans in order to reach maximum organizational effectiveness. *Planning* involves assessment of the environment for opportunities and threats in the foreseeable future, evaluation of the strengths and weaknesses of the enterprise, and the formulation of objectives and strategies designed to exploit the opportunities and combat the threats.

All planning is concerned with the future; it is concerned with deciding what an enterprise wants to be and wants to achieve, how to attain those aspirations, allocate resources, and implement designs. Russell L. Ackoff says, "Planning is the design of a desired future and of effective ways of bringing it about."[1] He goes on to say: "Planning is a process that involves making and evaluating each of the set of interrelated decisions before action is required, in a situation in which it is believed that unless action is taken a desired future state is not likely to occur, and that, if appropriate action is taken, the likelihood of a favorable outcome can be increased."[2] To George A. Steiner, "Planning deals with the futurity of present decisions."[3] This, he says, can mean one of two things—or both. "Planning examines future alternative courses of action which are open to a company. In choosing from among these courses of action an umbrella, a perspective, a frame of reference is established for current decisions. Also it can mean that planning examines the evolving chains of cause and effect likely to result from current decisions."[4]

WHAT IS GLOBAL PLANNING?

All the aspects of planning just mentioned are applicable to global planning as well. In addition, *global planning* is concerned with the assessment of the multinational environment; then, determining future worldwide opportunities and threats; and formulating the global objectives and strategies of the enterprise in light of this environmental assessment as well as an internal audit of the enterprise's strengths and weaknesses. Global planning includes the formulation of short- and long-term goals and objectives, and the allocation of resources, people, capital, technology, and information—globally—to achieve the enterprise's global aims.

THE ENVIRONMENT OF GLOBAL PLANNING

Planning in an international company is far more complicated than in a company that does not operate internationally. What makes it difficult is the complexity of the international environment. A domestic company—one that operates in the market of a single country—is required to monitor basically only the environment of one country, although it should also keep an eye on developments in other countries that may have an impact on its domestic environment. In an international company, a manager must monitor not only changes in the environments of every country in which the company currently has operations, but he or she must also determine how these environments are likely to affect one another, as well as how changes occurring in the global environment will affect the manager's domain.

Important Environmental Issues and Problems

Global planning evolves in response to two sets of environmental forces: changes in the external environment, particularly those over which the company management has little or no control, and changes in the internal environment of the company itself. In most companies, global planning is still in its infancy, but even plans that are developed and sophisticated still continue to encounter problems.

We shall first examine the external issues of most concern to international enterprises and the problems they create in the area of global planning. (In the next section, we shall look at internal issues and problems.) Some of the most significant external issues and problems international companies have to confront in their planning of global operations are listed below.

Political Instability and Risk

Many countries in which international companies have business operations have experienced frequent changes of government as well as unexpected modifications of a government's economic policies. Changes in government policies toward the industrial and commercial sector of the economy, and particularly toward foreign firms, foreign trade, and foreign investment, have had significant impact on the profits and other goals of international firms.

Currency Instability

Fluctuations in the exchange rates of currencies—especially those involving the U.S. dollar, the British pound, the German mark, the Swiss franc, and the Japanese yen—have been responsible for wild swings in the financial standing of many international companies. Some companies, such as Exxon, have been fortunate enough to have gained as much as $588 million in one year from foreign exchange transactions, whereas others, like Colgate, have lost $13 million or more from such transactions. Allied-Lyons, the British food and beverage company, has lost $269 million because of the 10 percent increase in the value of the U.S. dollar against the British pound and the German mark since the dollar's lows of February 1991. Allied-Lyons gets roughly 20 percent of its almost $8.4 billion in annual revenues from North American operations. The loss incurred by Allied-Lyons underscores precisely how costly an incorrect foreign-exchange position can be. In the opinion of London-based, foreign-exchange traders, the size of the "hit" stemmed mainly from exposure to forward currency contracts and risky money-market instruments, and not from day-to-day dealings in cash. This loss was one of the biggest foreign-exchange charges that a British industrial company has suffered in recent years. It wiped out roughly a quarter of Allied-Lyons' estimated pretax profit of about 630 British pounds for the fiscal year ending March 3, 1991.[5]

Competition from State-owned Enterprises

State-owned (government-owned) enterprises are presenting a growing competitive threat to international companies. State-owned companies—Aerospatiale of France in the aerospace industry; Montedison, which is 50 percent-owned by the Italian government, in the chemicals industry; and VIAG, a German company, in the aluminum industry—are rapidly changing the rules of the game in international competition. These companies are heavily subsidized by their respective governments and are not required to earn profits and returns on investments at levels comparable to those expected of privately owned competitors.[6]

Pressures from National Governments

International companies have come under severe criticism for their alleged conduct from the foreign governments of both developed and developing countries. They have been accused of such things as disrupting national economic plans, transferring obsolete or inappropriate technology abroad, avoiding taxes by manipulating transfer prices of goods and services, "exporting" jobs by establishing "runaway" plants in low-wage locales, and crushing indigenous competitors with their superior financial and technological power.

Nationalism

The desire for independence among nations, especially the developing ones, has promoted nationalism in many parts of the world. Nationalism does not subscribe to any one particular political ideology; a government having a right-wing political ideology can be just as nationalistic as one with a left-wing philosophy. Regardless of its ideological basis, nationalism does prompt the government to impose restrictive policies against foreign-owned companies—policies such as import controls, local equity requirements, local content requirements, restrictions on the hiring of foreign nationals, limitations on repatriation of profits and dividends, and so on.

Patent and Trademark Protection

Different countries have different laws for the protection of patents and trademarks. The recent trend in many countries is to reduce or completely abolish such protection granted to the industrial property rights of multinational enterprises. This trend is having a significant impact on research and development and on the product-planning activities of multinational companies, which are refusing to license or produce products in countries that do not provide adequate patent and trademark protection.

Intense Competition

As increasing numbers of companies become active internationally, competition among them for resources and markets is becoming increasingly severe. Until the late 1950's, international companies were predominantly U.S.-based, although there were at that time a few large companies—Unilever, Royal Dutch Shell, and Nestle—that were European in origin. Since the early 1960's, there has been a mushrooming of international companies based not only in the United States and Europe, but also in Japan and in the developing countries of Taiwan, South Korea, Brazil, and India.

Important Internal Issues and Problems

Multinational companies are continually confronted with several internal issues and problems in global planning. Some of the most significant of these are listed below.

Integrating the Foreign and Domestic Units

An international company can enjoy the benefits of economies of scale in each of the functional areas—production, marketing, finance, purchasing, and so on—if it can effectively coordinate its various foreign and domestic units and make them all work together as one system. To what degree should a company attempt such integration? Should integration of subsidiaries be attempted globally? Or should subsidiaries in just one region—Europe, for example—be grouped for integration purposes? And should all functions be involved in the integration, or merely one or two functions, such as production or finance? These are critical issues for the top management of an international company to resolve.

Centralized Control versus Decentralized Initiative

International corporations have a lot to gain from the initiative and drive of the management of their subsidiaries. Subsidiary managers, being close to where the action is in the subsidiary, are often in a better position than those at the parent company to make decisions on the basis of existing circumstances. There are times when decisions must be made on the spot in order to resolve a problem confronting the foreign subsidiary. Moreover, the geographic distance between the parent company and the foreign subsidiary means that decentralized decision making at the subsidiary level is almost a necessity. However, some degree of centralization of decision making helps to integrate the foreign subsidiaries, producing benefits that accrue from economies of scale. Top management at the parent company fears the dangers of fragmentation that would befall the multinational company system if each foreign affiliate were allowed to enjoy excessive autonomy. There is, therefore, a basic conflict between centralization and decentralization of authority that top managers at the parent company are obliged to resolve. The types of questions that parent company managers must answer are: What types of decisions should be made by the parent company? Should alternatives prior to the making of a decision be generated by the parent company, or should they originate from the foreign subsidiary? Are there any areas in which decisions should be made jointly by the parent company and foreign subsidiary managers? Finding answers that are acceptable to all parties and in the best interests of the international company as a whole is a challenge that managers in international companies have to face and handle effectively.

Developing Managers with an International Perspective

International companies need managers at all levels of the organization, parent and subsidiary, who can not only think, plan, and act strategically but do so from a worldwide perspective. For that capacity, a manager should have knowledge and appreciation of: (1) the differences—cultural, economic, political, sociological, technological, and so on—that exist among the various regions and countries of the world, and (2) the trends and events occurring, and how rapidly they are occurring, in the world. Having a global perspective also implies an ability and willingness on the part of managers to think and act on a company-wide basis. For example, a subsidiary manager in Egypt, if she or he is truly international in orientation, will make decisions that may not be in her or his subsidiary's best interests but that may benefit the entire international company. The loyalty of managers in an international company should be to the company as a whole and not to any one organizational unit within it. How to develop managers with an international perspective is a problem that top management of international companies must handle effectively.

Internalizing Environmental Information

International companies must search and identify, systematically and thoroughly, the important environmental factors, trends, and events which may have a significant impact on their worldwide operations. This activity is critical and should be conducted on the levels of the country, the region, and the whole corporation. In addition, information obtained from such environmental assessments must be used in the development of the company's strategies. Although the importance of environmental assessment and its use in planning is acknowledged by international managers, "most large companies have done a rather poor job of international environmental analysis"[7] and many dismal failures in international operations have been reported because companies did not properly perform the environmental assessment task. Managers are faced with the issue of choosing the best way of obtaining the necessary environmental data, deciding on the type of organization that can provide it most effectively, and ensuring that "the information itself can find its way into planning and decision making on a less haphazard and superficial basis than is often the case."[8]

Worldwide Resource Allocation

An issue that all international planners face involves the allocation of physical, financial, and human resources to old products versus the development of new products, and for the expansion of old country markets versus the development of new country markets. An ideal product/country portfolio would be one that provides the firm with a steady flow of cash for new product and market development and a rate of return on investment that is acceptable to top management. Achieving the proper balance between new and old products and markets is a challenging task for international planners.

CONSEQUENCES OF A LACK OF PLANNING

An international company should have an overall plan and a well designed strategy for entry into foreign markets. Too many companies have entered foreign markets via licensing, contract manufacturing, or production facilities without a deliberate plan for foreign-market penetration, only to find that the particular strategy chosen was wrong in light of later developments. For example, a company may begin its involvement in a foreign market in the form of export sales in response to inquiries from foreign distributors. As export sales grow, the company may begin to experience problems supplying the foreign market via exports because of a variety of tariff and non-tariff barriers and import restrictions imposed by the local government. Believing that the foreign market should be protected, the company management may resort to licensing a local company to produce the product. This may turn out to be the wrong strategy if, in fact, the market for the product expands and becomes large enough to support a local production facility. The option of production abroad would be unavailable to the company now because a local company is already producing the product. Had the company looked into the future and made sales forecasts for the product in the foreign market, it might not have given the license to the foreign company to produce the product, and instead could have commenced production itself.

Lack of planning may also "lead to a suboptimum deployment of corporate resources overseas and a consequent loss of the potential benefits of multinational operations. An important advantage of multinational business as contrasted with purely domestic operations is that it provides management with the broadest possible dimension of enterprise in which to take full advantage of worldwide investment opportunities that offer the highest returns. However, this strength can be realized only when alternatives are systematically examined and compared on a global basis."[9]

Absence of effective planning may result in the company's allocating its resources to ventures that may not represent the best among the available global market opportunities. A company that does not have a formalized program for the evaluation of foreign market opportunities is not likely to discover the best ones among the many available; therefore, it might make an unwise investment abroad merely because the prime opportunities were never identified as such. Proper timing of entry into foreign markets can often make the difference between success or failure of a foreign venture. Establishing a production facility before the market is large enough to support the required volume for optimum plant utilization results in excess plant capacity and higher per-unit production costs. However, waiting too long is always equally undesirable because the first entrant in the market has the distinct advantage of being able to capture a huge share of the total sales volume. And the experience of many companies has shown how difficult it is to take the sales and market share away from a competitor who already has a large portion of the total market. Timing of foreign-market entry is thus critical and needs very careful planning.

The availability of adequate resources, both financial and managerial, is often overlooked by firms when they decide to venture abroad. At issue is not the availability of such resources in absolute terms; companies with genuine opportunity can generally manage to find them. What is crucial is that the resources be at hand when they are needed. For instance, a company may be making fine profits, but if its capital is tied up in the development and marketing of many new products that experience a greater cash outflow than cash inflow, it may not have the necessary cash to start new ventures abroad, especially if it does not have a portfolio of mature products which can serve as cash cows. Or, a company could establish many foreign affiliates in rapid succession, only to find, to its dismay, that it does not have adequate managerial personnel to send out from the home office, or hire abroad, to manage these operations. Planning of foreign-market entry could avoid such problems.

Finally, lack of planning may cause numerous operating problems after the foreign venture gets under way. For example, a company may assume that marketing channels similar to those at home are available in the foreign market, only to find that there are no existing channels that it can use for marketing its products. In the United States and other advanced Western countries, a company has a choice between establishing its own distribution network or using one already there, such as a chain of department stores or retail food outlets. Most developing countries do not have such alternative distribution networks, so companies must set up their own, which can be quite expensive. Furthermore, the company may not have anticipated the need to hold a far greater stockpile of inventory of raw materials and components than the level generally kept in the home country. Such stockpiling could be necessary if the items must be imported because they are unavailable locally, and this stockpiling will probably mean higher inventory costs than anticipated.

STEPS IN DEVELOPING A GLOBAL CORPORATE STRATEGY

The aforementioned problems that arise from poor planning point out the acute need for the development of a strategy for international business operations. In the following pages we shall be concerned with how such a strategy may be developed by a company that is considering entering foreign markets, and we shall also look at some issues involved in the development of the strategy.

A company that is considering foreign-market opportunities should begin by asking the following basic question: Should we go international? If the answer to this question is in the affirmative, then the next questions to consider are: Where, throughout the world, should we look for opportunities? How soon should we embark on our first venture abroad? What is the best way of exploiting foreign opportunities? Although on the surface it may appear that there are many business opportunities abroad, it is important to recognize that such opportunities vary significantly among industries and individual firms. Besides, different firms have unequal abilities to exploit foreign markets successfully. Hence, in evaluating the value of entry into foreign markets, management should:

1. Evaluate the opportunities in foreign markets for the firm's products and technology, as well as the potential threats, problems, and risks related to these opportunities;
2. Evaluate the strengths and weaknesses of the firm's managerial, material, technical, and functional (finance, marketing, etc.) competence to determine the degree to which the firm has the resources to successfully exploit potential foreign opportunities

Step 1 is generally known as the *environmental analysis* and Step 2 as the *internal resource audit*.

The assessment of the international opportunities, and of the strengths and weaknesses of its resource base, should permit the company's management to define the scope of its international business involvement. The next step is to formulate company-wide global business objectives; then, develop pertinent global corporate strategies aimed at achieving company wide global business objectives.

To summarize, the development of a global corporate strategy involves the following steps:

1. Evaluate the opportunities, threats, problems, and risks.

2. Evaluate the strengths and weaknesses of the firm to exploit foreign opportunities.

3. Define the scope of the firm's global business involvement.

4. Formulate the firm's global corporate objectives.

5. Develop specific corporate strategies for the firm as a whole.

It should be noted that although the steps are listed sequentially in the preceding list, in practice the process is iterative. There is, typically, considerable backtracking as one progresses from one step to the next. For example, if global business objectives are formulated but then managers cannot develop creditable strategies to achieve them, the objectives must be changed and Steps 4 and 5 must be redone. The entire process is illustrated in Figure 3-1.

FIGURE 3-1 Global Corporate Strategy Process

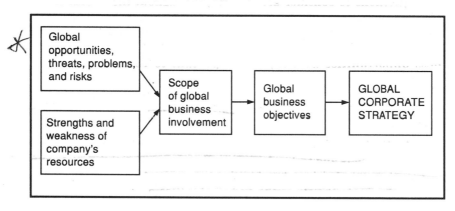

Let us now examine the steps in global corporate strategy formulation.

Analyzing the Global Environment

Environmental analysis focuses on the discovery and evaluation of business opportunities and on the threats, problems, and risks associated with them.

It involves the analysis of certain factors in the environment that could have a significant positive or negative impact on the operations of a firm, and over which the firm has little or no control. Environmental factors with a positive impact may create future opportunities, whereas those with a negative impact may represent future threats, risks, and problems for the firm. Such factors, which we shall call *critical environmental factors*, are the focus of an environmental analysis. Hence, when a firm conducts an environmental analysis, it should zero in on the critical factors in the economic, political, legal, and cultural segments of the total environment in which the firm operates.

Global environmental analysis is the conduct of this activity on an international scale. However, in an international company, environmental analysis should be conducted on at least three different levels: (1) multinational, (2) regional, and (3) country. At the *multinational level*, environmental analysts at the company headquarters are concerned with the identification, forecasting, and monitoring of critical environmental factors in the world at large. The analysis is of a very broad nature and devoid of much detail; its focus is on the significant trends and events unfolding over time. For example, corporate environmental analysts may study global technological developments, or trends in governmental intervention in the economies of nations, or the overall changes occurring in the values and life-styles of people in industrialized versus developing countries. Then the analysts would make judgments about the probable nature of these trends and the degree of impact on the internal operations of the company—now and in the future.

Environmental analysis at the *regional level* focuses on a more detailed study of the critical environmental factors within a specific geographic area such as Western Europe, the Middle East, or Southeast Asia. Here the intent is to identify opportunities for marketing the company's products, services, or technology in a particular region. Analysts also research the types of problems that may occur and the appropriate strategies to counter them. For example, an automobile company may find that significant growth anticipated in the gross national product and per capita incomes of a population has created a potentially large market for automobiles; however, because of the absence of good roads and skilled auto mechanics, cars sold in the region must be sturdy, with engines of a basic design that do not require complicated repair procedures. Similarly, a company making electronic equipment may find that low wages in the Far East or southern Asia provide an opportunity to significantly lower production costs by transferring labor-intensive operations to those areas. But it may also face problems in dealing with a labor force that has a different cultural background. Regional environmental analysis pinpoints countries in regions that seem to have the most market potential. These become the focus of country environmental analysis—the next level of analysis.

Environmental analysis at the *country level* is concerned with an in-depth analysis of the critical environmental factors—economic, legal, political, and cultural—in a small number of countries. In each country, an evaluation is made of the nature of the opportunities available. The kinds of questions analysts ask include: (1) How big is the country market for our products, services, or technology? (2) How can the market be served—by exports, licensing, contract manufacturing, or local production? (3) Which of these is the best strategy for entering the country market? (4) Can the country serve as a base for exports to other countries, including the company's home market?

Country analysis also identifies the nature of the potential threats, risks, and problems associated with each form of market entry. For instance, serving the local market through exports may carry with it the risk of government restraints in the future, such as higher tariffs or import quotas. However, establishing a local production facility may also be risky because the government may, in the future, insist that the equity of the foreign affiliate be shared with the local population. Thus, country environmental analysis must be oriented to each of the market entry strategies for it to be meaningful for planning purposes. A suggested procedure for conducting this analysis is as follows: First, identify the critical external conditions or factors that must exist for the success of a particular market entry strategy. Next, evaluate the critical environmental factors associated with each market entry strategy. A matrix similar to that shown in Exhibit 3-1 may be used for this purpose.

Evaluations of the critical environmental factors (economic, legal, political, cultural) that can affect each form of market entry are made and recorded symbolically in each cell in the matrix. The individual evaluations in each cell may be "averaged" to arrive at a cumulative index of the quality of the critical environmental factors for each market entry strategy, thus permitting a comparison among them. Similar market entry strategy evaluations may be conducted for each country under consideration. Examples of different types of critical environmental factors for each form of market entry strategy are presented in Exhibit 3-2 on page 97.

POLITICAL RISK AND GLOBAL CORPORATE STRATEGY

Of the many environmental factors an international manager examines, one of the most difficult to analyze is *political risk*. This analysis is difficult because the manager is usually unfamiliar with the political patterns and interrelationships in a foreign country, yet it is important because political problems have the potential to be both

EXHIBIT 3-1   Market Entry Strategy Evaluation Matrix

Critical Environmental Factors / Entry Strategy	Economic	Legal	Political	Cultural	Cumulative Strategy Index
Export	A	C	B	B	B
Licensing	B	A	A	E	A-
Contmanufacturing	C	B	A	E	B
Local Production	B	B	C	B	B-

A = Excellent   D = Poor
B = Good   E = Not acceptable
C = Fair

EXHIBIT 3-2   Examples of Critical Environmental Factors for Market Entry Strategies

Export	*Contract Manufacturing*
Import tariffs	Quality of local contractor
Import quotas	Capital repatriation
Distance from nearest supplier country	*Local Production*
Freight costs	Political stability
Licensing	Size of market
	Market structure
Patent and trademark protection	Currency stability
Quality of license	Capital repatriation
Legal limit on royalty rate structure	Local attitude toward foreign ownership

dramatic and costly.

   Political risk is the likelihood that political forces will cause dramatic, unforeseen changes in a business environment that will affect the profit and other goals of a business enterprise.[10] Political change, however, is not always negative. It can be positive, as in the case of the People's Republic of China, where foreign investment and free enterprise are now becoming accepted.[11] Therefore, a manager must continually scan the political environment, looking for opportunities as well as threats.

   One framework, put forth by Robock, analyzes political risk by dividing it into *macro* and *micro* components. A risk is of a macro nature when unanticipated and politically motivated environmental changes are broadly directed at all foreign enterprises. The risk is micro when the environmental changes affect only selected fields of business activity having specific characteristics.[12]

   Macro risk can be characterized by sweeping political edicts by the regime in power, such as the confiscation and nationalization of foreign firms by Cuba, China, the Eastern bloc countries, and other nations that have shifted from a private-enterprise to a socialist system.[13] Or, macro risk can be directed at the regime in power by opposing factions, but the opposition is actually expressed through foreign firms, as in the case of terrorist bombings of the offices of foreign companies. The Arab nations created a macro-risk situation when they declared a boycott of any foreign enterprise that had long-term business dealings with Israel.[14]

   Micro risk, on the other hand, is industry, firm, or project specific. The international manager is likely to encounter abrupt and politically motivated changes in the business environment that are selectively directed toward specific fields of business activity.[15] The types of business operations with high micro-risk vulnerability vary from nation to nation, over time, and with type of product, level of technology, and ownership structure.[16] At a particular point in time and for a specific country, it is theoretically possible to rank types of businesses according to their degree of political-risk vulnerability. However, these rankings keep changing.[17]

Public utilities, petroleum refining, mining industries, and, more recently, financial institutions have all had micro political difficulties in the form of industry-specific nationalizations in the last few decades. According to Robock's framework, these actions could have been better anticipated by examining the characteristics of these businesses which made them targets.

Two situations have the greatest potential for the development of political vulnerability over time. The first is dominance of a multinational enterprise in one of a country's major industries. One such situation resulted in Canada's 1980 policy reversal, which was intended to reduce foreign ownership in its petroleum industry from 75 to 50 percent.[18] The second potential danger for a multinational enterprise is the growing ability of the nationals to operate the business successfully. As countries accumulate capital and nationals gain management know-how and technical expertise, the pressures for curtailing foreign involvement are likely to increase.[19]

Political-risk vulnerability can originate in areas unrelated to characteristics of an industry or firm. Because international managers face a wide range of political risk factors, they need to be aware of both subtle changes in industry-specific conditions and cataclysmic events affecting all foreign firms.[20] As Simon points out, a variety of environments must continually be monitored when investing abroad.[21]

Exhibit 3-3 depicts a framework with four basic environments: *host country*, *home country*, *international arena*, and *global arena*.[22] The framework can help the international manager identify the key actors and developments affecting an analysis of political risk. One always first considers the host country, and the factors considered range from currency restrictions to expropriations. However, the many ways in which the home country can impact the multinational enterprise must also be considered.

The *home country* government can place restrictions on technology transfers, can change taxation policies, and can disallow customary payments to foreign officials. Other factors that can indirectly affect the international enterprise include a deterioration of trade relations, the imposition of economic sanctions, and trade barrier retaliation.[23] Nongovernmental influence include negative public opinion,

EXHIBIT 3-3   The Multinational Enterprise and Its Environments

Host Country Environment	Home Country Environment

Government actions/policies
Societal actions/attitudes
Local business community
  actions
Legal community rulings
Media reports
	Government actions/policies
	Societal actions/attitudes
	Local business community
	  actions
	Legal community rulings
	Media reports

MNE

International Environment	International Environment

Foreign policies (economic,
  military, diplomatic) of
  nation states
Regional organizations actions/
  policies
International activist groups'
  actions/policies
Internal developments in
  nation states
	Global organizations' actions/
	  policies
	Global developments (world-
	  wide inflation, recession, oil
	  crisis, commodity price
	  fluctuations, external debt
	  crises)

Source: Jeffrey D. Simon, "A Theoritical Perspective on Political Risk," *Journal of International Business Studies* (Winter 1984): 127.

pressure on the home-country to divest, and protests or demonstrations.[24] Environment must be carefully watched for developments that can affect foreign investments.

The *international environment* consists of policies and actions of other nation-states as well as nongovernmental influences such as international activist groups. Risks originating in the international arena include codes of conduct placed on the multinational enterprise, boycotts, terrorist attacks, and disruption of business activity stemming from border conflicts.[25]

The *global environment* incorporates those developments that transcend a particular country or group of countries and that affect nations simultaneously, such as an oil crisis, worldwide recession, external debt crises, and international economic sanctions. Also included in the global environment are the United Nations, the International Monetary Fund, and the World Bank.[26]

Simon's framework for political risk analysis further explains that the behaviors and interactions in each of the four environments are, to a large extent, shaped by the characteristics of the host country in which a firm is investing. Particularly key are the *stage of economic development* and the *degree of openness* in the host's sociopolitical system.[27] Awareness of these two factors can help a firm anticipate the types of political risk it is likely to encounter from each environment.

Industrialized and developing countries differ in their overall orientation toward foreign business. Developing countries certainly have more suspicion that large companies are potentially exploitative entities than do developed nations.[28] In developing countries, the need to promote indigenous business and manufacturing abilities as part of their development is reflected in risks such as technology transfer requirements, joint-venture pressure, local content rules, and, in extreme cases, nationalization and expropriation.[29] The risks encountered in industrialized countries are more moderate: environmental standards, licensing requirements, and price controls can be expected. In addition, pressures from home-societal and international groups to adhere to codes of conduct or to divest are greater for international firms in developing nations than in advanced ones.[30]

Variation in political risk cannot be explained by the differences between industrialized and developing countries alone. By considering another dimension, which distinguishes between an open and closed political climate, an international manager can better understand its origins.[31] An *open system* is characterized by the ability of all the members in a society to participate in the formal and informal political processes.[32] The United States, Great Britain, and Japan are examples of open societies. This degree of openness allows nongovernmental actors to shape events and express their views without violence in elections, protests, and boycotts. In a *closed system*, these avenues of expression are not available, and the repression of the populace can often erupt into violent activities.[33] South Korea, South Africa, and the territories under Israeli occupation have all experienced riots and terrorist activities perpetuated by repressed populations in closed systems. The multinational company in such a country will not only be prone to internal violent activity, but external international and home groups will pressure for disinvestment because investment in the country will be seen as tacit approval of or support for the repressive regime.[34]

Analysis of industrialized vs. developing and open vs. closed dimensions produces valuable insight into the risks a multinational firm is likely to face in different host countries. As can be seen in Exhibit 3-4, the host government's actions in an open, industrialized society

EXHIBIT 3-4 A Political Risk Framework

	Industrialized		Developing	
	Internal	*External*	*Internal*	*External*
Direct	Host government licensing, price controls, taxation Adverse legal rulings Negative Media Reports	Home government licensing, taxation policies Regional and global organizations' monitoring of MNE operations	Local content rules, joint venture pressure, technology transfer and import/export regulations Strikes, protests, boycotts, negative public opinion Adverse legal rulings Negative media reports	Home government licensing, taxation policies Regional and global organizations' code of conduct for MNE
Indirect	Bureaucratic delays and procedures Elections, public pressure for environmental controls Local business pressure for subsidies, favorable treatment	Host-home country trade disputes Bilateral/multilateral trade agreements detrimental to MNE Global economic developments	Intragovernmental friction General strikes, elections Local business pressure for subsidies, favorable tax rates	North-South issue disputes Anti-MNE public sentiment due to home country's foreign/military policy Regional/border wars High external debt, default Commodity price fluctuations
Open				

	Industrialized		Developing	
	Internal	External	Internal	External
Direct	Restrictions on remittances Strikes, terrorism, violent demonstrations/protests	Home government restrictions on operations Negative home and international public opinion, disinvestment pressure	Nationalization, expropriation Terrorism, riots, strikes	Home government restrictions on operations Negative home and international public opinion, disinvestment pressure
Indirect	Coups, radical regime change, leadership struggles Revolution, guerrilla war, riots	Deteriorating host-home relationships International economic sanctions/boycott International protests Global economic developments	Coups, radical regime change, leadership struggles Revolution, guerilla war, riots	North-South issue disputes Anti-MNE public sentiment due to home country's foreign/military policy Regional/border wars High external debt Commodity price fluctuations

Closed

are likely to be relatively moderate.[35] Because there is no need for rapid economic development, the political risks generated will be in the form of licensing requirements, taxation policies, adverse legal rulings, and unfavorable media reports. Host country societal pressures will be nonviolent and in the form of adverse election results, local businesses lobbying for legislation favorable to them, and public pressure for environmental controls.[36] Political risk on the international scene takes the form of protectionism and adverse global economic developments which must always be anticipated.

When a company invests in an industrialized, closed society, a new set of problems arises. The gap between societal aspirations and their realization is wide in this type of society because the advantages of the industrialized society are visible to all, but only a few are allowed to participate in them.[37] Without any peaceful means to express desire and exert pressure for change, dissatisfied groups must rely on violent demonstrations. A good example of this situation was in South Africa, where the black majority could not participate in the country's economic and political activities and was effectively shut out from the country's prosperity. In countries with nondemocratic and one-man governments, considerable uncertainty may also exist as to whether an orderly transition of power will take place.[38] During periods of instability, restrictions on moving profits or capital out of the country are likely. The lack of hard currency may also make the use of barter and countertrade arrangements necessary. The company may face negative public opinion in the home country and in international societies, while the home country government and international organizations may impose sanctions on the host country.[39]

As can be seen in Exhibit 3-4, a different set of political risks faces the international manager with an operation in an open, developing country. The country's need to promote economic self-sufficiency and to conserve foreign currency will increase the likelihood of local content laws of technology transfer, and of import/export regulations.[40] Societal dissatisfaction will yield strikes, boycotts, negative media, and the election of public officials antagonistic towards foreign business,[41] all of which have less violent overtones than counterpart responses in a closed system. Brazil, India, Mexico and Venezuela exemplify countries that are both open and developing.

Finally, a host country's environment might be both closed and developing. The risks escalate with this combination and involve local content requirements, joint venture pressure, nationalization, and expropriation.[42] In addition to being targets for the host government, foreign firms face threats internally from dissatisfied societal groups, threats that include terrorism, riots, illegal strikes, and, in extreme cases, revolution and guerrilla warfare.[43] Negative public opinion in the home and international communities will again be fueled by an impression that the international firm is in some way supporting the repressive regime.

From Simon's framework it can be seen that the multinational enterprise is exposed to a variety of risks from the different environments that it experiences when doing business globally. By analyzing the sociopolitical system and the level of economic development of the host country, international managers can get a better handle on the types of risks they are likely to encounter from each of these arenas. They can then isolate and identify the early signs of stress in each environment.[44]

Before closing the subject of global environmental analysis, we must stress that the external environment is always changing and hence the critical environmental factors favorable at one time may become unfavorable later, and vice versa. Therefore, multinational, regional, and country environmental analysis must be done continuously. Moreover, the focus of such analysis must be upon forecasting the characteristics of critical environmental factors in the future so that the company may have sufficient lead time to make appropriate modifications in its strategies.

Making an Internal Resources Audit

The focus of an external environmental analysis is on the environmental conditions that must be present for the successful implementation of a market entry strategy. Now our attention is turned to the internal resources audit, which is concerned with an evaluation of the conditions internal to the company that must exist if the company is to succeed in a specific business in a particular country. The aim of an internal resource audit is to match the company's managerial, technical, material, and financial resources with those required for success in a business.

The internal resource audit is business related rather than environment related. The *key business success factors* (KBSF) may be different from those needed in another business. For example, the factors needed to succeed in the baby food business are different from those required for success in the fast-food industry. The internal resource audit is also country related. For example, the total amount of resources that a firm must have at its command internally to succeed in a business in a country such as Mali may not be required to succeed in Japan. A well-developed capital market and banking industry in Japan, for instance, allows a firm to borrow locally for working capital or plant expansion purposes. It does not have to have this money internally. But the absence of such facilities in Mali would force the firm to finance the foreign affiliate's capital requirements from its internal sources, such as retained earnings. Thus, in order to succeed in a business in Mali, a firm must have the capacity to generate the required funds from internal sources.

Along the same lines, a firm in a business that requires effective channels of distribution—businesses such as vending machines or food markets (such as "Seven-Eleven")—for marketing its products must have the resources to develop its own distribution system. In a country that does not have well-developed channels of distribution, it will have to induce independent retail shop owners to carry and promote its products. Such a problem would not occur in an advanced country such as Germany, but would in a developing nation such as Sudan.

The preceding examples show that there is a close link between the strengths and weaknesses of a firm and the environment in which it does business; a firm may have ample resources to do business in one country but may match up very unsatisfactorily with the setting another country provides. Each environment places constraints on the

FIGURE 3-2   Relationship Between External Environmental Constraints and the Strengths and Weaknesses of a Firm

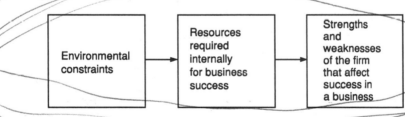

availability of resources required to succeed in the business in that country's market. These constraints determine the amount of resources that the firm must be able to generate on its own in order to succeed. The ability to generate resources determines the firm's strengths and weaknesses. This relationship between the environmental constraints and the firm's strengths and weaknesses is shown in Figure 3-2.

The conceptual process needed to evaluate the strengths and weaknesses of a company is this: (1) Determine the key business success factors; that is, those in which the firm must excel in order to succeed in the business. (2) Match the firm's available resources against those required to score high and do better than competitors in each of the areas identified by the key business success factors. (3) Assess the

FIGURE 3-3   Conceptual Process to Evaluate the Strengths and Weaknesses of a Firm

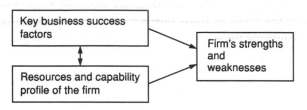

strengths and weaknesses of the firm. This process is illustrated in
Figure 3-3. Examples of key business success factors are presented in
Exhibit 3-5.

The key business success factors can and do change from one time
period to another. For example, fuel efficiency was not a critical
factor for success in the automobile industry prior to the oil crisis and
its resultant increases in the price of gasoline (since 1974), but now it
is. Therefore, a company must maintain an effective program for continuously monitoring and forecasting the key factors for success in each
of the businesses in which it is involved. And an international company must conduct an evaluation of its strengths and weaknesses to
succeed in every country in which it already has business operations
or is planning to start them in the near future.

EXHIBIT 3-5   Examples of Key Business Success Factors

Automobile Manufacturer	*Pharmaceutical Company*
Styling	Efficacy of products
Fuel efficiency	Product innovation
Quality	Patents
Price	Company image
Service	
Distribution system	

Soft Drinks Producer

Channels of distribution
Taste
Sales promotion
Brand identification
Price

Defining the Scope of Global Business Involvement

The next step in international corporate strategy formulation is the definition of the scope or basic perimeters of the firm's global business activities. Knowing the scope helps company management identify those foreign market opportunities that may be considered for an in-depth study before resources are committed for their exploitation. Those that clearly fall outside the scope can be ignored. A thorough investigation of a foreign market can be costly and time consuming; however, defining the company's scope of global business involvement helps the company weed out market opportunities that, given the company's strengths and weaknesses, it cannot exploit.

The scope of the company's global business may be defined in terms of the following dimensions: *geography*, *product*, *technology*, *ownership*, *size of commitment*, *risk*, *time span*, *form of market entry*, and *level of economic development*. The following questions must be answered for each dimension.

Geography. Should the company limit its international business involvement to certain geographic regions of the world, or should it become truly global by going after opportunities that are attractive irrespective of their geographic location?

Product. Should the company's global business involvement be limited to only some of its products? Should the stage in the product life cycle determine a product's global involvement—that is, should only mature products be involved in international business, leaving those that are at the development or growth stage for the home market first?

Technology. Shall the company limit its global activities to those opportunities that involve the use of older or nonproprietary technology? Or should the global thrust be founded on the superior and most advanced technology available? How important is patent protection in the transfer of technology abroad?

Ownership. Should foreign ventures be one hundred percent owned by the company, or can ownership be shared with local partners abroad? Is majority ownership acceptable in areas where complete ownership is not allowed by local legislation? Under what conditions will a minority ownership be acceptable?

Size of Commitment. Should there be limits placed on the magnitude of commitments the company is willing to consider in a given market? Should maximum and minimum limits be placed on the size of commitments that can be made in one country?

Risk.   How much risk is the company willing to assume in a venture, given the size of the commitment involved and benefits expected? What is the balance among risk, commitment, and benefits that is acceptable in each venture? Should risks be diversified by products and regions?

Time Span.   What proportion of the company's total resources should be committed to foreign opportunities in any given year? Should the company enter by phases into foreign markets?

Form of Market Entry.   Will the company consider only opportunities that are exploitable by local production or will it consider those that lend themselves to exporting, licensing, or other market-entry strategies?

Level of Economic Development.   Should the company limit its global involvement to developed countries only, or will it consider opportunities in both developed and developing countries?

A deliberate and careful study of these issues will serve to define and limit the scope of the company's global business involvement. For example, one firm may conclude that, given its strengths and weaknesses, it should limit its initial foreign involvement to establishing a firm foothold via licensing in the European Common Market, and it might limit such involvement in the early stages to only one of its major product lines. Another firm may decide to look worldwide for market opportunities, and to exploit them only by establishing wholly owned manufacturing facilities. Thus, defining the scope of global business involvement specifies the types of foreign business opportunities the firm is interested in, and allows it to ignore those that do not meet the chosen criteria.

Formulating Global Corporate Objectives

The next step in international corporate strategy formulation is the determination of what the company hopes to achieve from its international operations. Global corporate objectives are the objectives of the company as a whole. They serve as the umbrella under which the objectives of each of its corporate divisions and foreign affiliates are formulated. Divisional and affiliate objectives are expected to be consistent with, and contributory to, global corporate objectives. This relationship between global corporate, divisional, and affiliate objectives is presented in Figure 3-4.

Global corporate objectives are formulated in areas such as profitability, marketing, production, finance, technology, host government

FIGURE 3-4   The Hierarchy of Objectives

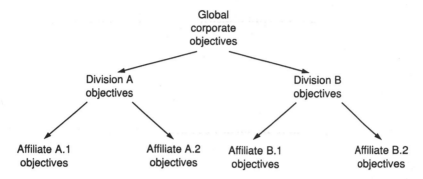

relations, personnel, research and development, and the environment. There may be other areas in which global corporate objectives can be formulated. The general guideline is to formulate objectives in areas that directly and vitally affect the survival and prosperity of the company. While developing corporate objectives, top management must recognize the objectives of the so-called claimants on the corporation— the stockholders, customers, employees, suppliers, and the public located in geographically dispersed regions. But most importantly, top management must make every effort to ensure that the company's foreign operations make positive contributions toward meeting the goals of each host country.

   Often the objectives of these various groups conflict with each other, in which case top management must establish their relative importance to the long-run survival and growth of the company. Management must also assess the comparative political influence of each claimant, then reformulate the international corporate objectives in the company's long-range interests. The importance of recognizing the objectives of the various claimants is brought into sharp focus when we realize that several American multinational companies in the 1950's and 1960's could have avoided expropriation of their properties in Latin America had they recognized the values and expectations of the host countries and incorporated them in their overall company objectives and plans.[45] The different areas in which a company may formulate (and revise) its global corporate objectives are presented in Exhibit 3-6.

   The next critical task for top management is deciding how the objectives are to be achieved. This decision involves the formulation of the company's corporate strategies.

EXHIBIT 3-6   Areas for Formulation of Global Corporate Objectives

---

Profitability

Level of profits
Return on assets, investment equity, sales
Yearly profit growth
Yearly earnings per share growth

Marketing

Total sales volume
Market share—worldwide, region, country
Growth in sales volume
Growth in market share
Integration of country markets for marketing efficiency and
  effectiveness

Production

Ratio of foreign to domestic production volume
Economics of scale via international production integration
Quality and cost control
Introduction of cost efficient production methods

Finance

Financing of foreign affiliates—retained earnings or local borrowing
Taxation—minimizing tax burden globally
Optimum capital structure
Foreign exchange management—minimizing losses from foreign
  fluctuations

Technology

Type of technology to be transferred abroad—new or old generation
Adaptation of technology to local needs and circumstances

Host Government Relations

Adapting affiliate plans to host government developmental plans
Adherence to local laws, customs, and ethical standards

Personnel

Development of managers with global orientation
Management development of host country nationals

(continued)

EXHIBIT 3-6   Continued

Research and Development

Innovation of patentable products
Innovation of patentable production technology
Geographical dispersion of research and development laboratories

Environment

Harmony with the physical and biological environment
Adherence to local environmental legislation

Developing Specific Corporate Strategies

A strategy may be defined as a course of action designed to achieve a desired end result. *Corporate strategy development* is concerned with the deployment of the company's resources in order to achieve its global corporate objectives. Corporate strategies, therefore, should be developed in each area in which corporate objectives have been developed.

A corporate strategy establishes the framework for the formulation of strategies at the divisional and foreign affiliate level. For example, a corporate financial strategy that states that all company growth objectives will be financed only by retained earnings implies a very conservative way of financing growth.

Therefore, all foreign affiliates must abide by this company wide strategy and finance their own growth plans only by retained earnings. Similarly, a corporate marketing strategy calling for the adaptation of products to suit local tastes and conditions allows foreign affiliates to make appropriate changes in the basic product, but it forbids the introduction of new products. For example, a company involved in the marketing of coffee worldwide may allow the local affiliates to modify its taste to suit local preferences, but it will not allow an affiliate to sell a product such as cocoa, which may be new to the company.

Corporate strategies affect the fundamental design of a company's overall operations. An analogy with the design of an aircraft may help to explain this concept. An aerospace engineer who changes the design of an airplane to achieve its performance objectives is involved in "corporate strategy" formulation, and the design of all components of the airplane must conform with the overall airplane design. Similarly, the design of the company's overall operations constrains and influences the design of the divisional and affiliate operations.

Although corporate strategies are formulated in areas that are of major concern to a company, and will therefore vary from one company to another, international companies do develop strategies in common in some areas. Consider the following:

- methods of entering foreign markets
- growth—internal development versus acquisitions
- geographical diversification
- product diversification
- product portfolio optimization
- foreign exchange risk management
- human resources development
- organization structure

The construction of corporate strategy is a difficult process. It requires an objective assessment of the strengths and weaknesses of the company's resources and of its managerial practices. Adoption of new strategies may mean the abandoning of old, familiar ways of running a business and therefore may, as a prerequisite, involve change in the fundamental attitudes of top management. However difficult the process may be, top management must evaluate corporate strategies periodically and keep them in tune with the dynamic environment.

To repeat a point that was made earlier in this chapter, the entire corporate strategy formulation process is by nature iterative. The essence of the entire process is to keep the organization adaptable and responsive to changes. Hence, every step in the corporate strategy formulation process we have discussed must be performed in view of both the present and forecasted characteristics of the firm's environment.

SUMMARY

This chapter was about the process of planning in an international company from the point of view of the top management personnel at the headquarters of an international company.

Planning is one of the basic functions of management. It is a process that involves the assessment of the environment for opportunities and threats, the evaluation of the strengths and weaknesses of the enterprise, and the formulation of objectives and strategies designed to exploit future opportunities and combat threats.

International planning is planning in an international context. Planning in an international company is far more complicated than in a domestic company because the multinational environment in which an international company's operations and activities occur is far more complex than that of its purely domestic counterpart.

International companies have to confront several significant external and internal issues and problems in global planning, such as political instability and risk, currency instability, competition from state-owned enterprises, pressures from national governments, nationalism, patent and trademark protection, and intense competition. Examples of internal problems and issues are: integration of foreign and domestic units, centralized control versus decentralized initiative development of managers with an international perspective, internalization of environmental information, and worldwide resource allocation.

After discussing briefly the nature of the problems created when a firm enters foreign markets without proper planning, the chapter was concluded with a coverage of the steps involved in the development of an international corporate strategy.

QUESTIONS

1. Discuss some of the issues and problems that international companies must confront in planning their global operations. Are any of these faced by companies that do not operate internationally?
2. Why is the formulation of an overall plan and a well-designed strategy for entry into foreign markets so critical for an international company?
3. Discuss the three levels at which environmental analysis must take place in an international company. Why should country environmental analysis be oriented to each market entry strategy?
4. The internal resource audit is both business- and country-related. Discuss this statement, giving examples.
5. a.) Go to the library and obtain information on the political system in South Africa.
   b.) Describe the types of risks that U.S. multinational companies such as Ford, General Motors, and Coca-Cola have experienced in South Africa.

FURTHER READING

Ackoff, Russell A. *A Concept of Corporate Planning*. New York: John Wiley & Sons, 1970.

Davidson, William H. *Global Strategic Management*. New York: John Wiley & Sons, 1982.

Hamel, Gary, and C. K. Prahalad. "Do You Really Have a Global Strategy?" *Harvard Business Review* (July-August 1985): 139-48.

Harrell, Gilbert D., and Richard O. Kiefer. "Multinational Strategic Market Portfolios." *MSU Business Topics* (Winter 1981): 5-15.

Planning in a Global Setting

LaPalombara, Joseph and Stephen Blank. *Multinational Corporations in Comparative Perspective.* New York: The Conference Board, 1977.

Phatak, Arvind V. *Managing Multinational Corporations.* New York: Praeger Publishers, 1974.

Schwendiman, John S. *Strategic and Long-Range Planning for the Multinational Corporation.* New York: Praeger Publishers, 1973.

Shanks, David C. "Strategic Planning for Global Competition." *Journal of Business Strategy* (Winter 1985): 80-89.

Simon, Jeffrey D. "A Theoretical Perspective on Political Risk." *Journal of International Business Studies* (Winter 1984): 123-43.

Steiner, George A. *Top Management Planning.* New York: Macmillan, 1969.

Walters, Kenneth D., and Monsen, R. Jose. "State-owned Business Abroad; New Competitive Threat." *Harvard Business Review* (March-April 1979).

Yoshino, M. Y. "International Business: What Is the Best Strategy?" *Business Quarterly* (Fall 1966).

NOTES

[1] Russell A. Ackoff, *A Concept of Corporate Planning* (New York: John Wiley Interscience, 1970), 1.

[2] Ibid., 4.

[3] George Steiner, *Top Management Planning* (New York: Macmillan, 1969), 6.

[4] Ibid.

[5] "Allied Lyons Says Foreign Exchange Costs It $269 Million," *Wall Street Journal*, March 20 1991, A17.

[6] Kenneth D. Walters and R. Joseph Monsen, "State-Owned Business Abroad: New Competetive Threat," *Harvard Business Review*, March-April 1979, 160-70.

[7] John Snow Schwendiman, *Strategic and Long Range Planning for the Multinational Corporation* (New York: Praeger Publishers, 1973), 87.

[8] Joseph LaPalombara and Stephen Blank, *Multinational Corporations in Comparative Perspective* (New York: The Conference Board, 1977), xiv.

[9] M. Y. Yoshino, "International Business: What Is the Best Strategy?" *Business Quarterly* (Fall 1966): 47.

[10] Stenfan H. Robock and Kenneth Simmonds, *International Business and Multinational Enterprises* (Homewood, Illinois: Irwin, 1983), 342.

[11] Ibid.

[12] Robock, Stenfan H., "Political Risk: Identification and Assessment," *Columbia Journal of World Business* (July-August 1979): 9.

[13] Robock and Simmonds, 345.

[14] Ibid.

[15] Robock, 10.

[16] Robock and Simmonds, 345.

[17] Ibid.

[18] Ibid.

[19] Robock, 10.

[20] Simon, Jeffrey D., "Political Risk Assessment: Past Trends and Future Prospects," *Columbia Journal of World Business* (Fall 1982): 66.

[21] Simon, Jeffrey D., "Theoritical Perspective on Political Risk," *Journal of International Business Studies* (Winter 1984): 126.

[22] Ibid.

[23] Ibid., 127.

[24] Ibid.

[25] Ibid., 126.

[26] Ibid., 127.

[27] Ibid.

[28] Ibid.

[29] Ibid.

[30] Ibid., 128.

[31] Ibid., 130.

[32] Ibid., 142.

[33] Ibid., 130.

[34] Ibid.

[35] Ibid.

[36] Ibid.

[37] Ibid., 131.

[38] Robock, 16.

[39] Simon, "Theoretical Perspective on Political Risk," 131.

[40] Ibid.

[41] Ibid.

[42] Ibid., 134.

[43] Ibid.

[44] Ibid.

[45] Arvind V. Phatak, *Managing Multinational Corporations* (New York: Praeger Publishers, 1974), 162.

Chapter **F O U R**

Strategies for Global Competitive Superiority

In the last chapter we examined the process of global planning. Now our focus will be on the content of strategies that global companies have embraced and implemented in search of a global competitive advantage in a variety of industries. We shall look at the following four types of strategies adopted by global companies:

- Strategic alliances
- Core competency leveraging
- Counterattack
- Glocalization

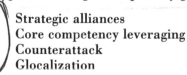

4 Strategies for ADVANTAGE in MKT.

STRATEGIC ALLIANCES

Not a week goes by without an announcement in the business press of a strategic alliance between two or more companies. Almost every internationally minded company trying to become global will consider forging a strategic alliance with another company as a fast track to that goal. A strategic alliance is a collaborative arrangement that a company makes with competitors, suppliers, customers, distributors, or firms in other industries in order to develop, produce, distribute, or market a product or service. A strategic alliance can take a variety of forms. Among the most common are the following:

- Collaboration without equity
- Joint venture
- Equity ownership
- Cash-neutral exchange of assets

Collaboration Without Equity

Here there is a loose association between the companies. An example is the alliance between the Japanese company Mitsubishi and the German company Daimler Benz. The two companies are working on eleven joint projects involving cars, aerospace, and integrated circuits. Sony, the dominant Japanese firm in the electronics and entertainment industries, has forged such alliances with several small, high-technology companies in the United States. The company is sharing its research staff, production facilities, and even business plans for specific products with small companies. Sony is working with Panavision Inc. to develop a lens for high-definition television cameras, with Compression Labs Inc. on a video-conferencing machine, and with Alphatronix Inc. to develop rewritable, optical-disk storage systems for computers.[1]

A Joint Venture

In this collaborative arrangement, a new venture firm is created, with its own identity and management structure in which each of the partners owns equity. For example, Texas Instruments (TI) and Acer Inc., the personal computer company in Taiwan, have formed a jointly owned company in Taiwan called Acer-TI to make 1 Mb and 4 Mb DRAMs. The plant will cost at least $250 million. The benefits of this alliance to TI are evident in their getting a new memory chip factory at little cost, as Acer is financing most of that cost. The benefits for Acer include getting an assured supply of parts that are critical to its core operations.[2]

In another joint venture, Japan's Mitsubishi Motors Corporation, AB Volvo, and the Dutch government each own 33 percent of a car production facility in the Netherlands. The trio jointly produce a new generation of midsize cars, replacing Volvo's 300 and 400 series currently produced at the Volvo plant in the Netherlands. The partners will invest a total of $3.7 billion to develop the new generation of cars. Mitsubishi will contribute its production and design expertise, a key weakness of Volvos. For Mitsubishi, buying into an existing factory in a joint venture arrangement was an attractive option, given the risk implied by the European Community having imposed quotas on Japanese car imports into Europe, and the strong likelihood that such quotas would include cars manufactured by Japanese transplant factories in Europe.[3]

In an unusual alliance, two of the world's largest global corporations, Coca-Cola Company and Nestle S.A., plan to form a joint venture to cash in on a potentially rich market in ready-to-drink coffees and teas. The venture, in which each company will invest $50 million, is designed to exploit the combined strengths of Nestle brand dry foods, like instant coffee and tea, with the massive, global distribution system of Coca-Cola. This venture will make possible the delivery of coffee and tea products to worldwide markets much faster than either company could alone.[4] Both companies stand to save considerable sums of money—Coca-Cola by not having to develop its own products, and Nestle by not having to develop the massive distribution channels required to compete effectively in the beverage industry.

Equity Ownership

This type of alliance involves either one-way or mutual purchase of equity. An example of the former is the 24 percent equity that Ford holds in Mazda, and Hong Kong's Semi-Tech (Global) Ltd., which owns 20 percent of Emerson Radio. Ford nameplates are on 12 percent of the cars Mazda makes and sells in Japan. The Semi-Tech and Emerson alliance gives Emerson a much needed cash infusion; and Semi-Tech, which owns Singer sewing machines' operations as well as its consumer electronic and durable outlets, gains access to Emerson's contract production facilities in the Far East. An example of mutual purchase of equity is the alliance involving alcoholic beverages between Japan's Suntory and Great Britain's Allied-Lyons. Suntory holds 2.5 percent in Allied-Lyons, while Allied-Lyons has a 1 percent stake in Suntory.

Cash-Neutral Exchange of Assets

In this type of alliance, the partnership does not involve any cash. Rather, each company has a stake in the other and they trade assets. It is believed that such cash-neutral transactions may become a trend in a credit sensitive, post-junk-bond era. An example of such an alliance is the one between Kodak's pharmaceutical unit, Sterling Drug, and Snofi, a majority state-owned French company. Kodak's Sterling Drug has been slow to develop new products. The companies plan to combine their pharmaceutical operations, which will provide each firm with both marketing and research power.

The agreement involves the division of the world into two segments. Snofi will take majority control of Sterling's operations in Europe while Sterling will do the same for Snofi's operations in both North and Latin America. For Snofi, this agreement represents an opportunity to sell products directly in the U.S. market through Kodak's well-established distribution system. It will also greatly broaden Snofi's reach into the U.S. market, which it has been trying to penetrate for quite some time. For Kodak's Sterling Drugs, the alliance could speed product introductions. Sterling has a strong over-the-counter presence, but Kodak is more interested in prescription drugs, which have a higher profit potential. Sterling, however, has not had the resources to move potential products through the pipeline fast enough for Kodak's liking.

The research and development budgets of Sterling and Snofi—$250 million each—would exceed the $300 million that experts say is the minimum amount required to reach the critical mass for creating and marketing drugs. With sales of Sterling-Snofi in excess of $3 billion, the alliance would have more marketing clout. It would make Snofi the largest pharmaceutical firm in Europe and enable Kodak to develop its pharmaceutical operations without taking on additional debt.[5]

Reasons for Creating Strategic Alliances

In the previous discussion regarding the variety of forms that strategic alliances could take, we have seen some of the reasons for the creation of strategic alliances. There are, of course, other reasons for strategic alliances, some of which are as follows:

- Penetrate new foreign markets
- Share the risk of giant investment
- Share research and development costs and risks
- Launch a counterattack against competitors
- Pool global resources
- Learn from partners

Penetrate New Foreign Markets.   Companies form strategic alliances because it is a cheap and more efficient way of entering either a partner's

home market or a third-country market in which a partner is especially strong. For example, General Mills and Switzerland's Nestle
S.A. have created a partnership in a newly formed company called
Cereal Partners Worldwide in order to launch General Mills' cereal
business in Europe. Nestle has strong distribution channels in
Europe; and its first assault will be on France, Spain, and Portugal
with General Mills' Golden Grahams and Honey Nut Cheerios. The
joint venture has also acquired the British breakfast cereal operations
of Ranks Hovis McDougall PLC, giving it a foothold in one of the
world's biggest cereal-eating countries. The average English person
eats thirteen pounds of cereal a year; the average French person one
pound a year; and in Japan, people eat less than one quarter of a
pound. An average American eats ten pounds of cereal a year. Therefore, the global cereal market is seen as fertile ground by the cereal
industry and the Nestle-General Mills venture expects sales of $31
billion in Europe by the year 2000. This partnership represents General Mills' first venture outside North America.[6]

Share the Risk of Giant Investment. Nowhere do we see the risk of
giant investment as strong a motive for forming alliances as in the
aircraft industry. The costs of creating jets are so enormous that aerospace companies are forced to join hands in coproduction agreements
with actual or potential rivals, even when they would prefer to invest
alone for fear of losing vital technological and other company secrets
to their partners. Boeing has formed an alliance with Fuji, Mitsubishi,
and Kawasaki—all Japanese companies—to help defray the estimated
$4 billion cost of building the new 777 jetliner. The Japanese will
build 20 percent of the airframe. By contracting out a large portion
of the design and manufacture, Boeing hopes to speed up market
introduction of the aircraft and beat the competition from Airbus A330
and A340 aircraft. Boeing has a contract with United Airlines to
deliver thirty-four planes worth $323 million each.

Larry Clarkson, the senior vice-president of Boeing's commercial
group, explains why such a dominant company needs partners: "The
day of an airplane being a sole Boeing product has passed," he says.
"What's unique about the big-jet business is that it takes a lot of
dollars and involves high risk, a long-term investment, and a limited
customer base. If we make another large airplane, we would have to
have international involvement."[7]

Share Research and Development Costs and Risks. This reason for a
strategic alliance has been the principal motive for linkups in the high
technology and biotechnology sectors. In 1988, Texas Instruments and

Japan's Hitachi Ltd. entered into a technology agreement to develop 16-megabyte (Mb) dynamic random access memories (DRAMs). Texas Instruments has several cross-licensing agreements with Fujitsu, Sharp, Toshiba, NEC, and Mitsubishi Electric. "No memory chip company can compete globally unless it has $1 billion of manufacturing plant,"[8] says Stan Shih, president and CEO of Acer, Taiwan's leading computer firm.

To underscore the importance of strategic alliances, consider that before such alliances became popular, companies were often forced to spend huge sums of money to acquire required technologies. For instance, in 1985 General Motors spent $5 billion to acquire Hughes Aircraft in order to obtain Hughes' advanced aerospace technologies. GM could have fulfilled the same goal through a strategic alliance and for no investment.[9]

The Big Three auto makers in America—General Motors, Ford Motor, and Chrysler—have undertaken joint projects to develop basic technologies which, upon development, each will share. The three companies have agreed to join hands because none has the resources to undertake alone the several expensive and risky basic research projects that must be financed in order to gain an edge over their Japanese rivals in state-of-the-art technologies. Practical Insight 4-1 explains how the three auto giants are sharing the costs of developing new technologies under the auspices of United States Council for Automotive Research (USCAR).

PRACTICAL INSIGHT 4-1

The Big Three Collaborate to Win Joint Patent

In what may be the first of many such future joint endeavors, the big three auto makers in America—General Motors, Ford Motor, and Chrysler—have achieved something that would have been unthinkable 10 years ago. The trio, better known for fierce competition with each other, have collaborated and successfully produced their first joint patent. The patent, a manufacturing process for a lightweight material that could replace steel in car bodies, is a milestone for the Big Three's accelerated efforts to pool basic research under the umbrella of the United States Council for Automotive Research (USCAR).

Why would the once cut-throat competitors agree to make peace with each other? There are several reasons. First, the U.S. auto makers must find a way to cut costs and improve global competitiveness. Second, no one company, including General Motors, has the financial clout to support the broad array of research projects that must be funded to develop the state-of-the-art technologies to get an edge on the Japanese. This was evident when General Motors scaled back its efforts to single-handedly build an electric car and instead started sharing its concepts with Ford and Chrysler. Third, there is a clear incentive to share costs for basic research whose payoff may be uncertain and far into the future. This is true of the process patent granted jointly to the Big Three auto makers which took five years of collaborative research, and which may not deliver a payoff in production for several more years.

The existence of USCAR has been made possible as a result of the relaxation of prohibitions against joint research under U.S. antitrust laws. There are now 10 consortia operating under the USCAR umbrella, and more are expected. One of the biggest is the U.S. Advanced Battery Consortium (USABC), a $225 million four-year project partly funded by the U.S. Government's Department of Energy, to research new technology to improve lead-acid battery technology. The goal of this project: to be the first in the race with Japan in developing a practical electric vehicle power supply. USCAR's existence is a clear signal that American auto makers cannot go it alone when it comes to funding expensive basic research projects whose prospects for success are uncertain and whose payoffs are unknown and in the long term.

Source: Adapted from Oscar Suris, "Big Three Win Joint Patent, Marking a First," *The Wall Street Journal*, April 13, 1993, B1 and B13.

Launch a Counterattack Against Competitors.

IBM, the powerful computer giant, found itself losing market share in the personal computer business in Europe to companies like Toshiba, Compaq, Hewlett-Packard, Olivetti, and Mitsubishi Electric. Simultaneously, it saw European rivals such as Netherlands' Phillips getting weaker, and in that situation there was a danger that IBM's rivals would fill the vacuum. In 1990, Fujitsu had acquired International Computers Ltd., Britain's flagship company, and Mitsubishi Electric had bought Apricot, the personal-computer manufacturer. In the mainframe market,

Hitachi was growing faster than IBM; and in April 1991, NEC Corporation was negotiating to buy a stake in France's troubled computer maker, Groupe Bull.

IBM perceived the battle for the European computer market as a winner-take-all contest against the Japanese. IBM's response has been to launch an all-out attack to hold its ground in Europe by forming several alliances with its European rivals. It has teamed up with Germany's Siemens to develop high capacity 64-megabyte chips. IBM will forge a critical research and development link between the United States and Europe as a new member of a European project called JESSI. The project is designed to conduct advanced chip research, an area in which the Japanese have a dominant position worldwide. As rivals like Toshiba, Compaq, and Olivetti have lured IBM's prized dealers away, IBM has sought to regain their loyalty by pumping equity capital into the dealerships. The company has invested $100 million in two years into nearly two hundred joint ventures and partnerships including European software suppliers, a Danish supplier of network services, and a German software maker. Says Fausto Talenti, IBM Europe's director of strategy and business development, "We're trying to put agreements in place with all the Europeans and challenge Japanese dominance with all our means."[10]

IBM's strategy of forming partnerships with rival European computer makers such as Siemens, and with software and service suppliers, is a classic example of a company launching a counterattack against aggressive, newer entrants into a market that it considers of vital importance to its global strategy.

Pool Global Resources. Companies in the same industry or line of business sometimes join together to eliminate unnecessary duplication or to share resources and facilities. This strategy is proving to be very popular in the airline industry. For example, United Airlines and British Airways have a strong alliance, especially on key flights through Chicago to London. In the airline industry, a formidable barrier to entry into the industry is the availability of gates at key airports in major world cities. No airline can land at an airport without a gate. Therefore, airlines of different countries are forging alliances in order to share gates. U.S. Air and British Airways share a terminal at Newark International Airport. British Airways and Scandinavian Airlines System (SAS) feed passengers to their U.S. partners, U.S. Air and Continental, through a practice called "code sharing." Under the code sharing system, when passengers take a U.S. Air flight from Philadelphia to London with a linkup to a London-bound British Airways plane in Newark, their tickets are listed in the reservation system as British Airways flights with one connection. This practice extends British Airways' reach deep into the heartland of the United States.[11]

As is true for many global industries, brand loyalty is most important as a competitive weapon for the airlines industry. Ideally, the airlines would prefer to acquire carriers around the world and merge them under one name. However, governments would block such mergers; so, in order to provide the necessary bonding, airlines have resorted to buying equity stakes in each other. For example, KLM Royal Dutch Airlines has a 20 percent equity stake in Northwest Airlines, and Delta and Singapore airlines have a 5 percent stake in each other. A larger picture of the type of network that alliances among airlines are creating is shown in Figure 4-1

Learn from Partners. The desire to learn critical aspects of a business from an alliance partner is a legitimate reason for consummating an alliance. An alliance that is famous as an example of this motive is the one between General Motors and Toyota who, in 1984, formed New United Motor Manufacturing Inc. (NUMMI). The alliance, which is managed by Toyota, took over an old General Motors plant in Fremont, California. Toyota's objective in the partnership was to learn from General Motors how to deal with plants, suppliers, and labor in the United States, while General Motor's goal was to learn the Toyota method of managing and manufacturing. Toyota has surely achieved its objective, considering that it has opened two more plants on its own in the United States since NUMMI was formed. How much did General Motors learn? It certainly learned a great deal from Toyota, but academics and consultants criticize General Motors for spreading NUMMI graduates too thinly throughout its huge bureaucracy. Rather than concentrating them in one place, GM has diluted their beneficial impact on the company as a whole.[12]

Some academics claim that, in the numerous alliances forged between American and Asian companies, it is the Asian companies that benefit the most because Asian companies enter into partnerships to learn from the other side. Such is not the case with most American companies, which often enter into alliances to avoid investments. They are more interested in reducing risks and costs of entering new businesses or markets, and not as much in acquiring new skills from their partners. The Japanese company NEC has been able to gain a leading position in telecommunications, computers, and semiconductors through a series of collaborative ventures. It has enhanced its technology and product competencies in spite of having invested less in research and development than competitors like Sweden's L.M.

FIGURE 4-1 The Airline Family Tree

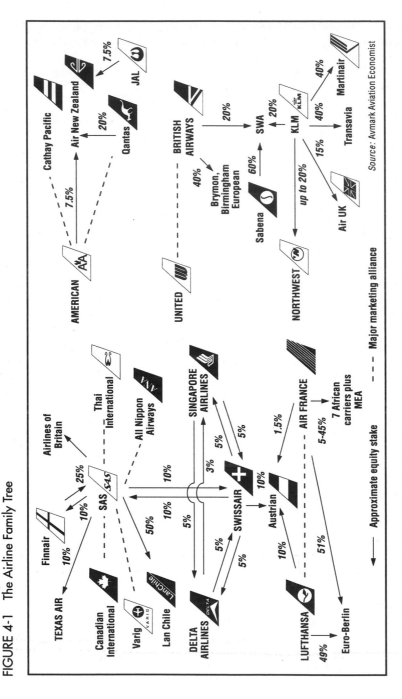

Source: Michael Westlake, "The Mating Planes," *Far Eastern Economic Review,* Hong Kong, February 15, 1990, 37-38.

126

Ericsson, Texas Instruments, and Canada's Northern Telecom. NEC astutely leveraged its in-house R&D over two decades via its string of alliances, especially with Honeywell.[13]

Risks and Problems in Managing Strategic Alliances

We have covered some of the most commonly observed reasons for forming strategic alliances. It is assumed, incorrectly of course, that all strategic alliances are successful. In fact, many alliances are terminated due to a variety of reasons. Among the most common reasons for the failure of alliances are the following:

(handwritten: Why Failed Alliances!)

- Clash of cultures
- Unrealized partner expectations
- Surrender of sovereignty
- Risk of losing core competence to a partner

Clash of Cultures.   When two companies from different countries with very different cultures come together in an alliance, problems can arise due to misunderstanding of the different ways of thinking, behaving, and communicating of each culture. For instance, in a Japanese-U.S. company alliance, the long-term orientation that is so typical of Japanese management could conflict with the relatively short-term orientation of American managers in decisions related to issues such as reinvesting profits in the business for long-term benefits versus declaring dividends in order to keep shareholders happy.

For the most part, Japanese companies are primarily interested in the welfare of their employees and not that of the shareholders; the opposite is the case with most American companies. Therefore, this fundamental difference in attitude toward employees versus shareholders impacts upon decisions that are made in almost all functional areas, from employee layoffs in production to financial decisions such as the expected pay-back period on a new investment in the plant and equipment that could have implications for employment.

Unrealized Partner Expectations.   Difficulties in partner relationships are often caused by one of the partners in the alliance thinking that the other partner is not doing its share or is not making the expected contributions to make the joint venture succeed. Sometimes such problems occur because it is difficult for the partners to accurately assess each other's capabilities during the negotiation stage of the alliance. Consequently, unrealistic expectations are created that lead to disillusionment later on.

Surrender of Sovereignty.   Big companies are increasingly turning to close alliances with small companies. Through joint ventures, equity investments, and other deals, big companies get quick access to new technology and entrepreneurship. The small companies get the much needed cash and credibility that a big corporate partner can provide. For example, Glaxo, the giant British pharmaceutical company, has forged an R&D deal with Gilead Sciences Inc., a biotechnology concern. Under this deal, Glaxo will fund Gilead's development of a new anticancer drug. In return, Glaxo obtains rights to market the drug internationally.[14]

However, there is always the danger of the larger partner buying out the smaller partner in the alliance when the smaller partner cannot keep up with an increasing demand for equity in order to maintain its share in the alliance as the venture grows. The larger partner's share in the venture grows as its contribution increases, and eventually the smaller partner is bought by the bigger company in the alliance.

The danger of a takeover is not limited just to small companies as was the case when, in 1990, Fujitsu bought 80 percent of the British computer company, ICL. Furthermore, a survey by McKinsey and Company, a management consulting firm, showed that of 150 companies involved in alliances, 75 percent had been taken over by the Japanese.

EXHIBIT 4-1   Some Strategic Alliances

Large Company	Small Company	Date	Type of Alliance
IBM	Geographic Systems	1989	Marketing and development
Motorola	Applied Intelligent Systems	1990	Product development
Sony	Panavision	1988	System development
Glaxo	Gilead Sciences	1990	Sales and marketing
Upjohn	Biopure	1990	Sales and marketing
Chesapeake	Stake Technology	1990	System development
Kodak	Immunex	1988	Technology development

Source: Udayan Gupta, "How Big Companies Are Joining Forces with Small Ones for Mutual Advantage," *Wall Street Journal,* February 25, 1991, B1. Reprinted by permission of the *Wall Street Journal,* © 1991 Dow Jones & Company, Inc. All Rights Reserved Worldwide.

Risk of Losing Core Competence to a Partner.   Earlier we discussed the desire to learn from a partner as being one of the reasons for forging strategic alliances.   However, unless there is mutual and equal learning by all parties involved in an alliance, the partner who learns the most from the partnership stands to emerge as the strongest among the alliance partners. The greatest danger is one partner learning the most critical or core skills from the other partner and later using the knowledge gained from the partnership to compete in the industry against its former allies.   This turn of events is precisely what happened in the case of Borden Inc. and Japan's Meiji Milk Products.

Borden and Meiji Milk had an enviable partnership. Under a licensing agreement with Meiji Milk, Borden marketed its premium ice cream throughout Japan through Meiji's vast distribution network. Meiji Milk, in the meantime, learned the technique of processing cheese, margarine, and ice cream, which were still unfamiliar to Japanese producers. In time Borden had over 50 percent of the Japanese market. But competition from Pillsbury Company's Haagen-Dazs, and a string of domestic brands, began to eat into Borden's market share.

Unhappy with Meiji Milk's efforts in fighting the competition to maintain market share, Borden decided to dissolve the partnership. However, much to Borden's dismay, Meiji Milk then introduced two competing brands of premium ice cream, one of which was named Breuges, a brand name that even Meiji Milk marketers concede is similar in price and content to Borden's "Lady Borden." Here is an example of a partner, in this case Meiji Milk, learning a core technology from its partner and then competing against it when the partnership sours.[15]

Making Strategic Alliances Work

Although there are no magical prescriptions to ensure the success of strategic alliances, there are some guidelines that could enhance the chances of their survival.

Trust Is Built in Small Steps.   Trust among partners is critical to the success of any alliance. But trust cannot be written into a legal document in the form of a contract. It is each other's observed behavior that builds trust in any relationship, and this fact is true in a strategic alliance as well. Alliance partners must keep trust in mind and behave in an open manner that enhances the bonds of that trust between them. Each of the partners must attempt to find ways of working together without either one feeling that the other is trying to steal technology or take advantage in any way. Such trust takes time to develop, and relationships based upon trust need to be developed in a deliberate fashion.

Pick a Compatible Partner.   To begin with, the alliance must be important enough to make a strategic impact on the future well-being of both partners. If one of the partners considers the alliance of merely peripheral importance, the seeds of dissolution are sown. Cultural compatibility is an absolute prerequisite for the success of any partnership. Therefore, if the partners in an alliance have greatly divergent cultures, it would be advisable to have one of the partners play a dominant role in the day-to-day management of the venture once the strategic intent of the alliance has been mutually agreed upon. This arrangement is the one under which the NUMMI partnership between General Motors and Toyota is being administered, with Toyota managing the venture on a daily basis.

Create and Maintain an Alliance with Equal Power.   An alliance in which one of the partners is more powerful than the other is in danger of collapsing unless the more powerful partner treats the weaker partner as an equal. Power derives from one's ability to deliver something—technology, capital, information, or resources—to another, something that the other party cannot obtain in the marketplace or develop by itself at an acceptable cost. The power that a company can muster in an alliance is not necessarily associated with its relative size vis-a-vis its partner. For example, a company that has the proprietary knowledge and expertise to develop a breakthrough drug for the treatment of a fatal disease, or that can develop a better and faster computer chip, will have the power to deal on equal terms with a much larger company. The power balance in an alliance is what matters. A small company may have the technology, but a large firm could provide the required capital to develop and commercialize it. As long as the relationship maintains a power balance, the partnership should not expect trouble. However, when a power imbalance develops in an alliance, the company emerging as the more powerful should be careful not to act as such in order for the alliance to survive.

Be Patient. An infinite amount of patience is needed on both sides during the various stages of an alliance. During the initial negotiation phase, patience is necessary to ensure that the alliance is properly structured in terms of who is responsible for what types of decisions, and so forth. Spending extra time and effort on ironing out such issues early in the alliance helps prevent future problems. Patience is also needed when the alliance begins to function. Expecting immediate results can prove fatal. Managers on both sides must recognize that delays and unexpected technical- and people-related problems will emerge in any organization, and that the chances of such problems arising when two companies are engaged in a collaborative effort are that much greater.

CORE COMPETENCY LEVERAGING :

Building strategic alliances is one of the principal strategies that astute multinational companies have successfully adopted in order to attain global competitive advantage and superiority. Another strategy is being used by companies that are gaining prominence in a variety of businesses, a strategy that is not readily apparent to their less perceptive competitors. This strategy is to gain superiority by building on one or more core competencies. Fundamental to the concept of core competence is the recognition of the distinction among core competence, core product, and end products.[16]
  Core competence may be defined as the distinctive ability to excel in a key area upon which a company can build a variety of businesses and develop new generations of products, some of which customers may need but have not yet imagined. Core products are the intermediate linkages between core competencies and end products. They are the subassemblies or components that actually make significant additions to the value of the end products. To be in a position of world leadership, a company must be in a position of strength at all three levels—core competencies, core products, and end products. For example, Honda developed core competence in engines and power-train technology that was physically embodied in its core product—the engine—which it skillfully incorporated in a variety of end products such as lawn mowers, generators, marine engines, motorcycles, and cars.
  At the core competence level, the goal is to attain state-of-the-art, world-class leadership in a key field. For example, Sony developed the capacity to miniaturize, and Canon's competencies are in optics, imaging, and microprocessor controls.
  At the core products level the goal is to maximize world manufacturing share. This goal is achieved by manufacturing a core product for sale to both internal and external customers. For instance, in the 1970's, the Japanese company JVC established several VCR supply relationships with American and European consumer electronics companies. Such arrangements enabled JVC to garner the cash and market feedback on its products and to surpass Sony and the Dutch company, Phillips. A similar strategy is being used by Korean companies such as Goldstar, Samsung, and Daewoo. They have set up supply

relationships with Western companies, their objectives being to build core product leadership in such diverse areas as displays, semiconductors, and automotive engines. Another strategic objective of the Korean companies is to prevent their potential American and European customer competitors from making manufacturing investments in the Korean companies' core products and thus displacing them from value-creating activities.

Serving as a manufacturing base for Western companies gives core product manufacturers like Goldstar and Samsung an opportunity to build manufacturing share without the risk and expense of building downstream brand share. Product feedback received from buyer companies provides free and invaluable market research data on customer preferences and market needs. Such information is used by a core product manufacturer to improve the core product. Furthermore, this kind of information serves as a lever to develop the end product by itself and to enter the end product market independently. This strategy was used quite effectively by Japanese television makers like Sony and Hitachi in their quest to enter the U.S. market. They first served as original equipment manufacturers (OEMs) of private-label, black and white television sets for American department stores. Then they used the experience and knowledge gained in the process to upgrade their presence in the United States from OEMs to independent marketers of color TV sets under their own brand names. More importantly, in doing so the Japanese companies managed to destroy American TV manufacturers like RCA, GE, and Sylvania.

A dominant world manufacturing share in a core product may not necessarily mean an equally strong position in the market for end products. For example, Canon supposedly has a dominating world manufacturing share in desktop laser printer engines; however, its brand share in the laser printer business is actually quite small. Similarly, Matsushita has a huge market share worldwide in compressors, its core product. Its brand share in the air conditioner and refrigerator businesses, however, is negligible. Clearly, the strategic objective for obtaining the maximum possible manufacturing market share for core products is to generate revenue and customer feedback, which in turn can be used to improve and extend core competencies. The focus should be fixed on enhancing and replenishing a company's core competencies and leveraging them to develop and market a variety of end products with core products serving as their backbone. Examples of companies that have effectively leveraged their core competencies are Casio, 3M, and Canon. Casio drew on its expertise in semiconductors and digital displays by producing calculators, small screen television sets, musical instruments, and watches. The 3M Company combined competencies in substrates, coatings, and adhesives to produce Post-it pads, magnetic tape, photographic film, pressure sensitive tapes, and coated abrasives—quite a diversified product portfolio driven by only a few shared core competencies. Canon has leveraged its competencies in optics, imaging, and microprocessor controls to produce copiers, laser printers, cameras, and image scanners.

Core competence is important because, in the short run, the quality of a company's product and its performance determine its competitiveness. In the long run, however, the global competitiveness of a company depends more upon its ability to grow through internal development, licensing deals, or strategic alliances. Its core competencies, however, are what give birth to new generations of products, and do so faster than the competition.

COUNTERATTACK

With the increasing globalization of industries, U.S. companies in such industries have come to realize that a competitive attack against their home market can be launched by foreign companies who, at the time of the attack, may have a relatively small presence in the U.S. market. In the past, the typical response of U.S. companies was to assume that foreign companies, especially those from Japan and the Pacific Basin countries, were able to effectively compete in the U.S. market because of lower costs derived from cheap labor rates in their own countries.

In response, U.S. companies established offshore assembly and manufacturing sites in Asia to lower their own production costs. American companies also observed that the Japanese were taking advantage of lower costs from scale economies derived from production in large world-scale plants. In response, American companies followed suit and also established world-scale plants. However, such strategies did not prevent a market share decline in the U.S. market of American companies as Japanese companies continued to take over the market share. What American companies did not recognize, and what Japanese companies apparently did, was that a strategy based on low labor costs was vulnerable to fluctuating exchange rates and rising labor costs. This phenomenon is exactly what has taken place in Japan. Wage rates there have risen significantly in the last three decades, high enough to make them noncompetitive in comparison to wage rates in other Asian countries such as Malaysia, Thailand, and Sri Lanka. Moreover, the strategy of lowering production costs through scale advantages derived from large-scale plants also proved to be vulnerable to technological improvements in the production process brought about by such factors as robotics and computer-aided, flexible manufacturing. Today, global competition is characterized by a series of competitive attacks and counterattacks by global companies in each other's home and third-country markets. Companies that cannot engage in such battles are doomed to lose market share, both at home and abroad.[17] For example, an American company that is attacked by a Japanese company cannot spend its resources only on defending its home market while the Japanese company faces no such threat in its own home market. The American company must be capable of attacking the Japanese company in the Japanese market or in a third-country market where the Japanese company is vulnerable. The Japanese aggressor, when attacked by the American defender on his (Japanese) home ground, is forced to divert his resources towards defending his home market and away from attacking the foreign American market. In actual military combat, a defender must be able to attack the enemy in the enemy's home territory in order to repel the enemy's attack. The same holds true in business warfare. In order to launch a counterattack, however, one must have the required "firepower" which, in business terms, is the cash flow to launch an attack.

Cash flows are needed to develop the various capabilities required to make an effective attack or counterattack. The types of capabilities needed are: (1) channels of distribution through which to direct an attack, (2) investment in key core competencies, and (3) a wide range of products that can benefit from the same distribution channels. With these capabilities in place in major world markets, companies can engage in cross-subsidizing across countries and markets.[18]

Cross-subsidization involves the deployment of resources generated in one area or country for use in another location. For instance, using cash flows generated in Japan or elsewhere, a Japanese company can launch an attack on an American company in the U.S. market or a third-country market in which the American company is weak. Such an attack might involve lowering the Japanese company's prices in the U.S. market just enough to squeeze the profit margins of the U.S. company. The objective here is to reduce the cash flows of the American company and drain them away from activities such as marketing and research and development. Without channels of distribution in the foreign company's home market, the American company is in no position to cross-subsidize and counterattack. The American company is thus weakened and unable to make necessary improvements in its products or launch expensive advertising and marketing campaigns. Consequently, the American company loses market share and the Japanese company then proceeds to raise its prices and increase its margins, which are, in turn, used to continue such attacks in other countries and markets.

Cash flows are also required to develop effective channels of distribution in major markets of the world. It is generally accepted that, to be a global player in a global industry, a company must have an effective presence in three areas of the world; namely, the United States, Europe, and Asia. Developing channels of distribution is an expensive endeavor for which enormous amounts of cash are needed.

Cash flows are also vitally needed to develop core technologies and core competencies, which, as just discussed, are key requisites of a global company's competitive advantage. Companies that can generate such competencies can leverage them in the ways that were discussed earlier.

Cash flows are also needed to develop a large enough portfolio of contiguous products that can be funneled through existing distribution channels in order to utilize the channels to their maximum capacity.

Each of the above activities, carried out on a global scale, requires cash flows. These activities, in turn, generate necessary cash flows, and the cycle of cross-subsidization, attack, and counterattack continues on a global scale. Companies that do not perceive the strategic intent of global companies playing the game of cross-subsidization—weakening the competition in one market after another in order to capture market share and accompanying cash flows—are paving the path to their own extinction. The strategic intent of global competitors is to wage battles worldwide. They want not only to capture world volume but to generate the cash flow necessary to support the creation of new core technologies; enhance core competencies; establish strong distribution channels; acquire or build world-class, efficient plants; and achieve global brand recognition through massive advertising and marketing campaigns. An excellent example of an effective counterattack strategy is the invasion by Eastman Kodak of the home market of Japan's Fuji Photo Film.[19] Kodak launched the attack against Fuji in response to Fuji's attack on Kodak's lucrative markets in America and Europe, where for decades Kodak had maintained a dominant market share in the color film business. Fuji's attack shrank Kodak's margins and forced it to cut prices. Realizing that it faced a global challenge from Fuji that would only grow stronger, Kodak struck back and invaded its rival's home market. The results have been dramatically favorable for Kodak. Kodak's sales have jumped sixfold to an estimated $1.3 billion in 1990. It has put Fuji on the defensive; Fuji's domestic margins have been squeezed, and some of Fuji's best executives have been recalled to Tokyo. In Kodak's estimation, its invasion of the Japanese market forced Fuji to divert its resources from overseas in order to defend its home market, where it had enjoyed a commanding 70 percent share of the market in color film. Practical Insight 4-2 presents a complete picture of Kodak's counterattack strategy.

PRACTICAL INSIGHT 4-2

The Revenge of Big Yellow

Eastman Kodak Has Struck Back at Fuji Photo Film Where It Hurts Most—at Home in Japan. Yes, It Can Be Done.

Throughout the 1980's, Eastman Kodak looked like just one more fat-and-unhappy American company incapable of defending itself against a Japanese onslaught. Fuji Photo Film attacked the American and European markets, where for decades Kodak had enjoyed a lucrative dominance in color film. It squeezed Kodak's margins and forced it into a divisive and not always successful panic to slash costs. "Big Yellow," as Kodak is known on Wall Street because of its bright yellow boxes of film, received the thumbs down from investors. Its share price underperformed the market for years, prompting rumors of eventual breakup.

Then Kodak struck back. Its executives in Rochester, New York, admitted to themselves that their company faced a global challenge from Fuji that would only grow. They decided to invade their rival's home market. Since reentering the Japanese market in 1984, Kodak's local operation has grown from a pokey office housing 15 people to a business with 4,500 employees, a fancy headquarters in Tokyo, a corporate laboratory in nearby Yokohama, manufacturing plants and dozens of affiliated companies.

Meanwhile, Kodak's sales in Japan have soared sixfold, to an estimated $1.3 billion this year. All this has been achieved against fierce resistance from Fuji and Konica, the entrenched Japanese film suppliers.

Kodak's push into the Japanese market has not been cheap. Its Japanese operations are now making an operating profit, but it may be years before they pay back the $500 million spent to build them up. But Kodak spotted that the Japanese market is the world's second largest. It judged that its invasion would put Fuji on the defensive, forcing it to divert resources from overseas in order to defend itself at home, where it had enjoyed a 70 percent share of the market in color film. Some of Fuji's best executives have now been pulled back to Tokyo. Fuji's domestic margins have been squeezed. Fuji has proved as vulnerable to attack in Japan as Kodak was in America. Kodak has been selling photographic materials in Japan since 1889. But after World War II, the American occupation forces persuaded most American firms, including Kodak, to leave Japan to give war-torn local industry a chance to recover. Kodak handed over the marketing of its products to Japanese distributors. Over the next four decades, Fuji gained its 70 percent share of the Japanese market and then launched its export drive. Konica, a latecomer, grabbed 20 percent of domestic sales, leaving Kodak and a handful of European firms to share a miserable 10 percent.

By 1984, repeated rounds of trade negotiations had dismantled most of the postwar barriers protecting the Japanese film market. Kodak set out to make its yellow-packaged boxes as familiar and friendly to Japanese customers as any local product. Its strategy was to boost:

Distribution. Kodak realized that it had to get control of its own distribution and marketing channels. "Using a trading company helps at the start," says Mr. Albert Seig, the president of Kodak's Japanese subsidiary, "but few trading companies take a strategic view." Rather than go it alone, Kodak established a joint venture with its distributor, Nagase Sangyo, an Osaka-based trading company specializing in chemicals. Kodak won the support of Nagase's 1,500 employees with two years of patient wooing.

Local investment. To nurture relations with its suppliers, Kodak also took equity stakes in them. It now has 20 percent of Chinon Industries, a supplier of 35mm cameras, videocamera lenses, printers and other computer accessories which Kodak sells under its own label. Kodak has acquired a good deal of manufacturing know-how from Chinon and is expected to increase its holding in it still further. When Kodak needed to hire 100 systems engineers quickly, it invested in Nippon Systems House. Likewise, Kodak Imagica, a photo-finisher that provides developing facilities around Japan, is 51 percent owned by Kodak. Kodak Information Systems, formerly part of a microfilm and electronic-imaging equipment supplier called Kusuda, is now a wholly-owned subsidiary.

Promotion. At a time when Fuji and Konica were committed to heavy spending on promotion abroad, Kodak spent three times more than both of them combined on advertising in Japan. It erected mammoth Sim neon signs as landmarks in many of Japan's big cities. Its sign in Sapporo, Hokkaido, is the highest in the country. It sponsored sumo wrestling, judo, tennis tournaments and even the Japanese team at the 1988 Seoul Olympics, a neat reversal of Fuji's 1984 coup when it won the race to become the official supplier to the Los Angeles Olympics.

Kodak's cheekiest ploy was to spend $1 million on an airship emblazoned with its logo. It cruised over Japanese cities for three years, mischievously circling over Fuji's Tokyo headquarters from time to time. To Fuji's chagrin, Japanese newspapers gleefully picked up the story. The Japanese firm was forced to spend twice as much bringing its own airship back from Europe for just two months of face-saving promotion in Tokyo.

Half of all Japanese consumers can now recognize Kodak's goods instantly. This brand awareness has helped Kodak grow in Japan at about twice the pace of Fuji or Konica. Kodak's share of sales to amateur photographers has grown by a steady 1 percent each year for the past six years. Kodak now has a 15 percent slice of that market and is expected to overtake second-place Konica within the next few years. Kodak's success in Tokyo has been even more impressive. It now has 35 percent of the amateur market there, even though amateur photography is not Kodak's biggest business in Japan. Medical x-ray film and photographic supplies to the graphic arts and publishing industries are bigger. In these markets Kodak's share reaches 85 percent.

Kodak's counterattack has been possible only because of an abrupt change in attitude back in Rochester. Kodak has shed the worst of its fabled parochialism, even though the parent company still has no foreigners on its main board. Technically brilliant, the company had become complacent and slipshod in marketing. It was not until 1984 that Kodak started printing in Japanese on its packaging in Japan—and not until 1988 that it launched a film (Kodacolor Gold) that offered the more garish colors which Japanese consumers prefer.

Today, Kodak thinks just like a Japanese company—at least in Japan. Apart from a small unit headed by Mr. Seig which liaises with Kodak's headquarters, the rest of the local subsidiary is entirely Japanese, complete with a Japanese boss and

Japanese management. There are only 30 foreigners among Kodak's 4,500 people in Japan. So thoroughly Japanese has Kodak become that it even has its own keiretsu—a family of firms with cross holdings in one another. And so thoroughly has it been accepted that some of Kodak's largest business customers are asking that Kodak take a small equity stake in them too. That is a significant gesture of both market anticipation and goodwill. The global battle with Fuji will continue, but it is now being waged on both sides of the world.

Source: *The Economist*, November 10, 1990, 77-78.

Implications of Counterattack Strategy

The implementation of a counterattack strategy has several critical implications for the management of a global company. This section examines some of the most important ones.

In order to assist a parent company in a global counterattack, the foreign affiliates in the company have to relinquish much of their autonomy to the parent company or to divisional management. The relationship between and among the affiliates and the parent company has to be one of resource interdependence rather than independence. The strategies and implementation plans of each affiliate have to be coordinated with those of the parent company and the other affiliates. This coordination is necessary so that resources required for launching offensive or preemptive cross-subsidization strikes against competitors can be marshalled from the most appropriate sources within the global network of the company. The managerial philosophy underlying a counterattack strategy is that in a global industry, competition in an affiliate country does not always emanate from other local companies; rather, it can come from affiliates of foreign companies that are members of powerful networks of global companies having worldwide access to resources. Therefore, a foreign affiliate left to fend for itself with only its own country-based resources would be no match for an aggressive global company's attack without help from sister affiliates or the parent company. Collaboration among the affiliates and the parent company in the sharing of resources through cross-subsidization is the only way to deflect an attack by a global company against a weak-sister affiliate.

At the parent company level, divisional management and strategic business units (SBUs) have to abandon a "my division" or "my business unit" attitude and think more in terms of interdivisional and cross-SBU relationships. Like foreign affiliates, they, too, have to collaborate and share resources among themselves and seek to agree on, and implement, strategies that add value and strength to the company as a global whole.

Investments abroad in manufacturing, research and development, marketing, and other functional areas have to be made for strategic reasons, such as establishing a beachhead in major markets of the world or in the home market of a foreign competitor. Such investments are based primarily on their strategic importance to any future offensive or defensive counterattack strategies and not necessarily on financial considerations, such as return on investment or profitability.

GLOCALIZATION

In discussing the three strategies above—strategic alliances, core competency leveraging, and counterattack—it is quite clear that the parent company plays a central role in coordinating its network of globally dispersed affiliates. The parent company makes the network operate as one integrated, collective global unit. Global companies, however, must be careful that, in their zealous pursuit of an effective global strategy, they do not neglect managerial initiative at lower levels in the organizational hierarchy, especially at the regional and subsidiary levels. *Glocalization*, which means thinking globally but acting locally, includes an optimal mix of parental control where it counts and local initiative at regional and subsidiary levels. This structural balance has proved to be most fruitful for well-managed, global companies.

A successful strategy incorporates the glocalization of the following interrelated elements:

- Management
- Foreign Affiliates
- Exports
- Products
- Production

Glocalization of Management

Adopting a global strategy that does not stifle local initiative involves a delicate balancing act. It often means giving regional and subsidiary managers the freedom to develop their own implementation plans for products, marketing, financing, and production that are consistent with local political, economic, legal, and cultural demands. For example, Levi Strauss & Company, the jeans maker, maintains tight headquarters control where it matters most. As a company that cherishes brand identity and quality, Levi's has organized several foreign manufacturing subsidiaries rather than rely on a patchwork of licensees that are hard to control. It has also exported its pioneering use of computers to track sales and manufacturing, and in so doing, keep a step ahead of fashion trends. Levi's also allows local managers to make decisions about adapting products to suit local tastes. In Brazil, Levi's local managers make decisions regarding distribution. For example, local initiative and knowledge of the market enabled Levi's to establish a chain of 400 Levi's Only stores, some of them in tiny, rural towns in Brazil's fragmented market. In 1990, the stores accounted for 65 percent of Levi's Brazilian sales. Levi's approach represents a slogan that is symbolic of what glocalization stands for: "Be global, act local."[20]

In the Sony Corporation, apart from the long-term strategy handed down from Tokyo, regional managers make all their own investment and product decisions on the spot. Top managers from Sony's subsidiaries around the world meet twice a year to hammer out the basic details of the company's operations.[21] Insiders say that this international-top-meeting arrangement is the main reason for Sony's ability to respond to market changes and launch new products so swiftly.

A glocalization of management philosophy is also evident in Toshiba and Matsushita Electric Industrial, which have delegated decision-making authority to regional headquarters. Toshiba has a tri-polar regional management structure for Asia, Europe, and the United States. Each area manager has decision-making authority for manufacturing, sales, and some research and development. At Matsushita Electric, which has regional headquarters for Asia, Europe, and the United States based in Singapore, London, and New Jersey respectively, most local decisions are now made locally, and the three top regional heads are all members of Matsushita Electric's board of directors. Again, each region has manufacturing, marketing, and product-related research and development capability, and Matsushita plans to develop some regional, basic-research facilities as well.[22]

Glocalization of Foreign Affiliates

Strong presence in a foreign market requires the physical presence of manufacturing facilities in the market itself. Governments are making it easier for companies to enter markets provided there is a commitment on the part of company management to base production of the product in the foreign country as soon as possible. Companies are also realizing that, as good corporate citizens, they ought to make a significant contribution to the economic development and social welfare of their host countries. Transferring production technology to the host country and increasing the ratio of locally produced items in the production process or the final product is one way to contribute to a host country's economic well-being. Training and developing local suppliers of components and subassemblies enhances the technological base of a nation. Such a transfer of technology could be brought about by entering into technical collaboration agreements with local partners, forming joint ventures with local capital, or establishing a wholly owned subsidiary—that is, owned by the parent company. The economic and political conditions in a country or region, as well as market size and the capabilities of the local partner, often dictate the mode of collaboration. For example, Japanese manufacturers have chosen to enter European markets mainly through joint ventures because of a preference, in Europe, for such collaborations and the hostility toward wholly owned Japanese plants exhibited by European governments. In the United States, Japanese companies have shown a preference for wholly owned plants, although they have also established several joint ventures with American companies. For example, Honda has wholly owned manufacturing subsidiaries in the United States, is collaborating with the Rover Group in Britain, and has a joint venture to produce motorcycles in Thailand.

Glocalization of Exports

Using foreign production plants as export bases to third-country markets is yet another way to become a "local" company in a foreign country. The Japanese have been exporting U.S.-made Japanese automobiles back to Japan and to European markets. Similar strategies have been adopted by global companies, which export from developing countries in Asia and other parts of the world. Following a glocalization-of-production strategy, Sony now has its own network of factories in each of the company's main markets—America, Europe, and Asia. Levi Strauss has a global manufacturing network with a mix of eleven sewing plants and contract manufacturers, enabling it to supply customers from nearby factories.

Glocalization of Products

Should a company standardize its product or service throughout the world—sell the same product without making variations to suit differences in local taste and use—or should the product or service be tailored and customized to comply with local taste and use? This issue has been debated ad infinitum, and the answer to the question is that, to the extent that standardization is possible, a company should attempt it. There are some products and services that can be standardized globally, such as fax machines and telephones. On the other side of the scale, however, are products, such as coffee and soups, which must be modified to make them more palatable to the tastes of people in various countries and cultures.

Companies are resolving this dilemma by realizing that some products have certain core technologies, subassemblies, or components that can be standardized on a worldwide basis, while other parts or configurations of the same product require adaptation to local conditions. For example, Whirlpool Corporation saw a growing market in India for washing machine sales to the growing number of middle-class, two income families in that country. The washing machines sold in Europe and America, however, were not suited to wash the traditional, five-yard-long saris worn by Indian women. Whirlpool formed a joint venture with an Indian partner to produce and market a Western-style automatic washing machine that is compact enough to fit into Indian homes and incorporates specially designed agitators that will not tangle saris. Variations of the same machine, internally dubbed the "World Washer," are also built and sold in Brazil and Mexico. In the aftermath of the glocalization-of-exports strategy discussed above, Whirlpool is considering the export of these machines from factories in those countries to other Asian and Latin American markets. Except for minor variations in controls, the three bare-bones washers are nearly identical; they all handle only eleven pounds of wash, which is about one half the capacity of the typical U.S. model.[23] Whirlpool illustrates the slogan of product glocalization, which is: Standardize worldwide what you can and adapt what you cannot.

Glocalization of Production

Companies are splitting up the production process and farming out parts of it to different countries. They are doing so in order to exploit the advantages of lower costs derived from scale economies, of international specialization—some countries are better at doing certain things than others—and of locational advantages such as proximity to markets, cheap labor, freedom from significant political risk, and local incentives such as tax holidays and government subsidies. Japanese automobile companies have targeted Asian countries for the expansion of their production activities because of the long-term growth potential of markets there. For example, one result of the Japanese expansion is the beginning of a parts-supply network that spans Southeast Asia. To achieve economies of scale, Japan's car makers produce different parts in different countries. Nissan, for example, wants to concentrate on production of diesel engines in Thailand, mechanical parts in Indonesia, wire harnesses in the Philippines, and clutches and electrical parts in Malaysia. Toyota has earmarked $215 million for investment in facilities to support a similar parts-production program.[24]

The farming out of production to different countries also extends to finished products. For instance, a company that produces a variety of models of the same product might assign a subsidiary in one country to specialize in the production of one model and a subsidiary in yet another country to specialize in a second model. The two subsidiaries then export to each other the models they produce. In this way, both subsidiaries have two models to market in their respective regions, but each is responsible for the production of only one of them. This strategy is quite common in the global automobile industry, and General Motors and Ford already practice it in Europe.

SUMMARY

This chapter was about the principal strategies that global companies have adopted to gain worldwide competitive superiority in global industries. Four such strategies were discussed: (1) strategic alliances, (2) core competency leveraging, (3) counterattack, and (4) glocalization.

Strategic alliances are collaborative agreements among firms in the same or different industries that are forged for a variety of reasons, including the following: necessity to penetrate foreign markets, share the risk of huge investments needed for various projects, share research and development costs and risks, launch an attack against a competitor by teaming up with a competitor's common enemy, and learn critical skills from the alliance partner. There are a variety of strategic alliances. Some involve collaboration without an investment in equity capital, while others are in the form of a joint venture between the partners in which a daughter company is formed, and in which both partners have an equity interest. Yet another type of strategic alliance is one in which there is either a one-way or mutual purchase of equity among the partners. A strategic alliance can also be cash neutral, meaning that each company trades assets with the others and no cash changes hands.

There are risks and problems with strategic alliances about which one should be cautious. Problems can and do arise, due to a clash of the divergent cultures of the partners, or because of unrealized expectations from the alliance, the surrender of sovereignty by one of the partners to the other, or the danger of losing core competence to a partner who later uses it to compete with its former alliance company. The strategy of leveraging core competencies is based on the premise that a company must have a core competence—some strength that it excels in vis-a-vis its competitors—in one or more areas, and that it can build a variety of businesses and new generations of products on that competence. A core product is the link between a core competence and the final product, and for a company to achieve a position of world leadership in a business, it must excel in all three aspects of leveraging—core competence, a core product, and end products.

Counterattack strategy is based on the premise that global competition is characterized by a series of competitive attacks and counterattacks by global companies in each other's home and third-country markets. Companies that cannot fight such battles risk losing market-share superiority both at home and abroad. In order to wage a counterattack strategy, companies must generate enough cash to cross-subsidize businesses and regions and to support and develop counterattack weapons that include the following: (1) strong distribution channels in major current and potential markets, (2) core technologies and core competencies, and (3) a portfolio of contiguous products that can also be funneled through the company's distribution channels in order to make maximum use of them.

The final global strategy discussed was glocalization, the essence of which is, "think globally, but act locally." To implement this strategy, companies must glocalize their managerial practices, foreign affiliates, exports, products, and production.

QUESTIONS

1. What is a strategic alliance? Discuss reasons for the formation of strategic alliances.
2. Identify and explain the different types of strategic alliances that are possible in a global business.
3. Scan some recent issues of *Business Week* and the *Wall Street Journal* and bring to class items that report on a new recently created strategic alliance. Identify and describe the type of alliance it is.
4. Discuss reasons that could cause an alliance to fail.
5. Explain the concept of core competence. What is the difference between a core competence and a core product?
6. Discuss the relationship among a core competence, core product, and end product.

7. Explain the meaning of cross-subsidization. How is cross-subsidization utilized globally in a firm's competitive battles?
8. What is the strategic intent of companies that engage in the practice of cross-subsidization?
9. Explain the relationship between cross-subsidization and global cash flows. Why is it important for companies to understand this relationship?
10. What is the meaning of the term glocalization? Can a company that is implementing a global strategy simultaneously implement a glocalization strategy?
11. Explain glocalization of each of the following aspects of a multinational company's business: management, foreign affiliates, exports, products, and production.

FURTHER READING

Babbar, Sunil and Arun Rai. "Competitive Intelligence for International Business." *Long Range Planning*, Vol. 26, no. 3 (June 1993): 103-113

Erdmann, Peter B. "When Businesses Cross International Borders: Strategic Alliances and Their Alternatives." *Columbia Journal of World Business*, Vol. 28, no. 2 (Summer 1993): 107-108.

Hamel, Gary, and C. K. Prahalad. "Do You Really Have a Global Strategy." *Harvard Business Review* (July-August 1985): 139-48.

Hamel, Gary; Yves L. Doz, and C. K. Prahalad. "Collaborate with Your Competitors and Win." *Harvard Business Review* (January-February 1989): 133-39.

Hamel, Gary, and C. K. Prahalad. "Strategic Intent." *Harvard Business Review* (May-June 1989): 63-76.

Maruyama, Magoroh. "Lessons from Japanese Management Failures in Foreign Countries." *Human Systems Management*, Vol. 11, no. 1 (1992): 41-48.

Ohmae, Kenichi. "The Global Logic of Strategic Alliances." *Harvard Business Review* (March-April 1989): 143-54.

Sugiura, Hideo. "How Honda Localizes Its Global Strategy." *Sloan Management Review* (Fall 1990): 77-82.

Turpin, Dominique. "Strategic Alliances with Japanese Firms: Myths and Realities." *Long Range Planning*, Vol. 26, no. 4 (August 1993): 11-15.

NOTES

[1] Udayan Gupta, "Sony Adopts Strategy to Broaden Ties with Small Firms," *Wall Street Journal*, February 28, 1991, B2.

[2] Stuart M. Dambrot, "Foreign Alliances that Make Sense," *Electronic Business*, September 3, 1990, 68.

[3] Stephen D. Moore, "Volvo Contract on Joint Facility Appears Near," *Wall Street Journal*, April 26, 1991, A12.

[4] Michael J. McCarthy, "Coke, Nestle' Get Together Over Coffee," *Wall Street Journal*, November 30, 1990, B1.

[5] Clare Ansberry, "Kodak, Snofi Plan Alliance in Drug Sector," *Wall Street Journal*, January 9, 1991, A3-A4.

[6] Richard Gibson, "Cereal Venture Is Planning Honey of a Battle in Europe," *Wall Street Journal*, November 14, 1990, B1 and B8.

[7] Jeremy Main, "Making Global Alliance Work," *Fortune*, December 17, 1990, 124.

[8] Michael Selwyn, "Making Marriages of Convenience," *Asian Business*, January 1991, 26.

[9] Jordan D. Lewis, "Competitive Alliances Redefine Companies," *Management Review*, April 1991, 14.

[10] Jonathan B. Levine and Gail E. Schares, "IBM Europe Starts Swinging Back," *Business Week*, May 6, 1991, 52-53.

[11] Tim Smart and Mark Maremont, "Birds of a Feather Are Doing Deals Together," *Business Week*, September 11, 1989, 32.

[12] Jeremy Main, "Making Global Alliances Work," *Fortune*, December 17, 1990, 124.

[13] Gary Hamel, Yves L. Doz and C. K. Prahalad, "Collaborate with Your Competitors and Win," *Harvard Business Review* (January-February 1989): 134.

[14] Jeremy Main, "Making Global Alliances Work," 121-22.

[15] Yumico Ono, "Borden's Breakup with Meiji Milk Shows How a Japanese Partnership Can Curdle," *Wall Street Journal*, February 2, 1991, B7.

[16] For an excellent expose of the concept of Core Competence, see C. K. Prahalad and Gary Hamel, "The Core Competence of the Corporation," *Harvard Business Review* (May-June 1990): 79-91.

[17] Craig M. Watson, "Counter-Competition Abroad to Protect Home Markets," *Harvard Business Review* (January-February 1992): 40-42.

[18] Gary Hamel and C. K. Prahalad, "Do You Really Have a Global Strategy," *Harvard Business Review* (July-August 1985): 139-148.

[19] "The Revenge of Big Yellow," *The Economist*, November 10, 1990, 77-78.

[20] Maria Shao, Robert Neff, and Jeffrey Ryser, "For Levi's, A Flattering Fit Overseas," *Business Week*, November 5, 1990, 76-77.

[21] Nicholas Valery, "Consumer Electronics Survey," *The Economist*, April 13, 1991, 17.

[22] "The Goal Is Genuine Internationalism," *Business Week*, July 16, 1990, 81.

[23] David Woodruff, "A Little Machine that Won't Shred a Sari," *Business Week*, June 3, 1991, 100.

[24] Amy Borrus, "Japan Streaks Ahead in East Asia," *Business Week*, May 7, 1990, 55.

Chapter F I V E

Organizing for
International Operations

Organizations are created to link the behavior of individuals; to collect and pool information, skills, or capital; to engage in related actions toward the achievement of a set of goals; and to monitor performance, initiate corrections, and define new goals.[1] In a strictly domestic enterprise, these aims can be achieved with a two-dimensional organization--an organization that concerns itself with resolving the potentially conflicting demands of functional (production, finance, marketing, etc.) and product-line requirements.

A two-dimensional organization is, however, not the appropriate structure for a multinational enterprise because a multinational enterprise must not only be able to resolve functional and product-line demands but must also to deal effectively with geographic area concerns. Thus, a more appropriate organizational form for a multinational enterprise should combine three dimensions: (1) functional expertise, (2) product and technical know-how, and (3) knowledge of the area and country. The manner in which these three dimensions are combined should and does differ from one international company

149

to another. There is no one best way for organizing an international company, and each company will combine these three dimensions in an organizational structure that it tries to make consistent with its particular strategy.

Michael Duerr and John Roach point out that a firm's international organization is generally determined as a response to three major strategic concerns:

- How to encourage a predominantly domestic organization to take full advantage of growth opportunities abroad.
- How to blend product knowledge and geographic area knowledge most efficiently in coordinating worldwide business.
- How to coordinate the activities of foreign units in many countries while permitting each to retain its own identity.[2]

Responses to each of these concerns will differ, depending on the firm's situation and the overall philosophy of top management. In this chapter we shall be focusing on the organizational design of international enterprises. That is, we will focus on the formal arrangement of relationships between the various domestic and foreign organizational units in the multinational network and the mechanisms provided for their coordination into a unified whole. The treatment will be limited to the level of the senior managers who report directly to the president's office. We shall not be concerned with the organizational structure of foreign affiliates; rather, the emphasis will be on the structure inside the parent company, whose purpose is to plan and control the multinational network, and on the structure of the network itself. Treatment of the organizational structure excludes recognition of the legal or statutory features of an enterprise. The legal structure is classified, in accordance with government regulations, for tax and cash-flow purposes. It seldom reflects the actual manner in which an enterprise is managed. Because this chapter is concerned with managerial aspects of an international company, the legal structure has been ignored.

Six basic organizational structures of multinational companies will be covered: (1) the preinternational division phase, (2) the structures of the international division, (3) the global product, (4) the global area, (5) the global functional, and (6) the multidimensional global form.

BASIC ORGANIZATIONAL DESIGN OF INTERNATIONAL ENTERPRISES

In most cases, a multinational firm's organizational structure is neither predetermined nor permanently fixed; rather, it evolves continuously to correspond with changes in the firm's strategy. As a firm's operations grow and spread to new foreign markets, its organizational structure typically becomes overburdened. As the strain intensifies and threatens organizational structure, the firm is normally compelled to experiment with alternate organizational forms.

Eventually the firm chooses an organizational structure consistent with its new international expansionist strategy and capable of handling its expanding operations. The replacement structure chosen is typically influenced by the structure that preceded it because the experience of the company with one structure provides a building block for future structures.

Although there is no one best organizational structure for multinational enterprises, it does not follow that every firm's organizational structure is completely unique or that there is no rationale for a firm's structural development. On the contrary, there are certain regular organizational patterns that firms of like strategy develop and through which multinational firms with changing strategies evolve.

PREINTERNATIONAL DIVISION PHASE

— Exports
— Few Products + MKTS

The early patterns of development of international firms appear to parallel the stages of development of the so-called product cycle.

According to this cycle (see Figure 5-1), a firm with a technologically advanced product in the new-product stage is well positioned to exploit foreign markets. Generally, initial exploitation occurs through exports--the first stage in the evolution of a multinational company. At this stage, the firm is relatively small by multinational enterprise standards, and its activities are generally confined to a few products and markets. (Different stages in the evolution of a multinational enterprise were covered in Chapter 1.) The firm has to deal with a comparatively limited number of strategic dimensions, most of which are related to the domestic market, and which can be addressed directly by the president with input from managers who report directly to her or him. Since the firm's technologically advanced product stands on its own, there is little need to develop expertise in the foreign markets in which the firm sells. Assistance in exporting is usually provided initially by an independent export management company and later by an in-house export manager. In most cases, an in-house export manager is regarded as an adjunct to marketing, whose principal communication needs are with the marketing vice president and others in the marketing group. The organizational arrangements for a firm in this stage of multinational development are rather simple, with an export manager reporting to the chief marketing officer in an organization with a narrow product

FIGURE 5-1   International Trade and Production in the Product Cycle

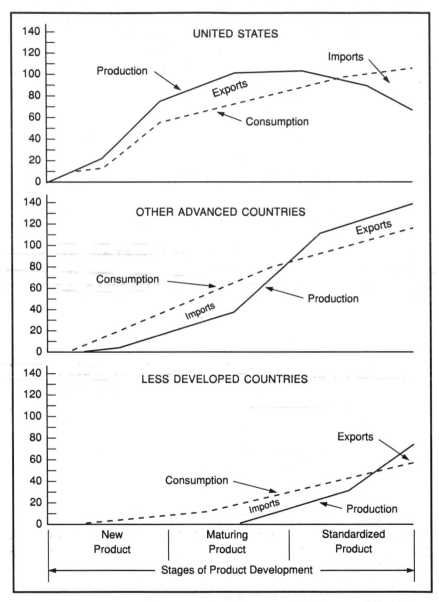

Source: Raymond Vernon and Louis T. Wells, Jr., *Manager in the International Economy*, 4th ed. (Englewood Cliffs, N.J.:   Prentice-Hall, Inc., 1981), 94.

line; or directly to the chief executive officer in an organization with a broad product line (see Figure 5-2).

As the firm's exports increase and its product matures, certain pressures develop that tend to threaten the firm's foreign market share. Such threats originate from two sources: (1) Others at home and abroad begin to share the firm's special knowledge and special skills. Thus the threat of competition becomes more tangible. (2) As local demand and sales volume increase in a country, an importing country begins to encourage local production by imposing "buy-local" policies on its government agencies and other public buyers and by enacting import restrictions such as tariffs and quotas.

Faced with increased competition from other producers and higher comparative costs resulting from freight and tariff costs, the exporting firm feels pressed to defend its foreign market position by establishing a production facility inside the foreign market. Once established, the

FIGURE 5-2   Typical Organization of International Company Primarily Engaged in Exporting to Foreign Markets

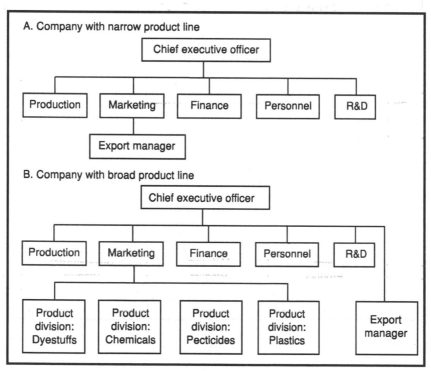

foreign production unit supplies the foreign market as the former technologically advanced product matures or makes its way through the maturity stage and into the standardized-product stage of the product cycle. The same cycle may be repeated by the firm in the markets of other nations as the firm tries to protect its market share by establishing local production units to supply local markets. At first the management of the newly formed foreign subsidiaries remains quite decentralized. A typical organizational arrangement for a firm at this early stage of foreign production is shown in Figure 5-3. Here the foreign subsidiaries report directly to the company president or other designated company officer, who carries out his responsibilities without assistance from a headquarters staff group. As the firm increases its investment in foreign operating units, however, and as these become more important to the firm's overall performance, greater emphasis is placed on international product coordination and operations control.

Thus, there is pressure to assemble a headquarters staff group to assist the officer in charge and to develop a specialized international expertise. While originally responsible for the firm's foreign operating units, the group essentially takes control of all international activities of the firm and evolves into a separate international division in a new and comparatively more complex organizational structure.

INTERNATIONAL DIVISION STRUCTURE

In the international division form of organization, all international activities are grouped into one separate division and assigned to a senior executive at corporate headquarters. The senior executive is often given the title of vice-president of the international division or

FIGURE 5-3   Typical Organization of Company at Early Foreign Production Stage

director of international operations and is at the same level as the other divisional and functional heads of the company in the organizational hierarchy (see Figure 5-4).

The head of the international division is generally given line authority over the subsidiaries abroad, and the international division is made into a profit center. The formation of the international division in effect segregates the company's overall operations into two differentiated parts--domestic and international. As far as the top management at headquarters is concerned, the international division is expected to manage the nondomestic operations and therefore to be the focus of whatever international expertise there is or should be in the company. There is not much contact or interaction between the domestic and international side, and whatever coordination there is between the two segments of the company occurs at the company's top-management level.

Organizationally, the formation of an international division lessens the autonomy of the foreign subsidiaries because authority to make strategic decisions is pulled up into the hands of the head of the international division. However, this change is also accompanied by a far greater measure of guidance and support from the top to the foreign subsidiaries.

Who Adopts the International Division Structure

In general, the companies that are still at the developmental stages of international business involvement are likely to adopt the international

FIGURE 5-4 International Division Structure

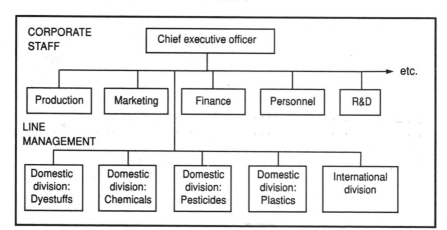

division structure. Other factors favoring the adoption of this structure are: limited product diversity, comparatively small sales (compared to domestic and export sales) generated by foreign subsidiaries, limited geographic diversity, and few executives with international expertise.

In the international division, executives are able to supervise the establishment and growth of one or more product lines in several foreign markets and, at the same time, develop new opportunities for expansion in others. In this structure, executives are providing the concentration of managerial expertise necessary for the effective promotion of the company's international efforts. During the period in which the company is establishing itself in international markets, international operations tend to remain, in the minds of the corporate executives of domestic operations, a sideline of minor importance. There are several advantages to the use of an international division structure. The concentration of international executives within the division ensures that the special needs of emerging foreign operations are met. The presence of the head of international operations as a member of the top management planning team serves as a constant reminder to top management of the global implications of all decisions. The international group provides a unified position regarding the company's activities in different countries and regions as it makes an effort to coordinate the operations of foreign subsidiaries with respect to the various functional areas—finance, marketing, purchasing, and production. For example, central coordination of international activities enables the company to make more secure and more economic decisions about where to purchase raw materials, where to locate new manufacture, and from where to supply world customers with products. Also, when the financial function of the international division is coordinated, investment decisions can be made on a global basis and overseas development can turn to international capital markets, instead of just local ones, for funds.[3] The international division also will not strain the capabilities of product or functional managers within the domestic divisions because these persons are not required to work in unfamiliar environments.

There are several drawbacks to the international division structure; hence, a company will use this structure only if the benefits from its adoption as a coordination mechanism clearly outweigh the costs. The principal disadvantages of the international division structure are the following: The separation and isolation of domestic managers from their international counterparts may prove to be a severe handicap as the company continues to expand abroad. If foreign operations should approach a level of equality with domestic operations in terms of size, sales, and profits, the ability of domestic managers to think and act strategically on a global scale could be critical to the success of the company. An independent international division may also put constraints on top management's effort to mobilize and allocate the resources of the company globally to achieve overall corporate objectives. Even with superb coordination at the corporate level, global planning for individual products or product lines is carried out, at best awkwardly, by two 'semiautonomous' organizations—the domestic company and the international division.[4]

Conflicts occasionally occur between the domestic product divisions and the international division, particularly when the international division asks for help from the domestic divisions and gets what it considers to be inadequate technical support and second-rate staff members for special assignments abroad. Still another problem with the international division is that the firm's research and development remains domestically oriented. Consequently, new ideas originating abroad for new products or processes are not easily transmitted to and enthusiastically tackled by the research and development personnel who remain, after all, in the domestic setting of the organization.

When Is an International Division No Longer Appropriate?

As international sales and production capacity grow, and as more markets are entered, product lines begin to diversify to serve a variety of end users. Then considerations such as transfer pricing (charging a higher or lower price between divisions than is charged to an outside buyer) come into play; the international division structure gets strained to its limits and is unable to fulfill its former role. Faced with this situation the company may continue to use the international division structure by subdividing further as a response to diversification either by product line, if product diversification is causing the problem, or by area, if regional diversification is straining the organization (see Figure 5-5). Product or area managers, reporting to the international division head, are then established within the division to coordinate the expansion of the firm into new markets.

Another alternative is to take the profit responsibility from the international division and reorganize the entire company on either a product or area division basis, keeping the international division in an advisory capacity. (Product and area based structures will be discussed later in the chapter.) If given an advisory role, executives in the division can function as generalists, monitoring environmental trends and conditions and advising their functional, product, or geographical counterparts in the company. If the firm chooses to

FIGURE 5-5   Divisions Within the International Division

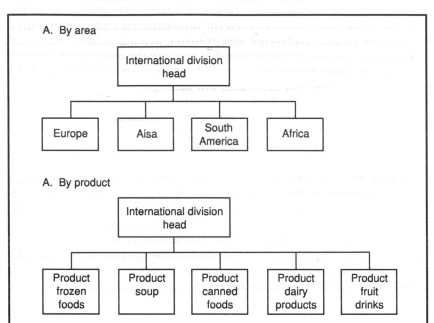

reorganize on a product basis, the international staff might be assigned to monitor the legal, political, cultural, and economic environments of major country and regional markets. If a geographically based structure is chosen, the international staff may serve as global coordinators, spotting trends and continuing to investigate the potential for new markets.

A *Business International* research report identifies the following factors as indicators that the international division is no longer an appropriate structure for an international company:

- The international market is as important as the domestic market.
- Senior officials of the corporation have both foreign and domestic experience.
- International sales represent 25 to 35 percent of total sales.
- The technology used in domestic divisions has far outstripped that of the international division.[5]

Other studies have shown that the pressures to reorganize on an integrated, worldwide basis by dismantling the international division mount when the division has grown large enough to be equal in size to the largest product division.[6] This is to a large extent because of the struggles that take place between the international and domestic divisions over capital budgeting and transfer pricing issues.[7] But most important, it is the structural conflict between the geographic orientation of the international division and the product orientation of the domestic divisions that motivates top management to reorganize the company in a fashion that merges the domestic and international sides of the business into one integrated global structure.

GLOBAL STRUCTURES

Up to this point we have been concentrating on the typical stages in the evolution of the organizational structure of a company as it becomes increasingly involved in international business activities. As the firm gains experience in operating internationally, the initially limited involvement in foreign direct investment gradually turns into a full-fledged commitment. Top management begins to perceive the company as a truly multinational enterprise. The company enters a new phase in its evolution: the domestic foreign bifurcation is abandoned in favor of an integrated, worldwide orientation.

Strategic decisions that previously were made separately for the domestic and international parts of the company are henceforth made at the corporate headquarters for the total enterprise, without any distinctions of domestic versus foreign. Top management considers the home market to be only one of many, and operational and staff groups are given global responsibility. Under such an attitudinal setup at corporate headquarters, corporate decisions are made with a total company perspective and for the purpose of achieving the company's overall mission and objectives. These decisions include where to establish a new production facility, where to raise capital, what business and products to be in, where to obtain resources, what methods to use for tapping foreign markets, what subsidiary ownership policies to adopt, and so on.

The shift to a global orientation in company management must be accompanied by the acquisition and allocation of company resources on the basis of global opportunities and threats. These changes require an organizational structure that is consistent with and supportive of this new managerial posture. The new organizational structure includes, as do all structures to varying degrees, three types of informational inputs: product, geography, and function. Although the structures adopted by various companies differ, the structure an international company adopts is certain to be based on one of these basic orientations: a worldwide area, a worldwide product, or occasionally, a worldwide function. Depending on which is chosen, delineation of the other dimension[s] "... are accounted for, in sequence. For these secondary and tertiary forces, they are subdivided (and hence duplicated) with each primary grouping, and/or they are centrally positioned in the form of corporate staff."[8]

We shall begin the study of global structures by first examining the product structure.

The Global Product Division

When the international division is discarded in favor of a global product division, the domestic divisions are given worldwide responsibility for product groups. The manager in charge of a product division is given line authority and responsibility for the worldwide management of all functional activities such as finance, marketing, production, and so on, related to a product or product group. Within each product division, there may exist an international unit or even a more refined subdivisionalization on an area basis (see Figure 5-6).

Each product division functions as a semiautonomous profit center. Divisional management has considerable decentralized authority to run the division because of the unique multinational environmental pressures under which it must operate. However, corporate headquarters provides an umbrella of company-wide plans and corporate strategy. This umbrella provides both the protection and the constraints under which product divisions are expected to formulate divisional plans and strategy. A product division receives general functional support from staff groups at the corporate level, but at the divisional level it may also have its own functional staff, specialized to provide services tailored to the division's unique market situation. The product division head is given worldwide responsibility to develop and promote his or her product line.

When Is a Global Product Division the Best Choice?

Conditions favoring a global product division are these: (1) The firm manufactures products that require different technologies and that have dissimilar end users. (2) There is little use of common marketing tools and channels of distribution among the firm's products. (3) There is a significant need to integrate production, marketing, and research related to the product. (4) Abroad, there is little need for local product knowledge and product adaptation. (5) The products involved need continuous technical service and inputs, and a high level of

FIGURE 5-6   Global Product Division Structure

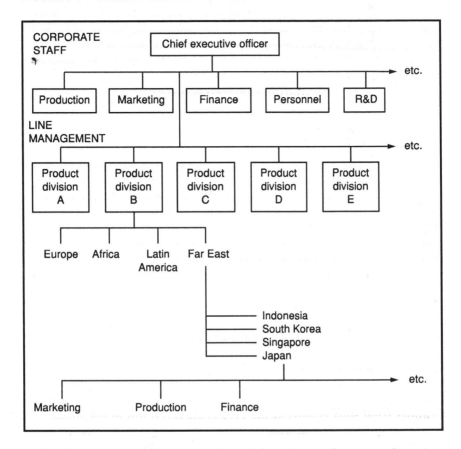

technological capability, requiring, therefore, close coordination between divisional staff groups and production centers abroad.

Some products require close, product-oriented technological and marketing coordination between the home market affiliates and foreign affiliates. This interdependence between the home and foreign affiliates—the latter needing help from the former in matters pertaining to the production and promotion of the growth product in a foreign market--calls for products, and not markets, as the primary organizing dimension.[9]

In order to maximize the benefits of divisionalization based on a global product structure, a firm must be able to produce a standardized product that requires very minor modifications for individual markets and for which world markets can be developed. Division managers are expected to take advantage of the structure to generate global economies of scale in production, resource acquisition, and market supply. This makes the structure particularly suited to firms that use capital-intensive technology.

The major advantages of this form of organization are the ease and directness of flow of technology and product knowledge from the divisional level to the foreign subsidiaries and back, which tends to put all facilities, regardless of location, on a comparable technological level. Other advantages of this structure are these: it preserves product emphasis and promotes product planning on a global basis; it provides a direct line of communication from the customer to those in the organization who have product knowledge and expertise, thus enabling research and development to work on the development of products that serve the needs of the world customer; and it permits line and staff managers within the division to gain expertise in the technical and marketing aspects of products assigned to them.[10]

In addition, the global product-division structure facilitates the coordination of domestic and foreign production facilities according to natural resource availability, local labor cost and skill level, tariff and tax regulations, shipping costs, and even climate, in order to produce the highest quality product possible at the lowest cost.

What Are the Drawbacks of a Global Product Division?

There are several critical problems associated with a global product structure. One is the duplication of facilities and staff groups that takes place as each division develops its own infrastructure to support its operations in various regions and countries of the world. Another is that division managers may pursue geographic areas that offer immediate growth prospects for their products and neglect other areas where the current prospects may not be as bright but may have a far greater long-run potential. A far more serious problem is that of "motivating product division managers to pursue the international market when the preponderance of their current profits comes from domestic business and most of their experience has been domestic."[11]

International companies have tried to alleviate these difficulties by adopting a multidimensional structure, which we will discuss later in this chapter.

The Global Area Division

Firms abandoning international division as a structure may choose to coordinate their global operations by using area (or geography) as the dominant organizational dimension.

In the international division structure, the company's worldwide operations are grouped into two regions--domestic and international. Thus, in a way, the international division structure is also an area-based structure. But in a truly area-based global structure, the company's worldwide operations are grouped into several coequal geographical areas, and the head of an area division is given line authority and responsibility over all affiliates in the area. There is no one fixed pattern for carving up the geographical areas. Obviously, each enterprise has its own circumstances and needs that determine how countries get grouped into regions. Factors such as locations of affiliates, customers, and sources of raw materials influence the grouping of countries into manageable geographic units.

The Domestic Market as One of Many

An area structure reflects a very significant change in the attitudes of top management towards international operations and the allocation of the company's resources. In the international division structure, the domestic and nondomestic bifurcation of the company's global operations reflects the point of view of top management that the domestic side of the business is as important as all the international operations together. The area structure embodies the attitude that the domestic market is just one of many markets in the world (see Figure 5-7).

The manager in charge of an area is responsible for the development of business in his or her region. However, his or her area plans and strategies have to be consistent with those of the company as a whole. Area managers and their counterparts participate in the formulation of company-wide plans and strategies. Such participation in total company planning gives each area manager an appreciation of how his or her area operations and results fit with total company plans and performance.

Companies using a product-division structure have products in foreign markets that are at the growth stage in the product life-cycle, whereas companies using an area-based structure have products in world markets that have already passed the growth stage. The products serve common end-user markets and are no longer unique; a competitive edge is no longer available from the possession of a distinctive technology. Hence, companies emphasize marketing rather than technology in their competitive strategies, with price and product differentiation being the dominant weapons for retaining market share and sales volume.

FIGURE 5-7   Global Area Division Structure

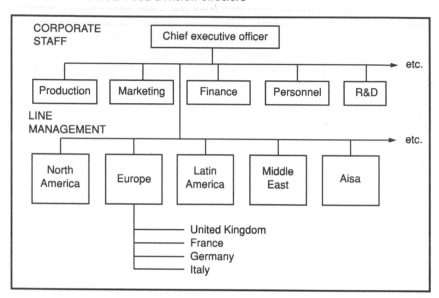

When Is Global Area Division the Best Choice?

A global area structure is most suited to companies having these characteristics: they are businesses with narrow product lines; they have
high levels of regional product differentiation which must obtain high
levels of economies of scale for production, marketing, and resource
purchase integration on a regional basis; and they feel the need to
lower manufacturing costs by utilizing large production runs. Industries with these characteristics which favor a global area structure
include pharmaceutical, cosmetic, food, beverage, automotive, and
container.

The principal advantage of an area structure is that the authority
to make decisions is pushed down to the regional headquarters. This
means that decisions on matters such as product adaptation, price,
channels of distribution, and promotion can be made near the scene of
action. For example, a company that makes soups, coffee, and prepared frozen foods must take into account regional and even country
differences. The Italians and Turks like dark, bitter coffee whereas
Americans like the lighter and less bitter variety. The English like bland
soups whereas the French prefer those with a blend of mild spices.

Different countries have different taste preferences. By and large, the peoples of the Middle East and Asia like their foods spiced whereas those in Europe and America like theirs bland. Information on such differences among regions and country markets can be considered at lower levels in the organizational hierarchy, which helps in making plans and strategies consistent with the existing regional and country conditions.

The other advantage of the area structure is that it promotes the finding of regional solutions to problems. Ideas and techniques that have worked in one country are easier to transfer to other countries in the region. And the area manager can resolve conflicts between subsidiaries by finding solutions that optimize the operations in the region as a whole. For example, when a new country market opens up, which subsidiary in the region is in the best position to serve it through exports? Conflicts could occur if more than one subsidiary attempts to export to the new market, but with the area structure, the area manager is in a position to resolve such problems.

What Are the Drawbacks of a Global Area Division?

The main disadvantage of the area structure is the difficulty encountered in reconciling product emphasis with a geographically oriented management approach. This can be particularly difficult if the company's product line is diverse and if it has to be marketed through different types of distribution channels. Since a certain amount of product expertise has to be developed by the area unit, a duplication of product development and technical knowledge is often required. At the same time there is an overlap of functional staff responsibilities with the worldwide headquarters. All of this adds to overhead costs and creates an additional tier of communications.

Other difficulties reported by executives in a study by the Conference Board are that "research and development programs are hard to coordinate, that global product-planning is difficult, that there is no consistent effort to apply newly developed domestic products to international markets, and that introduction to the domestic market of products developed overseas is too slow or simply that 'product knowledge is weak.'"[12]

In many respects, the advantages of a global area structure are the disadvantages of a global product division structure, and vice versa. The answer to the product/area dilemma may be in an organizational structure that incorporates in its authority, responsibility, and communications lines.

Global Functional Division

The functional division is not commonly used by international companies; however, an example of one important exception is the extractive industry companies that extract oil or metals.

In this form of organization, global operations are organized primarily on a functional basis and secondarily on an area or product basis, with marketing and production being the dominant functions.

The functional structure is most appropriate for firms with narrow, standardized product lines for which product knowledge is the significant factor (see Figure 5-8).

The main advantages of this form of organization are these: there is an emphasis on functional acumen; it provides tight, centralized controls, requiring a relatively lean managerial staff; and it ensures that the power and prestige of the basic activities of the enterprise will be defended by the top managers. The disadvantages of the structure are the following: coordination of manufacturing and marketing in an area (for example, Europe) is problematic; multiple product lines can become difficult to manage because of the separation of production and marketing into departments with parallel lines of authority to the top of the hierarchy; and only the chief executive officer can be held accountable for the profits.

A variant of the global functional structure is the functional process structure used by the petroleum industry. In it, specialized

FIGURE 5-8   Global Functional Structure

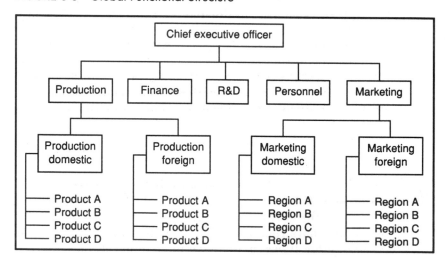

FIGURE 5-9 Global Functional Process Structure

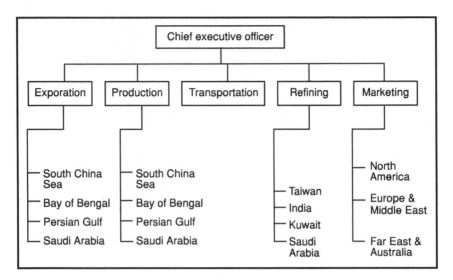

functions such as exploration, crude production, tanker and pipeline transportation, refining (manufacturing), and marketing are organized and managed on a global basis through centralized functional departments. These global functional departments may, in turn, be divisionalized on a geographic area basis (see Figure 5-9). In the functional process structure, all oil exploration in the different regions is centralized under the control and direction of the specialized exploration department. Similarly, production of crude oil is managed by the production department. The transportation of crude oil to the refineries located in different countries, and the shipping of gasoline and other petroleum distillates like kerosene, diesel oil, and lubricating oil to various world markets by railroads, ships, pipelines, and trucks is coordinated by the transportation department. The marketing of petroleum products in world markets is the responsibility of the marketing department.

Companies that favor the global functional process structure are those that need tight, centralized coordination and control of an integrated production process consisting of stages that are carried out on a global basis; and are involved in a major way in transporting products and raw materials across national boundaries, and from one geographic area of the world to another.

A global functional structure has proved to be quite unstable. Most companies that adopt it eventually have to abandon it, owing to the problems of integration of supply and distribution caused by a global dichotomy between production and sales. Commenting on the instability of this form of organizational structure, Stanley M. Davis says "The lesson is, don't organize global structures around functions unless you are in extractive raw materials industries, and even then you will find that they are unstable and will have to share primacy with geographic factors and, in some instances, with product differences."[13]

MULTIDIMENSIONAL GLOBAL STRUCTURE

In deciding whether to organize on a functional, product, or area basis, managers of international companies must weigh the benefits of each against the costs. The particular dimension that is chosen as the primary basis for organizing a company's operations is that which offers the best benefits/costs ratio. When one of these three dimensions--function, product, area--is chosen as the primary organizational form, management still tries to utilize the advantages of the remaining two dimensions at lower levels in the structure. For example, a company that is organized on a product-division basis may have its own functional staff at the divisional level, and each of the divisions may be further subdivided on a geographic basis. However, many international companies have found that none of the global structures discussed above is a totally satisfactory means of organizing because some problems remain untouchable, therefore unsolved. For instance, the problem of coordinating subsidiaries in different divisions on a regional basis in a global product division structure still remains. Similarly, in an organization based on global area, problems still occur in coordinating products on a global basis and across area division lines.

Some companies have attempted to cope with these problems by establishing product committees in area-based structures and area committees in product-based structures. Membership of such committees is comprised of divisional managers and staff specialists who are assigned the collective responsibility for coordinating transactions that cut across divisional lines.

Another alternative is to create staff positions for advisors and counselors. For instance, a product division structure might have area specialists for each of the major regions served by the company. These persons are given the task of exploring new opportunities and developing new markets for the company's products in their respective regions, thus maintaining the distinct advantages of the product structure without losing sight of the unique characteristics of each regional market. Similarly, in an area-based structure, the position of product manager would have responsibility for the coordination of the production and development of his or her product line across geographic areas.

In each of the preceding structural arrangements, there is an implicit assumption that an organizational structure can have only one dominant dimension. Because the advantages of the other dimensions are lost when only one is chosen, an attempt is sometimes made to correct the situation by overlaying the dominant dimension with some aspects of the others.

Some international companies are rejecting the notion that there must be a clear line of authority flowing from the top to the bottom in an organizational hierarchy, with a manager at a given level reporting to only one superior at the next highest level in hierarchy. This so called principle of the unity of command has been cast aside by companies that have adopted what is known as the matrix structure. In a matrix, the organization avoids choosing one dimension over another as the basis for grouping its operations; instead, it chooses two or more dimensions. "The foreign subsidiaries report simultaneously to more than one divisional headquarter; worldwide product divisions share with area divisions responsibility for the profits of the foreign subsidiaries."[14]

For instance, a subsidiary manager may report to an area manager as well as a product manager. In a pure product division or area

FIGURE 5-10   The Matrix Structure

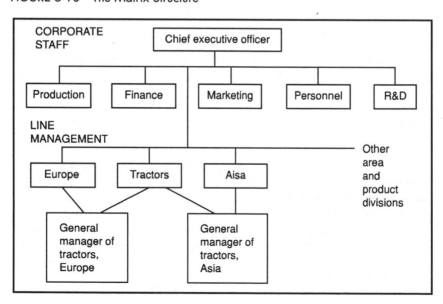

structure, only the manager in charge of the dominant dimension has line authority over a foreign subsidiary in her or his unit. In a matrix structure, both product and area managers have some measure of line authority over the subsidiary. Thus the unity-of-command principle is abrogated in favor of a coordinating mechanism that considers differences in products and areas to be of equal importance. Firms using the matrix structure are attempting to integrate their operations across more than one dimension simultaneously (see Figure 5-10).

Firms should consider adopting the matrix structure if conditions such as the following exist:

- There is substantial product and area diversification.
- There is a need to be responsive simultaneously to product and area demands.
- Constraints on resources require that they be shared by two or more divisions—product, area, or functional.
- Significant problems are created and opportunities are lost due to emphasis on just one dimension, product, or area.
- Formulation of corporate strategy requires the simultaneous consideration of functional, product, and area concerns.

Adoption of a matrix structure requires a commitment on the part of top management, not only to the structure itself but to the essential preparation required for it to be successful. Executive groundwork must be laid; executives must understand how the system works, and those who report to two or more superior managers, such as the subsidiary managers, must be prepared to work through the initial confusion created by dual reporting relationships. As noted by Davis and Lawrence, a "matrix organization is more than a matrix structure. It must be reinforced by matrix systems such as dual control and evaluation systems, by leaders who operate comfortably with lateral decision making, and by a culture that can negotiate open conflict and a balance of power."[15] Thus, the mere adoption of a matrix structure does not create a matrix organization.

Adoption must be followed by some fundamental changes in technical systems and management behavior. Managers must recognize the need to resolve issues and choices at the lowest possible level, without referring them to a higher authority. A delicate balance of power must be maintained among managers face to face. A tilt in favor of one organizational dimension or another would cause the organization to fall back to the old single-dimension, vertical hierarchy, with a resulting loss of the benefits of a matrix structure. Absence of cooperation between facing managers, even when a perfect power balance exists, could cause so many unresolved problems and disputes that must be referred up the hierarchy that top management would become over-loaded with interdivisional matters.

The benefits of a matrix structure flow directly from the conditions that induce enterprises to adopt it. An organization can respond simultaneously to all environmental factors that are critical to its success. Decision-making authority can be decentralized to an appropriate level. Policy decisions are made in concert with people who have relevant information, and the design also facilitates a flow of information that promotes better planning and the implementation of plans.

The matrix structure does take time, effort, and commitment by executives to make it work. Although Peter Drucker says that it "will never be a preferred form of organization; it is fiendishly difficult,"[16] he nevertheless concludes that "any manager in a multinational business will have to learn to understand it if he wants to function effectively himself."[17]

IBM, the giant computer company, has adopted a unique, multi-dimensional structure to manage its IBM-Europe operations. IBM has traditionally served its European customers on a country-by-country basis. This approach served the company handsomely when European country markets were fragmented. But now, with European countries increasingly integrating their markets into one unified market, the need for a unified European approach, mixed with local responsiveness, becomes acutely necessary.

The need to integrate its product, geography, and country inputs into a unified European strategy for IBM has brought about a reorganization of the company's managerial matrix. IBM has established a European management board consisting of the unit presidents, i.e., country managers, and others, specifically to involve them in central strategy formulation for Europe. In addition, the unit heads of the four biggest subsidiaries in Europe--Germany, the United Kingdom, France, and Italy--have been given specific, Europe-wide responsibilities for certain product groups and industry sectors. For instance, Germany has responsibility for mainframes and some other products, plus the industrial sector; and the United Kingdom subsidiary gets personal and AIX systems, as well as the service industries. With this new structure, IBM hopes to bring about effective cooperation among product divisions, geographical subsidiaries, and individuals.[18]

SUMMARY

This chapter was concerned with the typical stages in the evolution of the basic structures of international companies. Six organizational patterns were discussed: the preinternational division phase; international division structure; global product division structure; global area structure; global functional structure; and the multidimensional global structure. Reasons for the adoption of each of these organizational types, as well as the advantages and disadvantages of each, were explained.

Finding the organizational structure best suited to a company's global corporate strategy is a challenge that a multinational company's top management executives must meet effectively and efficiently. The imperative to coordinate the three dimensions--function, product, and area--has created problems and tensions in the internal transactions and management of multinational companies. Companies usually modify the structures and make trade-offs among the various approaches while attempting to integrate their geographically far-flung operations.

Another challenge facing multinational company managers is that, after finding a suitable structure for a particular global corporate strategy at a certain point in time, they must keep modifying the structure to suit evolving company strategy as well. This requirement for change is ever present in multinational enterprises.

QUESTIONS

1. Discuss the salient features of the international division structure. What factors are responsible for its adoption by an international company?

2. How does a global product division differ from a global area division? What conditions favor the adoption of each of these structures?

3. Why is the matrix structure adopted by multinational companies? What are the advantages of the matrix structure? What conditions must accompany the adoption of a matrix in order for it to be successful in an organization?

FURTHER READING

Business International. *Organizing the Worldwide Corporation*. Research Report No. 69-4. New York: Business International, 1970.

Clee, Gilvert H., and Wilbur M. Sachtjan. "Organizing a Worldwide Business." *Harvard Business Review* 42, no. 6 (November-December 1964).

Davis, Stanley M. "Trends in the Organization of Multinational Corporations." *Columbia Journal of World Business* (Summer 1976).

Davis, Stanley. *Managing and Organizing Multinational Corporations*. New York: Pergamon Press, 1979.

Davis, Stanley M., and Paul R. Lawrence. "Problems of Matrix Organizations." *Harvard Business Review* (May-June 1978).

Denalli, Jacquelyn. "Keeping Growth Under Control." *Nation's Business* Vol. 81, no. 7 (July 1993): 31-32.

Drucker, Peter. *Management: Tasks, Responsibilities, Practices.* New York: Harper & Row, 1974.

Duerr, Michael G., and John M. Roach. *Organization and Control of International Operations.* New York: The Conference Board, 1973.

Goggin, William C. "How the Multidimensional Structure Works at Dow Corning." *Harvard Business Review* (January-February 1974).

Phatak, Arvind V. *Managing Multinational Corporation.* New York: Praeger Publishers, 1974.

Stages of Global Development, *Chief Executive* (January-February 1993): 6-9.

Stopford, John M., and Louis T. Wells Jr. *Managing the Multinational Enterprise.* New York: Basic Books, 1972.

Vernon, Raymond, and Louis T. Wells, Jr. *Manager in the International Economy.* 4th ed. Englewood Cliffs, N.J.: Prentice-Hall, 1981.

Vincent, Edgar. "Developing Managers for an International Business," *Journal of Management Development.* Vol. 7, no. 6 (1988): 14-20

NOTES

[1] Raymond Vernon and Loius T. Wells, Jr., *Manager in the International Economy*, 3rd. ed. (Englewood Cliffs, N. J.: Prentice-Hall, 1976), 31.

[2] Michael G. Duerr and John M. Roach, *Organization and Control of International Operations* (New York: The Conference Board, 1973), 5.

[3] Stanley Davis, "Basic Structures of Multinational Corporations" in *Managing and Organizing Multinational Corporations*, ed. Stanley Davis (New York: Pergamon Press, 1979), 202.

[4] Gilbert H. Clee and Wilbur M. Sachjan, "Organizing a Worldwide Business," *Harvard Business Review* 42, no. 6 (November-December 1964): 60.

[5] Business International, *Organizing the Worldwide Corporation*, Research Report No. 69-4 (New York: Business International, 1970), p.

[6] John M. Stopford and Louis T. Wells, Jr., *Managing the Multinational Enterprise* (New York: Basic Books, 1972), 51.

[7] Stanley M. Davis, "Trends in the Organization of Multinational Corporations," *Columbia Journal of World Business* (Summer 1976): 60.

[8] Davis, "Basic Structures," 203.

[9] Ibid., 205.

[10] Arvind V. Phatak, *Managing Multinational Corporations* (New York: Praeger Publishers, 1974), 183.

[11] Duerr and Roach, *Organization and Control*, 12.

[12] Ibid., 10.

[13] Davis, "Trends in the Organization," 66.

[14] Stopford and Wells, *Managing the Multinational Enterprise*, 87.

[15] Stanley M. Davis and Paul R. Lawrence, "Problems of Matrix Organizations," *Harvard Business Review* (May-June 1978): 4.

[16] Peter Drucker, *Management: Tasks, Responsibilities*, Practices (New York: Harper & Row, 1974), 598.

[17] Ibid.

[18] Jonathan B. Levine and Gail E. Schares, "IBM Europe Starts Swinging Back," *Business Week* (May 6, 1991): 52; Tom Lester, "A Structure for Europe," *Management Today* (January 1991).

Chapter S I X

International Staffing

In this chapter, we shall consider the international staffing process. As the international business involvement of a company increases, so, too, does its need for well-qualified executives who are willing and able to be managers abroad. Not everyone who has been successful as a manager in one country can be as successful in another. It takes a person with a unique set of characteristics to succeed as a manager in diverse foreign environments. Many costly managerial failures abroad can be avoided by the use of effective selection methods and pre-departure training programs. Frequently, good managers who are also good candidates refuse to go abroad on managerial assignments because they fear that a foreign stint might have a negative impact on their career paths. To eliminate this problem, companies need a planned and a communicable program for the repatriation of the manager who serves abroad. A sound international, executive compensation program is another essential component of an international staffing program. Thus, we shall examine in this chapter the main features of compensation for foreign assignments.

SOURCES OF MANAGERS

There are three main sources from which managers can be recruited to fill international management positions both in the headquarters and the foreign subsidiaries. They are home-country nationals, host-country nationals, and third-country nationals. Home- (or parent-) country nationals are the citizens of the country in which the head-quarters of the multinational company is based. Citizens of the country that is hosting a foreign subsidiary are the host-country nationals. Third-country nationals are the citizens of a country other than the parent or the host country—for example, a French executive working in a German subsidiary of an American multinational company. Most multinational corporations use all three sources for staffing their international operations, although some companies exhibit a distinct bias for one of the three types.

Home-Country Nationals as Managers

Historically, multinational companies have had the tendency to staff the key positions in their foreign affiliates with home-country nationals. Some classic reasons include: the unavailability of host-country nationals having the required technical expertise; the desire to provide the company's more promising managers with international experience and thereby equip them for more responsible positions; the need to maintain and facilitate organizational coordination and control; the unavailability of managerial talent in the host country; the company's view of the foreign operation as short lived; the host country's multiracial population, which might mean that selecting a manager of any one race would result in political or social problems; the company's conviction that it must maintain a foreign image in the host country; and the belief of some companies that a home-country manager is the best person for the job.[1]

Research has shown that the most important motives for staffing foreign subsidiary management positions with home-country nationals are these: (1) they have greater technical expertise and (2) during the start-up phase, it is considered advantageous to have them there.[2] In a newly acquired subsidiary, the desire to ensure that the foreign subsidiary complies with overall company objectives and policies induces headquarters to staff it at the top with a home-country national.

Third-Country Nationals as Managers

Although the data on third-country nationals are not as extensive as those on home- and host-country nationals, the main advantages for using them are that they have greater technical expertise and the belief that the third-country national is the best person for the job.[3]

U.S. corporations tend to use third-country nationals only from advanced countries. The selection criteria for third-country nationals are identical to those applied in the selection of home-country nationals for foreign assignments. However, the company's final objectives for the two types of international managers are often different. In the case of the home-country manager, most often the objective is to train and develop her or him for a top management position in parent company headquarters. But for a third-country national, a top management position at the subsidiary is usually envisioned as the ultimate goal in her or his career development.

There are advantages and disadvantages in employing third-country nationals. One advantage is that the salary and benefit requirements of a third-country national may be significantly less than those of home-country nationals. However, the salary scales for the two groups are approaching parity—reflecting the rapidly evolving management salary structure in many industrialized countries, particularly those of Western Europe. This equalizing trend applies particularly to third-country nationals working in regional or international division headquarters.[4]

Another advantage of the third-country national is that she or he may be better informed about the host environment. For example, the candidate may speak the host country's language. A Belgian could work in France easily because French is the language spoken in both countries. Or a candidate's country may have a special relationship with the nation in which the subsidiary is located. Thus, a French citizen could adapt fairly readily to working in the Ivory Coast. For these reasons, many American companies have hired English or Scottish executives for top management positions in their subsidiaries in countries that were former British colonies, such as Jamaica, India, and Kenya.

Two distinct drawbacks may arise from the use of third-country nationals. First, in certain parts of the world, animosities of a national character exist between neighboring countries—for example, India and Pakistan, Greece and Turkey. Transfers of third-country nationals must take such factors into account because an oversight in this area could be disastrous. The second disadvantage is associated with the desire of the governments of developing countries to upgrade their own people into responsible managerial positions. It is often more palatable to these governments to accept a home-country national than to accept a third-country national, even though the third-country national might be better qualified for the position.

Host-Country Nationals as Managers

Most multinational corporations use host-country nationals in middle- and lower-level management positions in their foreign subsidiaries located in developing countries. This may be because local law requires that they do so. But, perhaps the corporation would fill all managerial positions with host-country nationals if there were not a scarcity of managers with the necessary qualifications for top jobs. In any event, it would be very difficult to staff the numerous middle-level positions totally with foreigners, even if local legislation permitted it.

When it comes to top management positions, the picture is not clear. Massey-Ferguson's Thornbrough asserts that "for all the talk, some North American companies still have the specific, rigid policy that key people in units abroad must be American."[5] This charge is refuted by a number of executives in other companies. The assistant general manager of the International Department at DuPont, David Cronklin, states, "Nationals head about half of our wholly owned subsidiaries in Europe and in only three of our eleven Latin-American subsidiaries are there American top executives on a long-term basis."[6] George Young, who is vice-president for International Operations at Abbott Laboratories, says, "Abbott starts out by hiring [host-country] nationals for foreign operations. Second choice is third-country nationals. Third preference is Americans. Out of 5,000 employees overseas, there are maybe three or four Americans at most."[7]

An important factor in determining to what extent host-country nationals are selected for management positions is the increasing pressure by some governments for foreign firms to expedite the "nativization" of management. This pressure takes the form of sophisticated government persuasion through administrative or legislative decrees. For example, Brazil requires that two-thirds of the employees in a Brazilian subsidiary be Brazilian nationals, and there are pressures on multinationals to staff upper management positions in Brazilian subsidiaries with Brazilian nationals. In response to such pressure, many multinational corporations are subscribing to a policy similar to that described by a Standard Oil Company executive:

> While in the past we did employ substantial numbers of people for assignment overseas on a career basis, today, in keeping with our policy of utilizing nationals of the host country to the maximum

extent possible, our practice is to assign domestic North American employees on a relatively short-term transfer or loan basis.[8]

Research by Rosalie Tung on U.S. multinational corporations throws more light on the staffing of foreign subsidiaries. She found that U.S. multinational corporations have a tendency to use host-country nationals at all levels of management to a much greater extent in the more advanced regions of the world than in the less advanced regions. This may be understandable, considering that the advanced countries are more likely to have a large pool of trained personnel with the necessary qualifications to occupy managerial positions. The executives in the survey said that the most important reasons for hiring host-country nationals were: (1) their familiarity with the local culture and language, (2) the lower costs incurred in hiring them as compared to home- or third-country nationals, and (3) the improved public relations that resulted from such a practice.[9]

There are other reasons as well for the hiring of host-country nationals to manage foreign subsidiaries. For instance, host-country managers are believed to be more effective in dealing with local employees and clients than their foreign counterparts because they adhere to local patterns of management. There is also greater continuity of management because host-country nationals tend to stay longer in their positions than managers from other countries. But more important is the avoidance of low morale that results when host-country managers are not given opportunities to move into upper management positions. The following argument by an Italian manager in a U.S. multinational company's subsidiary in Italy illustrates this point:

> We feel we are the hurt and wounded part of Italian management. In an earlier time having ... [Americans] here as managers was a good idea. As we have now developed our own management skills, some of those early advantages have disappeared. The right philosophy hasn't taken hold ... [and] the long hand of the parent is now a bad idea. I insist we who have been in the company ten, fifteen, or more years should have as much of the parent's confidence as do American managers. They sometimes come in here in fact for the ... reason of stopping in Italy as birds of passage on their way to brilliant careers with the parent.[10]

What Are the Trends in International Staffing?

Is there any pattern that can be detected in the international staffing practices of international companies? Research on this subject shows that changes in international staffing policies tend to coincide with predictable stages of internationalization of multinational corporations. It appears, however, that the issue of nationality mix in multinational companies has received surprisingly little attention from researchers in the field of international management. Descriptions of when, where, and why firms use native or imported managerial personnel are generally found only in company histories. Some of the best research on international staffing involving U.S. and European companies has been conducted by Franko.[11] It revealed that in the first stage of internationalization—exports—most companies preferred to hire host-country nationals. The company's greatest need was to adapt to local conditions, so local nationals were the logical choice. However, as the local market became large enough to support local manufacture of the product, home-country managers were sent abroad, at least during the first few years of the foreign manufacturing operation. After the start-up stage, the U.S. companies replaced home-country (American) nationals with host-country nationals. But in European companies, the home-country managers remained in the top foreign subsidiary positions, with many staying in the same country for the remainder of their working careers.

Franko did find, however, that American managers were often in charge of subsidiaries in those U.S. multinational corporations that followed a strategy of spreading a limited product line around the globe. As the limited product lines matured in successive markets, and as adaptation to local markets was replaced by a strategy of multinational product standardization, these firms pulled together the once relatively independent subsidiaries under the umbrella of a regional headquarters office. Then, U.S. managers were appointed both to head the regional divisions and to replace the host-country nationals as subsidiary chiefs. European companies have also followed these trends in their staffing practices. They, too, placed home-country managers in charge of regional divisions and subsidiaries.

As the process of nationalization was completed and as products and policies were standardized supranationally, host-country managers again replaced home-country managers as the senior staff of local subsidiaries in U.S. firms. Some even filled top managerial posts at regional division headquarters. Some host-country managers were also used to manage subsidiaries in third countries.

These findings from Franko's study are based on interviews and questionnaire responses from 25 European and U.S. firms, as well as a survey of literature covering about 60 European and 170 U.S. companies with manufacturing operations in seven or more countries. Clearly, one cannot arrive at definite conclusions about international staffing policies and practices from such a small sample. More research must be done in this area. However, one cannot discount the trends revealed by Franko's work.

As more and more companies become globalized, and their corporate agendas shift from a local focus to one that is regional or global, there is an increasing need for managers who can work effectively in several countries and cultures. This is especially true in Europe, where unification in 1992 is forcing many companies to focus several aspects of their businesses from a pan-European perspective. Because of all the changes that are already occurring in Europe, there is a need for what are now called *Euro managers*. These are executives who are able to think in terms of a Europe-wide, big picture, and at the same time appreciate and understand local nuances and differences in tastes and preferences. In many respects, they are "glocalized" in their attitudes and behavior (see Chapter 4). Among their other more important attributes are flexibility in managing people of a different cultural heritage and nationality, skills in bringing a diverse team together, and the willingness to learn at least one foreign language. Firms are facing difficulties finding Euro managers for their European operations. Practical Insight 6-1 is about the Euro-manager phenomenon and how global companies like ICI, Colgate-Palmolive, Unilever, 3M, and Honeywell are facing and handling the difficulties of hiring and keeping such managers.

PRACTICAL INSIGHT 6-1

Companies in Europe Seeking Executives Who Can Cross Borders in a Single Bound

When Vittorio Levi decided to leave the warmth of Italy for a job in Sweden, everyone told him he was crazy. Scandinavians may dream of working in a Mediterranean climate, but Italians aren't supposed to be willing to go north. Nonetheless, Mr. Levi says he made the right choice when he joined Oy Nokia's Stockholm-based computer division, where he became president early last year.

Expatriate executives are no novelty, of course. As more companies try to compete globally, more executives are crossing borders—not just as a brief detour but as a critical, and sometimes inevitable, stage in their careers. That trend is particularly pronounced in Europe, where plans for a unified market after 1992 are spurring companies to reorganize.

Responsibilities are rapidly shifting from national to regional or pan-European units. At the same time, companies want to stay in touch with local tastes. So they need managers who can think big while understanding local nuances.

Mastering that tricky mix often means hiring what some companies call Euro managers: people skilled at dealing with a variety of cultures and at bringing a diverse team together. And that means hiring and promoting more foreigners.

"You need as much cultural mix and diversity and experience as possible ... if you are running a global company," says Bob Poots, personnel director for the European division of London based Imperial Chemical Industries PLC. ICI's executive ranks were predominantly British 20 years ago; now, only 74 of the company's top 150 executives worldwide are British.

That sort of change isn't easy to effect. The problem, headhunters and personnel managers say, is that Europe has a shortage of good senior executives who are willing to move. Tax and pension hassles, family ties, and simple chauvinism keep many top managers in their own back yards.

"It's easy to say 'Euro manager'," notes Brian F. Bergin, president of the European division of Colgate-Palmolive Co. "In fact, [hiring them] is an extremely difficult task. But it's happening." To help realign its management, Colgate appointed a Pan-European human-resources director, Peter Dessau, a Dane who moved to Brussels in 1989. His job is to encourage mobility among managers in the U.S. company's European units.

Colgate quizzed all of its top European managers about what kind of executive works best in an international setting. Among the main attributes, Mr. Dessau says, is flexibility in managing. "You don't always go by the book," he says.

ICI's Mr. Poots says he looks for people who are good at getting along with colleagues at home. "That skill travels remarkably well," he says. Any problems an executive has in dealing with colleagues, he figures, will be magnified in a foreign setting, where much more effort is needed to build understanding and trust.

Unilever Group, the Anglo-Dutch food and soap giant, shies away from bossy executives. "We tend to look for people who can work in teams and understand the value of cooperation and consensus," says Floris Maljers, chairman of Unilever NV, the group's Dutch arm.

Some recruiters want candidates who have learned at least one foreign language besides English. Even if the foreign language won't be needed much in a particular job, having learned it "shows you are willing to dive into someone else's culture," says Marc Swaels, a Brussels-based partner for Korn/Ferry International, a U.S. executive-search firm.

Not surprisingly, many companies are above all looking for executives who have already succeeded in running at least one big operation outside their home countries.

Once the right kind of executive is found, companies wanting to move managers across borders must overcome differences in pay scales, pensions, and tax systems. In time, the European Community is expected to bring greater harmony in these areas, but for now the costs of solving such problems make some companies hold transfers to a minimum.

Even if the red tape can be cut, many European executives, especially senior ones with families, are reluctant to live abroad. British managers are often willing to leave their children in distant boarding schools, but Continental Europeans tend to want the family close together.

Another barrier to the free flow of executives is prejudice. Especially among older executives, history weighs heavily. Asked why his company wasn't moving into the German market, the chief of a Dutch retailer replied without hesitation, "Because we [in the company] don't like Germans."

To overcome these obstacles, companies are trying to be more flexible in managing people. Nokia Data, for instance, made it possible for the Italian, Mr. Levi, to keep his main residence in Turin. The company provides him with a small apartment in Stockholm and flies him home to Italy for weekends about twice a month.

Mr. Levi says such benefits have helped him make a smooth transition. At age 52, he is older than most executives in their first senior position abroad. Though he doesn't expect to spend the rest of his career in Stockholm, he says his international job gives him a better understanding of Europe's political and economic transformation. "In a time of great change," he says, "you get a closer view if you are in a position like this than if you stay home in Italy with your friends."

Companies also try to identify potential Euro managers at an early stage. ICI has long recruited heavily from British universities; now, it is trying harder to attract Continental students. A new program offered 20 university students two-month internships last summer at an ICI site outside their home country.

Rainer Goldammer, personnel chief for the European division of Minnesota Mining & Manufacturing Co., asks the company's local operating units for lists of young managers who might do well internationally. The company would like to send more young managers abroad for experience, but relocation and other expenses mean such managers cost about twice as much as local hires, Mr. Goldammer says.

An alternative is to give young managers international experience without moving them out of their home country. Both 3M and Colgate put managers on project teams with colleagues in other countries. "It's a way of seeing the light," says Colgate's Mr. Dessau. "You find out that you don't need to stay in the boundaries you're used to."

Honeywell Europe, a Brussels-based unit of Honeywell Inc., encourages managers to relocate by clearly showing them how such international experience could lead to promotions later on. Jean Pierre Rosso, a Frenchman who heads Honeywell Europe, says the company persuaded a reluctant Frenchman to take a post in Hong Kong by telling him that the next step would be a top job back in France. In general, it helps if foreign executives feel they have a chance to rise to the top. In Honeywell's European division, 12 of the top 13 jobs are held by non-Americans. Mr. Rosso, a Frenchman who in 1987 became the first non-American to head Honeywell Europe, says he hopes a European executive eventually will sit on the board of Honeywell in the U.S. Unilever has six nationalities on its board, but most companies' executive directors come almost exclusively from the home country. A boss's natural inclination, says Korn/Ferry's Mr. Swaels, is to surround himself with people from a similar background, speaking the same language. But Mr. Swaels and others say it will be vital for global companies to build up "an international culture" at the very top. Partly because true Euro managers are in short supply, some European companies turn to Americans or other non-Europeans who have worked for U.S.-based multinationals. U.S. companies sometimes have an edge in Europe because, whether through naivete or foresight, they have always tended to view Europe more as one big market than as a series of small nations. Colgate's top executive in Europe, Mr. Bergin, is Australian. The top finance man is Argentine.

At 3M, more Americans are filling top jobs in Europe these days. But Mr. Goldammer, a German who moved to Brussels a year ago, says the next generation of European managers will be more internationally minded and mobile. That would let 3M send more Americans back home.

Source: Bob Hagerty, "Companies in Europe Seeking Executives Who Can Cross Borders in a Single Bound," *Wall Street Journal*, January 25, 1991, B1 and B8.

Foreign Managers at Headquarters in Home Countries

More recently, foreign nationals have also come to occupy managerial jobs in the headquarters of U.S. and European multinational companies. Still, this is a rare occurrence. Multinationalization of headquarters management is a phenomenon that is taking place almost exclusively in the most mature industries and companies,[12] and in product areas with many years of international experience, such as oil, food processing, toiletries, synthetic fibers, and heavy electrical machinery.[13] It appears that the causes for this phenomenon are related to the following:

1. Horizontal mergers among competitors.
2. The nearly worldwide diffusion of skills in such industries.
3. The need for old firms in competitive industries to provide jobs "up the ladder" to foreign managers who could leave to join competitors.
4. The possibility of political pressure from foreign governments who feel that "competent local managers are now available."[14]

Some executives claim that the reason they do not have foreigners at headquarters is that many do not want to work at the headquarters because of language barriers and strong roots in their own countries. This may be true in some cases, but the real problem, says Howard Perlmutter, is "that U.S. companies prefer U.S. executives because they trust them more. They speak the language of corporate headquarters."[15]

CRITERIA FOR SELECTING MANAGERS
FOR FOREIGN ASSIGNMENTS

One of the most important factors in determining the success of a foreign operation, be it a branch or a fully integrated manufacturing subsidiary, is the quality of the home-country managers sent abroad to manage it. This is particularly true during the start-up phase of the foreign operation.

The problem facing multinational companies is finding a manager who can readily adapt to the demands of a foreign assignment. As yet, valid and reliable screening devices to identify, with certainty, managers who will succeed in a foreign assignment do not exist. What we do have is a set of criteria that a manager should be able to meet before he or she can even be considered for an assignment in a foreign country. Both home-country and third-country managers are expatriates, albeit willing ones. Therefore, the criteria we do have should apply in the selection of candidates for either of these two groups.

What are the ideal characteristics of an international manager? Following is one opinion on the subject:

> Ideally, it seems, he [or she] should have the stamina of an Olympic swimmer, the mental agility of an Einstein, the conversational skill of a professor of languages, the detachment of a judge, the tact of a diplomat, and the perseverance of an Egyptian pyramid builder.... And if he is going to measure up to the demands of living and working in a foreign country, he should also have a feeling for culture; his moral judgements should not be too rigid; he should be able to merge with the local environment with chameleon-like ease; and he should show no signs of prejudice.[16]

Of course, that is an idealized profile of what an international manager should be. There are, however, several more realistic traits or characteristics that most personnel executives would agree a candidate must possess if he or she is to succeed in an assignment abroad. Having some or most of these characteristics does not ensure success, but the lack of them vastly increases the chances of failure. The following paragraphs discuss some of these desirable traits.

Technical Ability

Obviously the candidate must have the technical knowledge and skills to do the job. Even though she or he may have each of the other attributes, if the candidate does not know what he or she is doing, there will be problems.

Managerial Skills

The candidate must know what it takes to be an effective manager. He or she must have knowledge of the art and science of management and the ability to put them into practice. A good indicator of a candidate's managerial ability is her or his past record as a manager. Someone who has not been an effective manager in the home setting is not likely to be successful abroad.

Cultural Empathy

All authorities agree that high on the list of desirable traits is cultural empathy, which refers to "an awareness of and a willingness to probe for the reasons people of another culture behave the way they do."[17] It is critical for success abroad that the candidate be sensitive to cultural differences and similarities between his or her own country and the host country. "He must have a personal philosophy that accepts value differences in other people and the ability to understand the inner logic and rationale of other people's way of life. He must be tolerant towards foreign cultural patterns and avoid judging others by his own values and criteria."[18] If one has cultural empathy, he or she will demonstrate "an openness to experience, a willingness to respond realistically to relevant cues; a lack of dogmatism and a capacity for responding to the world, flexibly and dynamically."[19] Cultural empathy is undoubtedly a very desirable trait, even though it is difficult to identify in a candidate.

Adaptability and Flexibility

The ability to adapt to new circumstances and situations and to respond flexibly to different and often strange ideas and viewpoints is a characteristic found in successful international managers. The following are some specific types of adaptability and flexibility—listed originally in an American Management Association's research study—of which an international manager should be capable of performing on the job:

1. A high degree of ability to integrate with other people, with other cultures, and with other types of business operations.
2. Adaptability to change; being able to sense developments in the host country; recognizing differences and being able to evaluate them; and being able to qualitatively and quantitatively express the factors affecting the operations with which he or she is entrusted.

3. Ability to solve problems within different frameworks and from different perspectives.
4. Sensitivity to the fine print of differences in culture, politics, religion, and ethics, in addition to industrial differences.
5. Flexibility in managing operations on a continuous basis, despite lack of assistance and gaps in information rationale.

All of the preceding items imply that there is a close association between cultural empathy and a manager's capacity to be adaptable and flexible. The candidate who lacks cultural empathy will find it extremely difficult to be adaptable and flexible in a foreign environment.

Diplomatic Skills

An international manager must be skilled in dealing with others. He or she must be able to represent the parent company in a foreign country as its ambassador and be effective in advocating the parent company's point of view to foreign business persons, government bureaucrats, and political leaders. The manager should be a skilled negotiator, particularly in obtaining the most favorable treatment possible for the foreign subsidiary from the host country's government. Diplomatic skills are particularly important in all countries where the manager has to interact often with politicians and government officials, but they are especially crucial in the developing nations of Asia, Africa, and Latin America, where the role of the government in managing the business sector is quite significant.

Language Aptitude

The ability to learn a foreign language quickly can be quite an asset for an international executive. It is possible that the foreign assignment may be in a country where one can get by with English. This is true of all countries that were once British colonies; for example, India, Kenya, Uganda, Guyana, Singapore, and Malaysia. However, the assignment may be to a country where English is not understood, in which case an aptitude for foreign languages could be of tremendous benefit.

The importance of foreign-language competency in international business is stressed by Michael H. Armacost, who, as the U.S. Ambassador to Japan, observed that a linguistic barrier is by far the most stubborn obstacle to a smoother economic relationship between the United States and Japan (see Exhibit 6-1).

Personal Motives

A candidate for an international assignment should have positive reasons for seeking it. Many persons apply for a foreign assignment because they believe that the higher salaries paid to international managers would make them rich quickly. A candidate who has money as a primary motive is not likely to be effective abroad unless she or he also has the other attributes discussed above.

The candidate's history is a good indicator of his or her interest in foreign countries and cultures and of his or her preparation for a foreign assignment. Has she or he studied foreign languages, taken courses in international business, spent some years in the Peace Corps, or traveled or lived abroad for extended periods of time?

Emotional Stability and Maturity

The emotional stability of a candidate has a direct bearing on that person's ability to survive in another culture. An emotionally stable person is one who is not subject to wide swings in mood. He or she does not get overly elated when good things happen nor lapse into a depression when things do not go well. A good candidate maintains

EXHIBIT 6-1

Failing in Our Language Requirements

Sustaining our global leadership and preserving the health of our economy will require more Americans who are knowledgeable about internal conditions, more skilled in foreign languages, more familiar with foreign markets and business practices and more capable of functioning abroad with professional skill and cultural sensitivity.

In my work in Tokyo, I observe trade barriers. But the linguistic barrier is, in many respects, the most formidable obstacle to a smoother economic relationship. . . . We are still one of the few nations where a student can graduate from a top-flight college without achieving proficiency in a second language.

Michael H. Armacost, U. S. Ambassador to Japan, commencement exercises, College of Wooster, Wooster, Ohio, May 13

Source: Philadelphia Inquirer, May 20, 1991, 11A.

emotional equilibrium at all times and is therefore able to cope constructively with adversity and to function day to day in various kinds of situations without being thrown off balance.

Emotional stability is a corollary of emotional maturity. The less judgmental a person is in his or her relationships with others, the more understanding she or he is of others and their perspectives. The emotionally mature person is not likely to consider his or her way of doing things or behaving as the best way. An emotionally mature person is most likely to be emotionally stable as well.

Adaptability of Family

The ability of a manager to be effective in a foreign subsidiary depends to a large extent upon how happy the manager's spouse and children are in the foreign environment. It is not always easy for a manager's family to feel comfortable in a country where so many things are different from those at home. For example, a family from the United States placed in Sri Lanka will find that the people look different, talk a strange language, eat spicy food, and dress differently.

Even the trees and shrubs, animals, birds, and insects are strange. To be transported to such an environment can be quite unsettling. The family might get homesick for people at home and for familiar surroundings. An unhappy family takes its toll on the effectiveness of a manager at work. The following account illustrates this problem:

> Some years ago, we chose a promising young man for a post in Nigeria. We were sure he was suited for the job. But the man had a family—two small children and a wife who had never been west of Pittsburgh. When they arrived in Nigeria, that young wife from Montclair discovered how big insects are in Lagos. Three weeks later we brought the family home at a cost of almost $15,000.[21]

Here is another example to illustrate the problem that non-adaptability of the family can create for a company:

> Several years ago a U.S. engineering company ran into trouble while working on a steel mill in Italy. The crisis stemmed neither from inexperienced Italian personnel nor from volatile Italian politics but from the inability of an American executive's wife to adapt to Italy. Frustrated by language, schooling, and shopping problems, she complained incessantly to other company wives, who began to feel that they, too, suffered hardships and started

complaining to their husbands. Morale got so bad that the company missed deadlines and, eventually, replaced almost every American on the job. [22]

What these examples imply is that no matter how gifted, competent, and suited a manager may be to work in a foreign country, that person's effectiveness as a manager will depend on the degree to which his or her family, and especially spouse, adjusts to the foreign country's environment. A manager cannot perform at the peak of her or his abilities if his or her family is unhappy and yearning to go back home.

The preceding criteria are all important in selecting a manager for a foreign assignment. But what criteria do companies actually use in their selection process? A study by RosalieTung classified overseas managerial assignments into four categories:

1. The chief executive officer, who is responsible for the entire foreign operation.
2. The functional head, who is assigned the job of establishing functional departments in a foreign subsidiary.
3. The troubleshooter, who analyzes and solves specific operational problems.
4. The operative.

Tung was interested in finding out whether the criteria used for selecting foreign personnel were contingent on the nature of the job they were expected to perform, the duration of stay in a foreign country, and the degree of contact with the local culture that the job entailed. For instance, the chief executive officer would normally have greater contact with the local community and a longer length of stay abroad than would a troubleshooter.

Tung found that U.S. multinational corporations consider the most important criteria for the selection of a chief executive officer of a foreign subsidiary to be these: communication skills, managerial talent, maturity, emotional stability, and adaptability to new environmental settings. For the category of functional head, the most important criteria were maturity, emotional stability, and technical knowledge of the business, along with the same criteria as would be required for the same job at home. Technical knowledge of the business, initiative, and creativity were the criteria most important in the selection of a troubleshooter. And in the selection of an operative, the criteria considered to be most important were maturity, emotional stability, and respect for the laws and people of the host country.[23]

SELECTION METHODS FOR FOREIGN ASSIGNMENTS

Once company executives agree on the attributes that a candidate must possess as prerequisites for a foreign assignment, the next step is determining who among the available candidates has these attributes. Selection methods that companies use include: (1) examination of past performance, (2) a battery of tests, and (3) extensive interviews.

It is generally accepted that past performance is not a sure indicator of future managerial success abroad. However, because of the very different circumstances in which a manager has to work in a foreign country, most executives do examine the work history of a candidate. The purpose of looking into a candidate's past performance is to weed out those who are clearly not suited for greater responsibilities, on the assumption that those who have not done well at home are not likely to succeed abroad.

Some companies like to use a battery of tests to determine a candidate's technical ability and psychological suitability. They seek to determine how a candidate measures up on the various desirable attributes discussed earlier, such as adaptability, emotional stability and maturity, and so on. However, not all companies are convinced that tests are useful as screening devices, so some choose to use them but do not rely heavily on them, and others do not use them at all.

There is widespread agreement that extensive interviews of candidates and their wives or husbands by senior executives are by far the best method available for obtaining necessary information in the selection process. In-depth interviews are conducted with the candidate to determine suitability for an assignment. The kinds of questions for which answers are sought are:

1. Why does the candidate want to be considered for a foreign assignment?
2. How keen is he [or she] about getting a posting abroad?
3. Does the candidate have a realistic perspective of the opportunities, problems, and risks involved in living and working abroad?
4. Is there evidence that the candidate is self-reliant, adaptable, and able to work independently?
5. What evidence is there that the candidate can learn foreign languages quickly?
6. Has he or she made career moves in the United States successfully?
7. Does the candidate's family have any medical problems?
8. How many children does he or she have and how old are they? Will the children move or stay home?
9. How enthusiastic is each member of the family about staying abroad?

These questions are just a few of the many that executives may ask when trying to determine how qualified a candidate is for a foreign posting.

Recognizing the importance of assessing the ability of executives and their families to adjust to life abroad, a growing number of companies are adopting a technique called adaptability screening. The program is conducted either by a professional psychologist or psychiatrist on the company's staff or by a personnel director trained in the technique. Two factors are generally measured during the screening: the family's success in handling transfers in the United States and its reactions to discussions of stresses that the transfer abroad and life in a particular foreign country may cause. The interviewer tries to alert the couple to personal issues involved in a transfer. For instance, the couple may have an aging, widowed, or ailing parent or close relative whom they may have to leave behind. They are told they may feel guilty and anxious about this. Or, family members might have strong bonds to their church or civic organizations. Such strong bonds could cause stresses after the family is physically separated from people and activities that are important to them. The frustrations of adjusting to a strange culture and learning to communicate in a new language are also highlighted during the interview.

The objective of adaptability screening is to make the family aware of the different types of potential stresses and crises that could arise in a transfer abroad and to prevent a failure abroad by giving the family a chance to say no to the transfer before it takes place. A failed foreign assignment costs a company anywhere from $250,000 to $350,000. It is estimated that U.S. companies lose between $ 2 billion and $ 2.5 billion a year from failed foreign assignments.[25] Hence, it is far more cost effective to prevent a bad transfer than it is to send family members abroad only to have them request a transfer back home again. In addition to alerting the family, the screening interview also permits the interviewer to assess the family's suitability for a stint overseas. There have been times when a family wants to go abroad but the interviewer does not recommend a transfer.

PREPARING MANAGERS FOR FOREIGN ASSIGNMENTS

Once a manager is selected for a foreign assignment, it is in the best interests of the company to ensure that this person and his or her family are prepared to handle the foreign assignment as effectively as possible. This goal may be met by having the family group attend a well-planned predeparture training program. Such a training program has the following two principal objectives: (1) to make it easier for the manager to assume her or his responsibilities and be effective on the job in the foreign environment as soon as possible, and (2) to facilitate the adaptation of the manager and his or her family to the foreign culture with as few problems as possible. The best program will probably have two phases. The executive alone should be involved in the first phase of the program, and both the executive and his or her family should be included in phase two.

For the Manager

Phase one of the program, which is just for the executive, should include study and discussion of at least the following elements:

- The characteristics of the economy, political structure, political stability, and legal environment of the host country.
- The relationship between the subsidiary and the rest of the company. The extent to which the subsidiary's operations are interlocked with the operations of other subsidiaries and of the parent company should be discussed.
- The economic and political aspirations of the host country as reflected in the government's policies, and what it expects of the subsidiary in areas such as creation of more jobs, exports, development of local resources, and so on.
- The management practices peculiar to the host country (for example, the practice of permanent employment and consensual decision making, both of which are typical of Japanese management).
- A comprehensive job description that specifies the authority, responsibilities, duties, and tasks of a manager's position in the foreign subsidiary.
- The overall objectives and goals a manager is expected to achieve.

For the Manager and Family

Phase two of the program, which includes the executive and family, should focus on helping the participants to adapt to the foreign environment as effectively and quickly as possible. To achieve this goal, the program should at least have the following elements: (1) language training, (2) area study, and (3) cross-cultural training.

Language Training

Language training is a must for the entire family. It gives them a start in becoming acclimated to their new country. The goal of language training is to provide the family with an elementary knowledge of vocabulary so that they can communicate with others on arrival in the host country. Simple things, such as ordering a meal in a restaurant, asking for directions, or reading street signs can be quite bewildering. Even a few hours of instruction prior to departure—as little as twenty to thirty hours—can make a tremendous difference, and will provide the family with the very basic vocabulary required to get started.[26]

Area Study

This element of training includes an intensive study of the host country's culture, politics, geography, climate, food, currency, and attitude toward foreigners. The family may be given books to read on this subject. Lectures by area experts, accompanied by film presentations, have been useful because they give participants the opportunity to ask experts questions about specific areas of concern.

Cross-Cultural Training

This training has as its purpose the preparation of executives and family to interact and communicate effectively in other cultures. Individuals learn how to work with people who think, behave, and perceive things differently, and who hold different beliefs and values. There are four basic models of cross-cultural training.[27]

Intellectual Model.   This training model consists of lectures and reading about the host country. The premise of this model is that factual knowledge about another culture should prepare an executive for living or working in that culture.

Area Simulation Model.   This is a program tailored to the specific culture in which the executive and her or his family will be immersed. Attempts are made to create a variety of situations that the participants are likely to face in the foreign culture. The premise is that exposure to these situations will teach the family how to function in the new culture.

Self-Awareness Model.   Programs using this model are based on the premise that understanding oneself and the motivations for one's own behavior is critical to understanding other persons, particularly those of another culture. Sensitivity training is the main ingredient of this method.

Cultural Awareness Model.   This training technique assumes that for an individual to function successfully in another culture, he or she must first learn universal principles of behavior that exist across cultures. The program attempts to make participants aware of the influence of culture on an individual and of how participants differ from the peoples of other countries because of cultural differences. The focus of the program is on improving participants' ability to recognize cultural influences in personal values, behaviors, and cognitions. This ability should enhance a person's skill at diagnosing difficulties in intercultural communication and lower his or her inclination to make judgments when confronted with behavior that appears strange.

There are many different methods of cross-cultural training, such as the Cultural Assimilator or the Contrast-American Method of Cross-Cultural Training. It is beyond the scope of this chapter to discuss these techniques in detail; but we can say that, regardless of the type of method used, the objectives of all cross-cultural training programs are similar:

1. They encourage more astute observations in new situations, as well as greater sensitivity toward people who are culturally different.

2. They foster greater understanding in dealing with representatives of microcultures within one's own country.

3. They improve employee and customer relations by creating an awareness of cultural differences and the influence on behavior of these differences.

4. They develop more cosmopolitan organizational representatives who not only understand the concept of culture but can apply this knowledge to interpersonal relations and organizational culture.

5. They increase managerial effectiveness in international operations, especially with regard to cross-cultural control systems, negotiations, decision-making, customer relations, and other vital administrative processes.

6. They improve cross-cultural skills of employees on overseas assignments or of representatives of microcultures in our own country.

7. They reduce culture shock when on foreign deployment and enhance the intercultural experience for employees.

8. They apply the behavioral sciences to international business and   management.

9. They increase job effectiveness through training in human behavior, particularly in the area of managing cultural differences.

10. They improve employee skills as professional intercultural communicators.[28]

Cross-cultural training programs may be conducted by professionals who understand cross-cultural education and challenges. Such professionals may include psychologists; cultural anthropologists; communications specialists; and human resources development specialists, trainers, and facilitators. Nationals of the host country, third-country nationals experienced in the particular culture, and local professors with relevant expertise can all be drafted to assist in such a program. There are management consulting organizations, universities, and agencies that specialize in cross-cultural education who may also be called upon for assistance. A few final comments are called for on training programs designed to prepare managers for foreign assignments. If a foreign assignment involves a great deal of interaction with the local community and if great differences exist between the home and host cultures, the manager should be subjected to as many cross-cultural training programs as possible, in addition to language training and area studies. However, area study alone may be sufficient if contact with the local community is low (e.g., the troubleshooter) and minimal cultural differences exist between the home and host countries (e.g., the United States and Canada). Between these two extremes there exist situations involving degrees of cultural differences between the home and host countries.[29]

The number of cross-cultural training programs is growing in American companies. A survey of 200 corporate clients by Berlitz International found that they needed cultural orientation more than foreign-language training. A senior vice-president of personnel at Reynolds Metals Company says that "American businesses are dumb if they don't use cross-cultural training." Reynolds Metal's expatriate burnout fell to almost zero after the company began using cross-cultural training in the late 1970's. General Motors, despite massive cost cutting in the late 1980's and early 1990's, still spends nearly $500,000 a year on cross-cultural training for about 150 Americans and their families who live abroad. General Motors expatriate failure rate of less than 1 percent compares very favorably with a 25 percent failure rate at companies that do not have adequate cross-cultural training programs.[30]

MANAGING DUAL-CAREER PERSONNEL

Practical Insight 6-2 gives examples of four dual-career families in which both spouses have independent careers. The phenomenon of dual careers is building rapidly. The number of dual-career couples has grown from 52 percent of all couples in 1980 to 59 percent in 1992. A survey of 127 U.S. and foreign multinational businesses conducted in May 1992 by Windham International and the National Foreign Trade

Council has shown that about 41 percent of employees transferred abroad have spouses who worked before locating.[31]

The dual-career expatriate couple issue has become a major concern for global companies that require, or sometimes insist, that experience in working in foreign cultures is a required qualification for promotions to senior positions. Commuter marriages, while not uncommon within the U.S., now sometimes span the globe as married women with careers of their own become less accepting of the idea that they ought to give up their careers for their spouses.

Global companies must have sound policies to ensure that a fast-track, bright male or female manager does not leave the company because of the hazards of separation from his or her spouse when asked to undertake an assignment abroad. Here are some policy suggestions:

1. Make the pangs of separation more bearable by paying for frequent visitation trips. One trip every two months is not unreasonable.
2. Give a very generous allowance for long-distance phone calls. A phone conversation can do wonders to remove loneliness.
3. Try to find a job for the spouse within the company in the foreign location if the spouse is willing to quit his or her job at home. The U.S. State Department has the practice of finding jobs for spouses of U.S. foreign service personnel in U.S Embassies and Consulates abroad.
4. Network in the foreign location with other global companies for spousal jobs. For example, the Hong Kong subsidiary of a company like Proctor and Gamble might be in a position to hire the spouse of an expatriate Colgate-Palmolive manager working in Hong Kong.

The stresses and strains of working in different countries and cultures can be brutal for dual-career couples. Therefore, global companies must realize that, in order to retain competent managers, they must do everything within their grasp to enable dual-career couples to effectively cope with their difficulties and problems.

PRACTICAL INSIGHT 6-2

Married But Worlds Apart

Michael and Judy Casper hoped to be together for their 25th wedding anniversary. They had planned a romantic three-week vacation in Alaska. But alas the company called. Michael spent the anniversary watching a rented videotape. He could not get away from his new job as General manager of Gulf Bank in Kuwait City. Judy lives 7,700 miles away in Houston, Texas. She had been following Michael around the world for 17 years. Now she has a job of her own, her first for which she gets paid. Judy owns a successful home-interior shop. She celebrated the anniversary dining in an Italian restaurant with her three college-age children.

Ed and Rebecca Rolfes both had jobs in Brussels, Belgium, until Ed was sent packing for Chicago by his company. Rebecca is a researcher with the Conference Board in Brussels; Ed is an export manager with Navistar International Corporation. Rebecca stayed back in Brussels for 18 months with their teenage daughter while Ed spent every other month in Brussels for a year. Rebecca claims that although staying in Brussels has helped her career it has not done their marriage any good.

Ingrid Ma works in Taipei, Taiwan. She is the first U.S. female manager sent abroad by Stride Rite Corporation. She runs the company's Taiwan operations. She left behind her husband and two daughters. Her husband Hansan is a top toy designer for Tonka Corporation's Parker Brothers division in Beverly, Massachusetts. Stride Rite pays for her personal calls and agreed to fly her home three times a year and fly her husband to Taipei four times a year. This enabled the couple to spend their 25th anniversary together in their Marblehead, Massachusetts, home.

Elizabeth McElroy is a marketing manager with Ameritech Corp. She has been transferred to Warsaw, Poland. Husband Robert runs a light-fixture distributorship in Chicago. Ameritech pays for the couple to visit each other three times a year provided they fly coach. Robert is not very happy with his "commuter marriage". He complains that he is used to having her around in their home, and that he finds weekends especially difficult. He thinks that Ameritech could have done much more for them, such as giving them trips to visit each other at least once every two months.

Source: Adapted from Joann S. Lubin, "Spouses Find Themselves Worlds Apart As Global Commuter Marriages Increase," *The Wall Street Journal*, August 19, 1992, B1 and B5.

Until now, we have been looking at the strategy an international company should implement to improve the chances of a manager's success in a foreign assignment. But executives at the parent company cannot sit back and assume that, having prepared the manager for the foreign posting, they have done their part and now it is up to the manager to perform. The manager abroad may experience many anxieties that are not related to the environment in the foreign country but that emanate from his or her being physically and emotionally separated from the parent company. Such anxieties can have a detrimental impact on job performance.

There are things that executives in the parent company can do— some before the manager's departure and some during his or her tenure abroad—to help alleviate those anxieties. We shall examine this subject in the following section.

REPATRIATING THE INTERNATIONAL MANAGER

A problem that has become of increasing concern to both managers abroad and their companies is the reentry of managers into their home-country organizations. Most expatriates take foreign assignments for several years, under the assumption that they will eventually return to their home company, either to headquarters or to a subsidiary in the home country. More often than not, the move back home is a source of potential anxiety for a manager.

What are the reasons for the anxiety about returning home? Among the foremost reasons is the fear that the company has not planned adequately for the manager's return. Perhaps he or she will be placed temporarily—which may mean months—in a mediocre or makeshift job.[32] There is also anxiety because an extended foreign stay may have caused the manager loss of visibility in, and isolation from, the parent company factors which may have an adverse effect upon the manager's career and upward mobility in the organization. The expatriate manager is anxious that, despite access to the formal power structure he or she had from the foreign post, a manager abroad still loses contact with the informal power structure within the company.[33] Managers have apprehension, too, that they may miss opportunities for advancement at home, and that peers will be promoted ahead of them. Another source of anxiety is the possibility of failure in a foreign assignment and its impact upon a once-promising career. If a manager fails at her or his foreign assignment, he or she is usually penalized indirectly by a change in the company's attitude, which expresses disfavor with such failures. This attitude is exemplified in the following comment by the director of employee relations of Dow Chemical, U.S.A. "If a person flunks out overseas ... we bring him home.... He's penalized indirectly because the odds are that if he flunked out over there, he's in trouble over here. But we bring him back and, generally, he has a tough row to hoe."[34] This attitude is neither fair nor logical, considering that the problems, both work-related and personal, and the environment of an expatriate manager, are very different and usually more difficult than those facing his or her domestic counterpart.

Getting used to working under organizational constraints may be hard for some expatriates when they come back home. Abroad, the manager had a great deal more autonomy. Physical distance from the parent company permitted the manager to function independently and to demonstrate what she or he could accomplish without much corporate assistance. When the manager returns home, even if it means coming back to a bigger job in the organizational hierarchy, he or she still must operate as a member of an organization that constrains the freedom to act. In other words, "One minute he is Patton roaring across the desert ... and the next he is on Eisenhower's staff, where the moves must be made an inch at a time."[35]

A sense of loss of status may also be experienced by the executive upon coming home. Abroad, especially for a local general manager or senior executive, a manager was probably a very prominent member in the local community. Back home she or he is apt to be just another executive.

An expatriate manager may have to incur financial burdens when he or she returns. For instance, the returning manager may find that he or she no longer can afford to buy a home similar to the one sold a few years before. In addition, the abundant benefits and perquisites received as an inducement to accept the foreign post are eliminated upon an executive's return. Even if promoted, the returning manager may in essence be taking a pay cut.

What can companies do to ease the reentry of expatriate managers? Some companies, such as Westinghouse Electric, Dow Chemical, and Union Carbide, use repatriation agreements—written guarantees that a manager will not be kept abroad longer than two to five years and that, upon return, he or she will be placed in a job that is mutually acceptable. The written agreement does not promise the expatriate any promotion or specific salary increase upon return. However, it may state that the manager may be given a job equal to, if not better than, the one he or she had abroad. Such repatriation agreements could be of great value in alleviating the career-related anxieties of expatriate managers.

Another strategy to ease repatriation is to make senior executives serve as sponsors of managers abroad. It is the responsibility of a sponsor to monitor the performance, compensation, and career paths of expatriate managers who are under his or her wing, and to plan for their return. Sponsors begin scouting anywhere from six months to a year prior to an expatriate's return for a suitable position to which he or she can come back.[36] Union Carbide and IBM are two companies that make use of such sponsors, but there are others as well. Dow Chemical has a cadre of ten full-time counselors who act as "godfathers" of expatriates. Once a year they travel abroad to meet each of the foreign-based managers to explore and understand the manager's career goals and how any changes in such goals could be accommodated. The counselors also act as advocates for the managers back home to ensure that they are given due consideration for any promotional opportunities that may occur during their foreign stay.[37] Sponsors and counselors are helpful in keeping the expatriate manager in touch with developments at home, and they help to ease the career oriented concerns of expatriates.

Other methods of keeping the expatriate manager plugged into the informal power structure include corporate management meetings around the world, regularly scheduled meetings at the headquarters, and combining home leave with an extended stay at the headquarters to work on specific problems or projects.[38]

To lessen the financial difficulties caused by inflation in the housing market, companies such as Aluminum Company of American and Union Carbide have established programs to rent or otherwise maintain an expatriate's home while she or he is away. Union Carbide pays real estate and legal fees to help most of its international executives rent their homes. Such a program can erase the problem an executive would otherwise face on returning home—finding that a home similar to the one he or she used to live in has become unaffordable!

THE HOST-COUNTRY NATIONAL

It is not uncommon for host-country governments to put restrictions on the employment of foreign nationals. Such restrictions reflect a desire to ensure full employment among their own workforce. These restrictions may appear to be unnecessary and inconvenient to the multinational corporation that wants to utilize the best human resources available; but the multinational corporation must realize that, just as it is seeking to maximize the return on its investment, so is the host government. As a result of these requirements, it is becoming increasingly common for local nationals to rise to top executive positions.

Advantages of Host-Country Managers

A local manager does in fact have an advantage over an expatriate. Cultural differences may be difficult to overcome for the expatriate, but a local manager is very familiar with the local environment, business people, and government officials. In the area of public relations, a local manager can be extremely helpful. Knowledge of local customs is essential for minimizing the inevitable bureaucratic red tape. In Latin America and Asia, it is not uncommon for local officials to refuse to conduct business with anyone other than a local national of managerial status.[39]

A local manager helps to minimize any bad feelings a foreign government may have toward a multinational operation. A company having a responsible attitude toward the local community should alleviate many of the fears the local government might have. A company with a policy of training local nationals to assume greater responsibility within the corporation would be received enthusiastically and should have good relations with the local community.

Recruitment and Selection

Problems are often encountered by multinational corporations seeking to recruit and select local nationals for positions within the corporation. Local customs and educational opportunities, particularly in underdeveloped countries, often produce individuals deficient in aptitudes traditionally regarded by Western management as essential to top management performance. Economic growth concepts and the role of capital, profits, savings, and investment are often misunderstood and unacceptable to those raised in developing countries. Consequently, the likelihood of finding suitable managerial candidates is reduced. This situation is not often a difficulty to the same degree in developed or industrialized countries.

Under the best of circumstances, finding acceptable local managers is a difficult and time-consuming assignment. There are four basic sources to choose from: (1) the present workforce, (2) local and foreign university graduates, (3) government agencies, and (4) local businesses. The first and most obvious place to look within an operating subsidiary is to the present workforce. Someone from the non-management ranks or a lower supervisory position may be prepared to assume greater responsibility.

Until the subsidiary is established, the executive search goes into the local business community. Local managers may feel that working for a foreign-owned organization poses certain threats; hence salary, fringe benefits, working conditions, and advancement opportunities must be comparable to or better than those offered by other local firms. When strong nationalistic feelings are part of a culture, a local manager may be viewed as a bit of an economic traitor. This is especially true when the firm is in competition with a national company. Conditions must be attractive enough to make the adjustment worthwhile.

Finding the right person for a specific job in a foreign subsidiary is not easy. Few local managers have the experience or training desired by the multinational. In addition, local managers are not as accustomed to changing jobs frequently as are managers in the United States. An effective selection interview must be tailored to the local culture. For instance, in many countries questions regarding a person's family, hobbies, parents, or religious convictions are often considered unacceptable.[40] In general, these areas are private and not subject to questioning by a stranger. An effective interview must probe, instead, into the candidate's motivations, ambitions, communication abilities, and management style. The multinational home management must also keep in mind that it is extremely difficult, if not impossible, to terminate an employee in most developing countries, where an employee is practically guaranteed a job for life.[41] Strong unions and government regulations restrict a company's actions when an employee proves unsuited for a given job.

Finally, the success of a local manager is necessary for the long-run success of the foreign subsidiary, for it is ultimately the local manager who will replace the managers from the home country and third countries.

MULTINATIONAL STAFFING PHILOSOPHIES

The multinational staffing practices of a company are influenced significantly by the attitude of top-management executives at headquarters toward doing business around the world, and particularly, toward foreign executives in headquarters and subsidiaries. Howard Perlmutter has identified three primary attitudes among international executives that can be inferred from examining the managerial practices of companies that have substantial foreign operations. He has labeled them as ethnocentric, polycentric, and geocentric.[42]

A multinational company of any country may exhibit ethnocentric, polycentric, or geocentric attitudes. In an *ethnocentric corporation*, the prevailing attitude is that home-country attitudes, management style, knowledge, evaluation criteria, and managers are superior to anything the host country might have to offer. Consequently, top management executives at headquarters and at all subsidiaries are from the home country exclusively. A *polycentric corporation* treats each of its subsidiaries as distinct national entities. There is a conscious belief that only host-country managers can ever really understand the culture and behavior of the host-country market; therefore, a foreign subsidiary should be managed by local people. However, no local manager can ever hope to be promoted to a position at headquarters, which is staffed exclusively with home-country people.

The third attitude, which is still rarely observed today among multinational corporations, is geocentrism. *Geocentrism* is based on a policy of searching for management candidates on a global basis. A geocentric philosophy of staffing must be accompanied by a worldwide, integrated business philosophy to be successful. Thus, the selection and training of management at the international level must take place without regard to the managers' nationalities. Management potential from anywhere in the world can be employed to the advantage of the multinational company as a whole and, wherever it is necessary, at headquarters as well as in the subsidiaries.

It is true that geocentrism is limited in some countries by legal and political factors. Despite this fact, it is very important for a company operating as a true multinational entity to have a personnel policy that is also multinational. In view of the demands on a multinational company's management, it is necessary to have an internationally employable "fire brigade." Moreover, because the environment of a multinational company is truly global, the result of multinational recruiting should be a cadre of top management at headquarters, one that is not only internationally oriented but also composed of nationals of various countries.[43]

The feasibility of implementing a geocentric policy is based on the following five related assumptions:

1. Highly competent employees are available not only at headquarters but also in the subsidiaries.
2. International experience is a condition for success in top positions.
3. Managers with high potential and ambition for promotion are constantly ready to be transferred from one country to another.
4. Competent and mobile managers have an open disposition and high adaptability to different conditions in their various assignments.
5. Those not blessed initially with an open disposition and high adaptability can acquire these qualities as their experience abroad accumulates.[44]

These five assumptions hold true in varying-degrees, depending on a company's particular circumstances. In most cases, multinational firms with a truly global outlook realize the need to combine different nationalities in managing their operations. However, despite these beliefs and the desire to become geocentric, a large number of companies are still a long way from internationalizing their staff.

There is still a strong emotional attachment to an enterprise's original country, reflecting the attitude that the quality of management and the cohesion of an organization require at least a certain proportion of experienced people from the home country.[45] Nevertheless, ideally the goal of a company's international staffing policy should be a corporate pool of experienced international executives who are available for assignment wherever their skills are needed. In other words, to operate as a truly geocentric company, a multinational firm must have geocentric managers.

INTERNATIONAL EXECUTIVE COMPENSATION

If there is one area of multinational personnel policy that can be designated the most complex, it has to be the area of compensation. The problems to date defy a simple solution and cause much intra-organizational resentment. The basic compensation strategy of international companies is to pay a base salary and apply to it the base differentials determined by the country of location of the affiliate. Problems arise in determining the base salary, the type and amount of the differentials, and the countries to which they apply. The following discussion covers some standard approaches to compensation developed by multinational companies, some methods of determining the salaries of home-, host-, and third-country nationals, and a review of various differentials.

Evolution of Compensation Systems

The development of multinational compensation systems in effect today has been quite haphazard. The American businessman has been working abroad since this country began. In the early days, a manager received the same salary abroad that she or he would have received at home; there was no compensation for additional expenses. This policy fell apart when the oil companies began sending employees to the Middle East, where they were often obliged to live and work in primitive conditions. Consequently, the companies had a difficult time convincing qualified people to accept such positions. The idea of premium pay was then developed and other companies followed the lead.

In those early days of premium pay, there was no set percentage allowed for foreign service; rather, the embarking employee negotiated the amount of the premium. Understandably, the resultant variation in pay for one company's employees working in the same country caused some discontent. The policy eventually evolved into a standard percentage for premium pay anywhere abroad. Finally it became a premium designed to maintain the expatriate's "real" salary in his or her particular foreign post.[46]

Today, expatriate compensation can roughly be categorized into three standard approaches. The first approach is based on headquarters scale plus affiliate differentials. The base salary of the home-country national is determined by the salary for that job at headquarters. With many companies now using the balance sheet method of determining differentials, an affiliate differential can be a positive addition to an expatriate's salary, or it can be a negative allowance to account for any extra benefits associated with the particular foreign assignment. Under this system, host-country nationals are entitled neither to the base salary nor to the differentials allotted to home-country nationals; rather, their salaries are based on local salary standards. Third-country nationals pose a problem, however. The company may either treat them as host-country nationals or home-country nationals; in either case, inequities are possible. This system is undoubtedly the most ethnocentric of the three.[47]

The citizenship salary system solves the problem of what to do about the third-country national. An executive's regular salary is based on the standard for her or his country of citizenship or native residence. An appropriate affiliate differential is then added, based on comparative factors between the executive's native country and the host country. This system works well as long as expatriates with similar positions do not come from countries with different salary scales. As affiliate staffing becomes more internationalized, it has become harder to avoid precisely this problem. Consequently, the inequities arising from different salary scales for the same position do not go unnoticed.[48]

The global compensation system is a move toward a more geocentric personnel policy, although it, too, has its constraints. Under this system, the same job has the same base salary, regardless of country. Affiliate differentials are then added to the base. Differentials are determined by affiliate location and job or rank but are unrelated to the home country of the expatriate. The resultant system allows for no unexplained inequities among employees performing the same job in the same subsidiary. A prerequisite for this type of compensation scale is a global system of job classification. The task of measuring comparable job elements across cultural boundaries is awesome, and no company has completely succeeded in this respect. Nevertheless, efforts are being made in this direction, and a global salary structure seems surely to be the system of the future.[49]

Dealing with Dissatisfaction

Until a global salary system becomes a reality, most multinational companies are operating under one of the first two compensation systems. Under these systems, the most troublesome problem has been the host-country national's salary. In the past, the remuneration of local nationals has been ruled by local salary levels. This practice stems from the multinational companies' fear of raising the salary standards for the entire area and thus raising the affiliate's costs of operation. The pressure to utilize more native managers and local statutory limitations on expatriate employment have increased the demand for capable host-country nationals. Increased competition among companies with subsidiaries in the same country has led to a gradual upgrading of local managers' salaries.

One company has divided its employees into two classifications. If a local employee meets certain established performance standards, she or he is shifted from local management status to the international executive corps. His or her pay is then adjusted to the new, higher salary scale of the other international executives, including Americans. The promoted local manager, in turn, agrees to be available for transfer to any other country where his or her services may be needed.

Another approach is to shift all local managers above a certain level to the headquarters scale. Under this system, junior and lower middle management personnel may remain on a local salary standard, while upper level management is moved to a higher standard.

A third approach is to use management by objectives to determine local salaries. While this system does not necessarily eliminate the difference between local and expatriate salaries, it does provide a more rational explanation for the difference. Overall, however, international firms are moving toward a narrowing of the salary gap between the host-country national and the expatriate.[50]

As the number of third-country nationals in multinational companies increases, their compensation level approaches that of the home-country expatriate.[51] One of the problems peculiar to third-country nationals, however, is defining them. The most common definition is "one who works outside his home country for a company based in still another country."[52] But, is a Frenchman working for a Spanish-based company in Geneva or an Argentine working for a U.S.-based firm in Santiago really an expatriate, third-country national? And why do most U.S.-based companies consider Canadian nationals working abroad as U.S. expatriates and not third-country nationals?[53] Some countries are using cultural zones rather than nations to define third-country nationals. For example, Western Europe may be one zone, Africa, another, and so on.[54] Other companies use a combination of geographic and language zones. Thus an employee remains a local national (not a third-country national) unless he or she moves to a different geographic zone and a different language zone as well.[55]

Salary Differentials

The final section of this discussion on compensation is a brief review of the different types of salary differentials. It is not meant to be an exhaustive examination of each area, but simply an introduction to their different components and some of their problems.

Overseas Premium (OP)

This differential is usually paid as a percentage of the executive's base salary. There are a number of reasons companies still use the OP, but three basic rationalizations emerge: (1) the executive is being compensated for the various emotional, cultural, and physical adjustments he or she will have to make; (2) the executive is being given an incentive to accept a foreign assignment; and (3) the company must offer an OP because its competitors are offering one.[56] Some sources feel that the OP is practical since it indicates to the employee that the company realizes the inconvenience she or he is undergoing. The company avoids the administrative costs of analyzing and pricing each inconvenience separately. The alternative would be to increase the base salary, distort the firm's salary structure, and increase the costs of pension and other salary-based expenditures.[57]

Many industrial relations specialists assert that paying the same flat percentage of base salary to the executive going from Peoria to the deserts of Saudi Arabia as that paid to the executive going from New York to Paris is preposterous, and a number of companies have considered eliminating or modifying their OP. One suggested modification is the reduction of the OP over time. Another is that the percentage should be based on the degree of contrast between the home-country environment and host-country environment.[58]

Reimbursement for Payments into Host-Country Welfare Plans

Most developed countries require workers to contribute to some type of state welfare plan, whether it be a pension plan, a medical plan, or an unemployment plan. Since the expatriate is almost always making payments concurrently to a pension fund in the United States, and because any benefits accruing to him or her abroad will probably not be claimed, companies often leave local payment to the expatriate and compensate for it in the cost-of-living allowance. This situation occurs particularly when local tax regulations treat the company's contribution to the host-country program on behalf of an individual as a taxable fringe benefit. In the case of company pension plans, some companies "forgive" the employee's contributions while overseas. Where mandatory state medical plans exist, a company may reimburse the employee only for those expenses that are not provided free by the state.[59]

Housing Allowance

A housing allowance is provided by companies to permit executives to maintain living accommodations comparable to what they had at home, and to house them in a fashion comparable to their foreign peers. Some companies simply pay the difference (or a portion of the difference) between normal housing costs at home and the cost of housing in the foreign country. The problem with this method is determining the cost of normal domestic housing. Another common approach is to require the employee to pay up to a certain percentage of his or her salary for housing and make the company responsible for the difference. In these types of plans, the company may set a ceiling on the amount it will contribute in order to discourage excessively lavish choices of housing by the manager living abroad.[60]

Cost-of-Living (COL) Allowance

This differential is probably the most controversial of the differentials. Critics claim that good international managers choose to experience the novel conditions of a foreign life-style, and that their families will eventually adjust their consumption patterns and tastes to the foreign environment. By this reasoning, a COL allowance is not needed or can at least be decreased over time.

Proponents of the COL allowance counter that an expatriate has the right to live in a foreign country as she or he does at home. In addition, maintaining a familiar life-style may be essential to a family's satisfaction with a foreign assignment. The biggest problem here is determining cost-of-living indexes. The most easily available resource is the U.S. State Department's index, but it is often out of date and contains cultural biases. Many companies develop their own indexes or turn to private research firms for one.[61]

Education and Perquisites

This allowance includes schooling for children, club memberships, and home leave, among other amenities. Education is probably the most commonly provided expense, and the policy is usually uniform among companies. The company attempts to provide the means whereby an expatriate can educate his or her children in their mother tongue up to the level required for university entrance in their home country, and at a cost to him or her no greater than it would have been at home. Implementation of this policy, particularly regarding transportation and the determination of an acceptable school, varies according to the parent country and local facilities.

   Clubs are an essential feature of business life in some countries, and fees can be expensive. Some firms provide nothing for club membership; others pay the entrance fee but not the dues. Very few pay all membership fees.

   Home leave also varies among companies, but the most common policy is to grant thirty days home leave after eleven or twelve months abroad. The class of travel allowed is usually determined by the amount of time spent in the air (e.g., first class for a flight exceeding ten hours, tourist for a shorter journey).[62]

Income Taxes

Taxes can be an extremely complex area of international compensation. In some countries, only locally paid compensation is taxable, but in most, worldwide compensation is taxable. U.S.-based companies tend to prefer tax equalization plans in which the company withholds from the employee her or his U.S. tax liability and pays local taxes. British companies, on the other hand, vary their policy depending on the affiliate country. The tax equalization policy presents the danger of paying multiple taxes; that is, in many countries a tax paid by a company on behalf of an employee is also taxable. It has been suggested that a company with operations in many countries would be better off adopting a tax equalization policy. It would gain in some countries while losing in others. But if the company operates in only a few countries, it would be best to leave local taxes to the employee and adjust other local allowances accordingly.[63]

Fluctuations in Exchange Rates

The fluctuations in exchange rates between parent and host countries are provided for by the inclusion of a currency cushion in the overseas premium—if the fluctuations are minor. Major currency changes are dealt with through special allowances. To avoid unnecessary problems and costs, local price reviews are sometimes delayed for six months after a major change; third-country nationals are paid in home-country currency; a proportion of the expatriate's salary is retained in his or her home country; and any special allowance is reduced over time.[64]

In conclusion, a good compensation program must meet the needs of two groups: the corporation and its employees. "A multinational company that needs to widen its horizons to get the best managers regardless of citizenship must structure a salary plan equitable enough to compensate all managers fairly, and attractive enough to draw the top managers it needs."[65]

COMPENSATING THE HOST-COUNTRY NATIONAL

In general, U.S. corporations have not offered local nationals compensation packages that are equal to those offered to home- and third-country expatriates. Local nationals are typically compensated in accordance with local standards. In other words, the total compensation package of the local manager often amounts to as little as one-half or even one-third of that of an expatriate manager with identical credentials doing essentially the same job.

In order to attract and retain high-quality local managers, multinational companies must ensure that a total compensation package is not only internally equitable but also externally competitive. The various components of the package must consider local conditions, such as the tax structure; cultural variables, such as status symbols; and governmentally legislated social welfare schemes, such as health insurance and pension plans. Consideration of such factors, which vary from country to country, would enable the company to design a compensation package for a local manager that is most beneficial to her or him in terms of specific local conditions.

Comparative Executive Life-styles in the United States, Japan, Germany, and Great Britain

Many differences exist in the life-styles of executives in the major world economies such as the United States, Japan, Germany, and Great Britain. Differences exist with respect to salaries and benefits, taxation, housing, food and clothing, medical care and education. By far, the most affluent life-style an upper-middle manager (earning between $75,000 and $150,000 per year) can attain is found not in Paris, Tokyo, London, New York, or Los Angeles, but in cities like Omaha, Atlanta, and Seattle, far from large and costly coastal cities. Some of these major differences will be discussed in the following sections.

Income

Although U.S. executive salaries are not the highest of their European or Japanese counterparts, differences in taxation and purchasing power afford them the maximum return on their dollar. As a result, American managers have more of everything: larger houses and property, more cars, appliances, electronic devices, and so on. Europeans in particular are penalized by high sales taxes (up to 15 percent in some countries) and protectionism (agricultural subsidies and import restrictions) that significantly diminish purchasing power for goods and services. The Japanese pay only 3 percent in sales taxes, but their cost of living is high due to extreme protectionism. To make up for lower disposable incomes, Europeans and Japanese enhance compensation packages with generous, company-provided perquisites, such as company cars.

Pensions and Other Benefits

When it comes to pensions, most Europeans are given more generous plans than are the Americans. In addition, American managers are more likely to be fired than are their counterparts anywhere else in the world. They are also more likely to change jobs, making their future financial security less certain than that of Japanese executives who are "employees for life" in their organizations.

Vacation time also varies among different countries. Europeans in general take four to six weeks vacation each year, while Americans average three weeks, and some managers feel guilty about taking any time off at all. In Japan, leisure time is frowned upon and managers often do not use all of their vacation time.

Health Care

Executives in the United States spend about as much on health care as do their foreign counterparts. The British, however, have the best system, and executives there can take advantage of the features of both the National Health Service and private plans.

Housing

Except in cities like New York, Los Angeles, Washington, D.C., and other places where real estate values and rents are excessive, Americans have by far the best advantage in housing. Americans can purchase much more square footage and land than is possible for their European and Japanese counterparts. In Germany, for example, zoning restrictions favor farming over construction, and city codes impose strict requirements on building materials and insulation. As a result, many Germans cannot afford a detached house; so, like the British, they live in row houses having much less space. The Japanese are in the worst position with respect to housing. In Tokyo, for example, the smallest detached home located within an hour's distance of the city cannot be purchased for less than $500,000. Middle managers who are fortunate enough to own homes either inherited them or bought them many years ago. To help ease their employees' housing burdens and to help them save money, Japanese corporations provide inexpensive, subsidized housing for their young managers. When employees are ready to purchase their own homes, the companies also help them with subsidized mortgages.

Education

Despite American executives' affluence, they are the only ones of their foreign counterparts who are daunted by the prospect of financing their children's education. Nowhere else in the world is this burden as heavy, although it does vary from country to country. In Germany, the government pays for tuition, as almost all colleges and high schools are state-sponsored. In Great Britain, where the public school system is not favored, private elementary and secondary schools present a financial burden for families concerned with the quality of their children's education. In Japan, education is less costly than in the United States but not nearly as inexpensive as in Germany. Executives tend to send their children to private high schools and colleges, but costs for this education are heavily subsidized by the government.

While the components that contribute to life-style vary from country to country, and although tastes differ dramatically, the United States still appears to offer executives the greatest amount of economic diversity and the widest variety of choices.[66]

SUMMARY

International companies have three main sources from which they can draw their pool of international managers—the home country, the host country and a third country. Home-country nationals are the citizens of the country in which the headquarters of the company is located; nationals of the country in which the foreign affiliate is situated are the host-country nationals; nationals of a country that is neither the home nor host country are third-country nationals. For instance, an Italian working in the French subsidiary of an American company would be classified as a third-country national.

Multinational companies have a tendency to staff the key positions in their foreign affiliates with home-country nationals. Third-country nationals are also used frequently, but most companies prefer to use nationals of advanced countries in this capacity. Most multinationals use host-country nationals in middle- and lower-level positions in subsidiaries that are located in developing countries. In more advanced countries, they employ host-country nationals to a far greater extent at all levels of management. This is probably because more qualified personnel are available in advanced countries than in developing countries.

Recently, foreign nationals have been named to managerial positions in the headquarters of U.S. and European multinational corporations. However, this is still a rare occurrence.

Most personnel executives would agree that a candidate for a foreign assignment must possess a few key characteristics if he or she is to be successful abroad. Having these features does not ensure success, but not having them greatly increases the probability of failure. These characteristics are: technical ability, managerial skills, cultural empathy, adaptability and flexibility, diplomatic skills, language aptitude, positive motives, emotional stability and maturity, and a family capable of living in a foreign country. Selection methods used by companies to determine which candidates have these attributes include: an examination of each candidate's past performance, a battery of tests, and extensive interviews of the candidate and spouse.

The selected candidate should undergo a well-planned predeparture program, the purpose of which is to make a manager capable of assuming her or his new job abroad quickly and effectively. Such a program also facilitates a manager's, and his or her family's, adaptation to a foreign culture. The problem of personnel with dual-careers, wherein both spouses work and have independent careers, has gained considerable importance in global companies. Global companies must develop and implement policies that would facilitate dual-career personnel retention because many fast-track managers belong to dual-career families. Increasingly, the human assets of a company are becoming one of the most critical ingredients for its competitive success. Therefore, it is incumbent that companies develop effective personnel policies and programs to prevent the turnover of their best managers. Companies should also have effective programs to facilitate the reentry of the expatriate manager into the home-country organization at the completion of a foreign assignment.

Companies exhibit ethnocentric, polycentric, or geocentric staffing philosophies. Companies that have an ethnocentric staffing philosophy staff their foreign affiliates almost exclusively with home-country nationals. Host-country nationals are employed predominantly by those companies that have a polycentric philosophy. Companies with a geocentric staffing philosophy adopt the strategy of selecting and placing the right candidate in the right job, anywhere in the world, regardless of the nationality of the candidate.

Probably the most complex aspect of international staffing is international executive compensation. The basic compensation strategy of international companies is to pay a base salary and apply to it base differentials contingent on the location of the affiliate.

QUESTIONS

1. "Changes in international staffing policies tend to coincide with predictable stages of internationalization of multinational corporations." Discuss why this is so.

2. Does the nature of the job and the length of stay abroad influence the criteria for selection of candidates for a foreign assignment? What are the traits that an international manager should possess if she or he were to be appointed chief executive of a foreign affiliate?

3. Why is the preparation of a manager and her or his family for a foreign assignment just as important as the selection of the right candidate? What should be the objective and essential features of a predeparture training program?

4. Suggest policies that global companies should implement to ensure that fast-track managers, when given a foreign assignment, do not leave the company because of dual-career problems.

5. "Planning to bring an executive back home after a foreign assignment is as important as planning to send her or him abroad." Discuss this statement.

6. Discuss the salient differences between an ethnocentric, polycentric, and geocentric staffing policy.

7. Explain the assumptions underlying an effective geocentric staffing policy.

8. How would you approach the problem of determining an equitable compensation package for an American and an Egyptian who have been assigned to work on similar jobs in the Japanese subsidiary of an American multinational company?

9. Compare and contrast the executive life-styles in the United States, Japan, Germany, and Great Britain in terms of income, pensions, vacation time, health care, housing, and education.

FURTHER READING

Black, Stewart J., and Hal B. Gregersen. "The Other Half of the Picture: Antecedents of Spouse Cross-Cultural Adjustment," *Journal of International Business Studies*, Vol. 22, no. 3 (Third Quarter, 1991): 461-477.

Borrman, W. A. "The Problem of Expatriate Personnel and Their Selection in International Enterprises," *Management International Review* no. 4-5 (1968).

Boyacigiller, Nakiye. "The Role of Expatriates in the Management of Interdependence, Complexity, and Risk in Multinational Corporations," *Journal of International Business Studies*, Vol. 21, no. 3 (Third Quarter, 1990): 357-381.

Compensating International Executives. New York: Business International Corporation, 1970.

Crystal, Graef S. *Compensating U.S. Expatriates Abroad: An AMA Management Briefing*. New York: American Management Association, 1972.

Desatnick, R. L., and M. L. Bennett. *Human Resource Management in the Multinational Company*. New York: Nichols, 1977.

Domsch, M. and B. Lichtenberger. "Managing the Global Manager: Pre-Departure Training and Development for German Expatriates in China and Brazil." *Journal of Management Development*, Vol. 10, no. 7 (1991): 41-52.

Feldman, Daniel C. and Holly B. Tompson. "Entry Shock, Culture Shock: Socializing the New Breed of Global Managers." *Human Resource Management*, Vol. 31, no. 4 (Winter 1992): 345-362.

Franko, Lawrence G. "Who Manages Multinational Enterprises?" *Columbia Journal of World Business* 8, no. 2 (Summer 1973).

Harris, Philip R., and Robert T. Moran. *Managing Cultural Differences*. Houston: Gulf Publishing Co., 1979.

Heller, Jean E. "Criteria for Selecting an International Manager." *Personnel* 57 (May-June 1980).

Howard, Cecil G. "The Multinational Corporation: Impact on Nativization." *Personnel* (January-February 1972).

Illman, Paul E. *Developing Overseas Managers—And Managers Overseas*. New York: AMACOM, 1980.

Lanier, Alison R. "Selecting and Preparing Personnel for Overseas Transfers." *Personnel Journal* (March 1979).

LaPalombara, Joseph, and Stephen Blank. *Multinational Corporations and National Elites: A Study of Tensions*. New York: The Conference Board, 1976.

Maddox, Robert C. "Solving the Overseas Personnel Problem." *Personnel Journal* (June 1975).

McClenahen, John S. "The Overseas Manager: Not Actually a World Away." *Industry Week*, November 1, 1976.

Miller, Edwin L., and Joseph L. C. Cheng. "A Closer Look at the Decision to Accept an Overseas Position." *Management International Review* 18 (1978).

Moskowitz, Daniel B. "How to Cut It Overseas." *International Business*, Vol. 5, no. 10 (October 1992): 76, 78.

Perlmutter, Howard W. "The Fortuitous Evolution of the Multinational Corporation." *Columbia Journal of World Business* (January-February 1969).

Phatak, Arvind V. *Managing Multinational Corporations*. New York: Praeger Publishers, 1974.

Rose, Stanford. "The Rewarding Strategies of Multinationalism." *Fortune*, September 15, 1968.

Smith, Lee. "The Hazards of Coming Home." *Dun's Review*, October 1975.

Tung, Rosalie L. "U.S. Multinationals: A Study of Their Selection and Training Procedures for Overseas Assignments." *Academy of Management Proceedings*, 1979.

Tung, Rosalie L. "Selection and Training of Personnel for Overseas Assignments." *Columbia Journal of World Business* (Winter 1981).

Voris, William. "Considerations in Staffing for Overseas Management Needs." *Personnel Journal* (June 1975).

Young, David. "Fair Compensation for Expatriates." *Harvard Business Review* (July-August 1973).

Zeria, Yoram, and Ehud Harari. "Genuine Multinational Staffing Policy: Expectations and Realities." *Academy of Management Journal* 20, no. 2 (1977).

NOTES

[1]Edwin L. Miller and Joseph L. C. Cheng, "A Closer Look at the Decision to Accept an Overseas Position," *Management International Review* 18 (1978): 25-27.

[2]Rosalie L. Tung, "U. S. Multinationals: A Study of Their Selection and Training Procedures for Overseas Assignments," *Academy of Management Proceedings*, 1979, 298.

[3]Ibid.

[4]R. L. Desatnick and M. L. Bennett, *Human Resource Management in the Multinational Company* (New York: Nichols Publishing Co., 1977), 233-234.

[5]Sanford Rose, "The Rewarding Strategies of Multinationalism," *Fortune*, September 15, 1986, 180.

[6]Ibid.

[7]Ibid.

[8]Cecil G. Howard, "The Multinational Corporation: Impact on Nativization," *Personnel* (January-February 1972): 42.

[9]Tung, "U. S. Multinationals."

[10]Joseph LaPalombara and Stephen Black, *Multinational Corporations and National Elites: A Study of Tensions* (New York: The Conference Board, 1976), 57.

[11]Lawrence G. Franko, "Who Manages Multinational Enterprises?" *Columbia Journal of World Consumers* 8, no. 2 (Summer 1973): 30-42.

[12]Ibid., 39.

[13]Ibid.

[14]Ibid.

[15]"American Standard's Executive Melting Pot," *Business Week*, July 2, 1979, 93.

[16]Jean E. Heller, "Criteria for Selecting an International Manager," *Personnel* 57 (May-June 1980): 48.

[17]Ibid.

[18]Arvind V. Phatak, *Managing Multinational Corporations* (New York: Praeger Publishers, 1974), 194.

[19]William Voris, "Considerations in Staffing for Overseas Management Needs," *Personnel Journal* (June 1975): 354.

[20]Heller, "Criteria for Selecting and International Manager," 49.

[21]Robert C. Maddox, "Solving the Overseas Personnel Problem," *Personnel Journal* 44, no. 2 (February 1965): 93.

[22]"Gauging a Family's Suitability for a Stint Overseas," *Business Week*, April 16, 1979, 127.

[23]Tung, "U. S. Multinationals," 298-299.

[24]"Gauging a Family's Suitability," 127-130.

[25]Joann S. Lubin, "Companies Use Cross-Cultural Training to Help Their Employees Adjust Abroad," *The Wall Street Journal*, August 4, 1992, B1.

[26]Alison R. Lanier, "Selecting and Preparing Personnel for Overseas Transfers," *Personnel Journal*, 58 (March 1979): 162-163.

[27]Philip R. Harris and Robert T. Moran, *Managing Cultural Differences* (Houston: Gulf Publishing Co., 1979), 149.

[28]Ibid., 128-129. Reprinted by permission.

[29]"How to Ease Re-Entry after Overseas Duty," *Business Week*, June 11, 1979, 82.

[30]Joann S. Lubin, "Companies Use Cross-Cultural Training to Help Their Employees Adjust Abroad," *The Wall Street Journal*, August 19, 1992, B1.

[31]Joann S. Lubin, "Spouses Find Themselves Worlds Apart as Global Commuter Marriages Increase," *The Wall Street Journal*, August 19, 1992, B1.

[32]Rosalie L. Tung, "Selection and Training of Personnel for Overseas Assignments," *Columbia Journal of World Business*, Spring 1981, 74.

[33]John S. McClenahan, "The Overseas Manager: Not Actually a World Away," *Industry Week*, November 1, 1976, 53.

[34]Ibid.

[35]Lee Smith, "The Hazards of Coming Home," *Dun's Review*, October 1975, 72.

[36]"How to Ease Reentry."

[37]Ibid., 84.

[38]McClenahan, "The Overseas Manager" 53.

[39]Desatnick and Bennet, *Human Resources Management*, 168.

[40]Paul E. Illman, *Developing Overseas Managers—And Managers Overseas* (New York: AMACOM, 1980), 178.

[41]Ibid., 176.

[42]Howard W. Perlmutter, "The Tortous Evolution of the Multinational Corporation," *Columbia Journal of World Business*, 3, no. 1 (January-February 1969): 11-14.

[43]W. A. Borrman, "The Problem of Expatriate Personnel and Their Selection in International Enterprises," *Management International Review* 8, no. 4-5 (1968): 37-38.

[44]Yoram Zeira and Ehud Harari, "Genuine Multinational Staffing Policy Expectations and Realities," *Academy of Management Journal* 20, no. 2 (1977): 328.

[45]Borrman, "The Problems of Expatriate Personnel, 40.

[46]Graef S. Crystal, *Compensating U. S. Expatriates Abroad: An AMA Management Briefing* (New York: American Management Association, 1972), 1-3.

[47]E. J. Kolde, *The Multinational Company* (Lexington, Mass.: Lexington Books, 1974), 176-78.

[48]Ibid., 178-79.

[49]Ibid., 179-80.

[50]Ibid., 180-81.

[51]*Compensating International Executives* (New York: Business International Corporation, 1970), 33.

[52]Ibid.

[53]Ibid.

[54]Crystal, *Compensating U. S. Expatriates Abroad*, 44.

[55]Ibid.

[56]Ibid., 9.

[57]David Young, "Fair Compensation for Expatriates," *Harvard Business Review* 51, no. 4 (July-August 1973): 119.

[58]Ibid., 119-20.

[59]Ibid., 120-21.

[60]*Compensating International Executives*, 23-25.

[61]Crystal, *Compensating U. S. Expatriates Abroad*, 18-19.

[62]Young, "Fair Compensation for Expatriates," 123-45.

[63]Ibid.

[64]Ibid.

[65]Crystal, *Compensating U. S. Expatriates Abroad*, 10.

[66]Shawn Tully, "Where People Live Best," *Fortune*, March 11, 1991, 44-54.

Chapter S E V E N

The Control Process in an International Context

A multinational company derives its strength from being able to recognize and capitalize on opportunities anywhere in the world, and from its capacity to respond to global threats to its business operations in a timely fashion. On the basis of an evaluation of global opportunities and threats, and of a company's strengths and weaknesses, top management executives of a multinational at the parent company level formulate corporate strategy for the whole company. The objectives of a multinational company serve as the umbrella under which the objectives of divisions and subsidiaries are developed. There is considerable amount of give and take among the parent company, divisions, and subsidiaries before the divisional and subsidiary objectives are finally agreed upon by executives at all three levels.

The objective of managerial control is to ensure that plans are implemented correctly. In this chapter, the focus will be on the parent company's managerial control over its foreign subsidiaries. We shall examine first the salient features of the managerial control process. Then, because multinational companies experience problems controlling their far-flung operations, we shall look at those problems and their causes. The chapter next includes a review of the typical characteristics of control systems used by international companies. It concludes with some suggestions for improving the international control process.

THE MANAGERIAL CONTROL PROCESS

Managerial control is a process directed toward ensuring that operations and personnel adhere to parent company plans. A control system is essential because the future is uncertain. Assumptions about the internal and external environment that were at one time the basis of a forecast may prove invalid, strategies may not be applicable, and budgets and programs may not be effective. Managerial control is a process that evaluates performance and takes corrective action when performance differs significantly from the company's plans. With managerial control, any deviations from forecasts, objectives, or plans can be detected early and corrected with minimum difficulty.

Managerial control involves several management skills: planning, coordinating, communicating, processing and evaluating information, and influencing people.

There are four main elements in the managerial control process:[1]

1. The setting of standards.
2. The development of devices or techniques to monitor the performance of an individual or an organizational system.
3. The comparison of performance measures obtained from monitoring devices to the company's plans in order to determine if current performance is sufficiently close to what was planned.
4. The employment of effectuating or action devices that can be used to correct significant deviations in performance.

There is a close relationship between managerial control and planning. Managerial control depends on the objectives set forth in tactical plans, which in turn are derived from the strategic plans of the organization. Tactical plans are for short-term contributions of each functional area to the strategic plans, goals, and objectives.

Setting the Standards

The first step in the control process is the setting of standards. These standards are derived from the objectives defined in the planning process. Without a definition of objectives, there can be no formulation of standards.

After standards are formulated, a hierarchy of degrees of importance needs to be established. However, it would be inefficient and unrealistic to set specific standards for every organizational activity. Instead, management should continuously monitor the performance of activities in key areas, or those it considers to be essential. Whatever is not considered essential to the attainment of a company's objectives could be controlled by "exception," whereby monitoring is periodic and on a sample basis.[2] In key areas, standards need to be as concrete and as specific as possible while taking into consideration the fact that some key areas, such as management development, cannot be expressed in specific and concrete terms.[3]

Monitoring Performance

Once standards have been established, the next step is the development of techniques to monitor and accurately describe performance. Budgets, managerial audits, and financial statements are the main measuring devices used to assess the performance of organizational systems. A *budget* is a "detailed listing of the resources or money assigned to a particular project or unit."[4] Here, standards of performance are translated into dollar amounts for each item in the budget. However, the dynamic, changing character of a business environment necessitates some flexibility with budgets.

There are several methods for making budgets flexible without eventually losing managerial control, such as the adoption of supplemental budgets, alternative budgets, and variable expense budgets. *Supplemental budgets* are used with budgets that establish limits on expenditures, such as for plant expansion, capital improvements, and so on. If a capital expenditure budget proves to be too low because of inaccurate costing in the planning stage, a supplemental budget can be prepared and added to the original budget.[5]

Alternative budgeting is another form of controlled budgeting. A budget is usually prepared on the basis of an organization's assessment of the most probable future conditions. However, if there is a real possibility that, for example, future sales may be lower (or higher), *alternative budgets* are also prepared based on the implications of specific lower or bigger sales figures.

A third type of budgeting is the variable expense budget found mostly in manufacturing organizations. *Variable expense budgets* are devised to ensure proper coordination of activities as changes take place in sales of manufactured goods.

These budgets are "schedules of costs of production that tell managers what levels of critical activities actually should be established as changes occur in sales and output volume."[6]

All these budgetary techniques require accurate and timely communication. Variable expense budgets, in particular, depend on accurate and prompt reports from production and sales.

Another typical control mechanism of organizational systems is financial statements, particularly the income statement, which details the sources of revenues and expenses for a given year and comprises the profit and loss statement, balance sheets, and so on.

Comparing Performance to Plans

The third step in the managerial control process is comparing the performance measures obtained from the different monitoring devices to the company's objectives, and evaluating whether current performance is sufficiently close to the company's original plan. Management must decide how much variation between the standard and actual performance is tolerable and what "sufficiently close" means for the organization.

Changes in the external environment may affect the limits of possible performance, which in turn may necessitate a change in the performance standards. Once the limits of possible performance are altered, management must decide how the standards of measurement should be altered. Naturally, when the external environment does not deviate from the forecast, the task of managerial control is simply to evaluate whether performance is within acceptable limits.

Another aspect of the evaluation phase of the control process is related to feedback and feedforward controls. With *feedback controls*, the focus is on information about events that have already occurred, such as production and actual sales. This information is compared with a standard of performance in order to make necessary corrections for the future. For example, feedback control is typically used to monitor the productivity and performance of a factory worker against a preset production rate.

Feedforward controls are different in that the deviations from standards are anticipated or predicted before they occur. When those conditions do occur, certain actions are scheduled to take place in anticipation of the outcome of the first occurrence. For example, when sales volume reaches a predetermined level, management is automatically obliged to increase the level of inventory. This action is taken to prevent inventories from running out, a situation that would otherwise occur as the result of the first occurrence—the sales increase. "Feedback control cures problems: feedforward control prevents them." Companies use both types of controls, although feedback is more common because it is less complicated and requires less forecasting.

From the discussion above, it is apparent that accurate communication and a pervasive managerial information system are essential in management control. Management cannot appraise, compare, or correct performance without the proper reporting of appropriate and meaningful information.

Correcting the Deviations

The fourth step in the control process is correcting significant deviations from the standards. For this step, effectuating or action devices must be employed. The application of action devices requires many management skills, such as decision-making, persuading, effectively communicating, and so on. When a subsystem of an organization needs help, the corrective action might be to use different budgeting techniques, or to impose control mechanisms on costs, expenses, and so on. When the deviation concerns organizational personnel, the action devices could be either positive (promotions, salary increases, increased responsibility, and special privileges) or negative (reprimands, withdrawal of privileges, demotions, salary reductions, and termination of employment).[8]

It is essential to recognize the overriding human dimension in the managerial control process. The steps or elements in the control process are not automatic but are activated by management. Monitoring, comparing, and action devices depend on human intervention. The necessary communication is between people. The effectiveness of the control system depends on the acceptance of the system as necessary, legitimate, and appropriate by the members of the organization. This human dimension is most significant in the managerial process in a multinational company.

PROBLEMS OF CONTROL IN AN INTERNATIONAL COMPANY

Control and the problems associated with it are far more complex in a multinational company than in one that is purely domestic because the multinational operates in more than one cultural, economic, political, and legal environment. Let us examine a few of the most important international variables having a major negative impact on the flow of information between headquarters and subsidiaries. These variables, in turn, influence the effectiveness of the multinational company's control system.

Despite the sophistication and speed of contemporary communication systems, the *geographic distance* between a parent company and a foreign affiliate continues to cause communication distortion. Differences in language between the parent company and its foreign affiliates are also responsible for distortions in communication. *Language barriers* caused by language differences involve both the content and the meaning of messages. Many ideas and concepts are not easily translatable from one language to another. Because of geographic distances, there is little face-to-face communication and the messages of non-verbal communication are lost. Problems are also caused by misunderstanding the *communication habits* of people in other cultures. Managers of different cultures may interact and yet may block out important messages because the manner in which the message is presented may mean something different in the sending and receiving cultures. For example, a manager may make a wrong judgment about a subordinate's performance because he or she is unaware of culturally different communications habits. As an illustration, consider that the aborigines in Australia exhibit attention by listening intently with their faces and bodies turned away from the speaker and with no eye contact.[9] This behavior could easily be misread by a member of a different culture—one who is accustomed to associating body posture and eye contact with attention.

Cultural distance is as significant as geographic distance in creating communication distortions. Lack of understanding and acceptance of the cultural values of a group may impair a manager's ability to evaluate information accurately, to judge performance fairly, and to make valid decisions about performance. This failure could create problems in a multinational company in the area of employee performance appraisal.

In some cultures, one does not make criticism bluntly but discusses critical areas in an oblique fashion. And in the Mexican culture, responsibility is viewed as being tied to fate. It is therefore deeply offensive to a Mexican to be told that he or she is personally responsible for some failure.[10] In contrast, the American style of managerial control fixes responsibilities for achieving certain organizational goals on specific members in the organization. Other control mechanisms are also affected by cultural differences. The detailed reporting required by some "tight" managerial control systems is not acceptable to some cultures. Also, the degree of harmony valued in a culture may make the accurate reporting of problems difficult.[11]

For example, in the Japanese culture, maintaining group cohesiveness is considered to be far more important than reporting a problem to a superior who would place blame on the group or an individual within the group. It is therefore not unusual for Japanese supervisors not to report a problem to upper management in the hope that it can be resolved at the group level.

Communication distortion between the parent company and a foreign affiliate may occur because of the *differing frames of reference* of these two organizational units. The parent company may perceive each foreign affiliate as just one of many, and therefore may have a tendency to view each affiliate's problems in light of the company's entire global network of operations. However, foreign affiliate heads may view the problems of their operations as being very important to them and their affiliates. Both the parent company and the affiliate heads may try to communicate their feelings and views to each other without much success because each could be communicating from a different frame of reference.

CHARACTERISTICS OF CONTROL SYSTEMS IN INTERNATIONAL COMPANIES

Multinational companies use a variety of control systems to monitor and change the performance of their foreign subsidiaries. Some of these controls are direct controls, whereas others can be categorized as indirect.

Direct Controls

Direct controls include the use of such devices as periodic meetings, visits by home-country executives to foreign affiliates, and the staffing of foreign affiliates by home-country nationals. Controls can be exercised by holding management meetings to discuss the performance of foreign affiliates.

Some companies, such as International Telephone and Telegraph Corporation, hold monthly management meetings. ITT holds monthly meetings at its headquarters in New York, at which each ITT manager of every profit-and-loss division, however small, is in attendance. The meeting is presided over by the chief executive officer of the company, and reports submitted by each ITT unit head from around the world are discussed. Each report contains all facts concerning the performance of the unit, such as financial analyses of sales, profits, return on investment, and virtually every other measurement used in business. The report is also expected to contain a description of every existing and potential problem affecting the operation. A description of the problem, however, is not enough. The report must also explain how and why the problem arose and how the executive in charge of the unit plans to solve it. Other multinational companies also resort to meetings, similar to ITT'S, for controlling their foreign affiliates. The focus of such meetings is on direct, face-to-face communications and direct feedback.

Visits by top executives from corporate headquarters to each foreign affiliate also serve as control devices. It is not unusual for the chief executive officer and a group of top headquarters executives to spend several days sitting across the table each month from subsidiary and regional managers. Such visits are held so that problems, such as competition problems, performance problems, or others, can be dealt with face to face.

The international staffing practices of some multinational companies are also aimed at ensuring adequate control over foreign affiliates. The practice adopted by many companies of staffing the top management slot of a foreign subsidiary with a manager from the home country is for this purpose. Whether the reason is a lack of trust of foreign nationals or a belief that home-country nationals are better managers and are more knowledgeable about the company's overall philosophies, policies, and strategies than are managers of foreign nationality, putting a home-country national in charge of a foreign subsidiary is supposed to provide the subsidiary with the type and kind of management that the parent company wants. The idea is that the better a foreign subsidiary is managed, the fewer deviations from planned performance will occur, and therefore there will be fewer problems associated with controlling its operations.

The organizational structure of the company is yet another control mechanism. In an earlier chapter we examined the various types of organizational structures that multinational companies have used to coordinate and control their global operations. No two companies have the same organizational structure because companies need different types of information flows in order to control their far-flung operations. For example, the creation of regional management units in a product division structure reflects an attempt by companies to shorten the distance between headquarters and the foreign affiliates, thereby promoting better control over foreign operations.

Indirect Controls

The preceding paragraphs dealt with so-called direct controls. Companies also use *indirect controls* to control foreign subsidiaries. These include various reports, similar to those required by ITT from each foreign unit head, that each foreign subsidiary is expected to submit to top management detailing its performance during a certain period. Other forms of indirect controls include a whole range of budgetary and financial controls that are imposed through budgets, and various types of financial statements such as a balance sheet, profit-and-loss statement, cash budget, and an exhaustive set of financial ratios depicting the financial health of the subsidiary.

Three different sets of financial statements are usually required from subsidiaries to meet different needs. The first set of statements is prepared to meet the national accounting standards and procedures prescribed by law and other professional organizations in the host country. Use of national accounting standards also facilitates management's evaluation of a subsidiary's performance against its local competitors.

The second set of financial statements is prepared to comply with the accounting principles and standards required by the home country. For this compliance, accounts have to be restated and modified according to the home country's requirements. Only after these adjustments are made can financial statements of subsidiaries be deemed adequate for consolidation with those of the parent company and for comparison with the relative performance of several subsidiaries.

A subsidiary prepares a third set of statements to meet the financial consolidation requirements of the home country. For consolidation, financial statements denominated in the host country's currency need to be translated into the currency of the home country. In this way, financial statements have a common basis of valuation. International Accounting Standard No. 3, adopted in the United States, requires a foreign subsidiary's financial statements to be consolidated line by line with those of the parent company. Subsidiaries are defined as entities over which the parent company exercises control by ownership, majority equity capital, or control of the board. Although the parent company is not required to consolidate the financial statements of its foreign associates with its own accounts, under the equity method it is required to record them. This method requires the value of an investment to be increased or decreased in the parent company's books in order to recognize the parent's share of profit or loss after the acquisition. A foreign associate is defined as a company over which the parent company exercises significant influence by holding at least 20 percent of its voting power.

Any other corporate equity holdings are required to be recorded at cost in the balance sheet of a parent company. However, the dividends received from these investments are recorded in the parent company's income statement. Presently, FAS-52 requires U.S. multinationals to translate all assets and liabilities of a foreign subsidiary into dollar amounts at the current rate of exchange. Under this method, all assets and liabilities are first restated at their current price levels, then translated in the parent company's book at current exchange rates.

Most companies use returns on investment and profits as the dominant criteria for an evaluation of the performance of a foreign affiliate. A study conducted by Robins and Stobaugh of 150 companies with foreign operations showed that 95 percent of them judge their foreign subsidiaries on precisely the same basis as domestic subsidiaries; and, almost without exception, they use a form of return on investment (ROI) as their main measure of performance.[12] However, the reported profits of a foreign subsidiary and its ROI may not, and very rarely do, reflect its true performance. What follows is a discussion of why this is the case.

MEASURES OF PERFORMANCE: REPORTED PROFITS AND ROI

There are many decisions made above the subsidiary level at the parent company or regional headquarters that affect the operations of a subsidiary. Take, for example, the manipulation by the parent company or regional headquarters of the transfer prices of raw materials, components, or products in intracompany transactions. A higher-than-arm's-length price might be charged on exports made by a subsidiary located in a low income tax country to a subsidiary located in a country that has high income tax rates. Other things being equal, this maneuver would result in lower profits for the importing subsidiary, and lower taxes. The exporting subsidiary, on the other hand, would make higher profits. However, the important point is that the difference in tax rates could result in maximizing overall corporate profits.

It is alleged that the United States government is losing each year between $20 and $30 billion in unpaid taxes by foreign corporations doing business in the Unites States. It is further alleged by the U.S. Internal Revenue Service (IRS) that foreign companies are able to evade paying U.S. taxes by manipulating the prices charged for goods and services to their U.S. subsidiaries. Officials in the IRS also charge that U.S. multinationals could easily account for $5 billion in unpaid taxes as a result of transfer pricing strategies that minimize the total tax burden on the corporation.[13]

Practical Insight 7-1 gives examples of how companies like Toyota, Yamaha, and Westinghouse Electric have used transfer pricing to minimize their U.S. federal tax burden.

PRACTICAL INSIGHT 7-1

The Corporate Shell Game

How Multinational Firms Use 'Transfer Pricing' to Evade at Least $20 Billion in U.S. Taxes

Abuses in pricing across borders—"transfer pricing" in corporate jargon—are illegal, if they can be proved. Corporations dealing with their own subsidiaries are required to set prices at "arm's length," just as they would for unrelated customers. And there's no question that abuses can be enormous. In its biggest known victory, the IRS made its case that Japan's Toyota had been systematically overcharging its U.S. subsidiary for years on most of the cars, trucks, and parts sold in the United States. What would have been profits from the United States had wafted back to Japan. Toyota denied improprieties but agreed to a reported $1 billion settlement, paid in part with tax rebates from the government of Japan.

Some abuses are blatant. One foreign manufacturer, for instance, sold TV sets to its U.S. subsidiary for $250 each, but charged an unrelated company just $150. Most cases are nowhere near as clear. What if the set sold outside has a slight change in the casing? Which subsidiary gets charged for shipping and insurance? In one current case, the IRS says Japan's Yamaha forced Yamaha Motor Corp., U.S.A., to overstock motorcycles and all-terrain vehicles in the early '80s, and then made the subsidiary pay for discounts and promotions to unload the excess inventory. The result, says the tax agency, was that Yamaha Motor U.S.A. paid only $5,272 in corporate tax to Washington over four years. Proper accounting would have shown a profit of $500 million and taxes of $127 million, the agency says. But Yamaha argues that the IRS case ignores the colossal reality of the 1982 recession, which caught the company just as unprepared as its U.S. competitors. The U.S. Tax Court is mulling the case.

American based multinationals have also been accused of squirreling profits away. Tax agents find it easier to monitor their books, since they're all in this country and follow SEC standards. As Wheeler explains it, "It's the difference between examining the head and several arms of an octopus, rather than just one tentacle." Even so, he thinks the U.S. multinationals could easily account for an additional $5 billion in lost taxes on profits dubiously allocated to tax havens. Wheeler and Richard Weber say they've found one case that is suggestive: Westinghouse Electric managed to book 27 percent of its 1986 domestic profit in Puerto Rico, where its final sales are tiny.

To spur the Puerto Rican economy, Washington has set the corporate-tax rate there at zero. (Westinghouse says the accounting is proper, since its "highest-profit products are made in Puerto Rico.")

Who's Got the Profits?

By using tax havens and "trick" pricing, a corporation could slash its U. S. tax bill by transferring profits to low-tax countries. This typical transaction follows one trail.

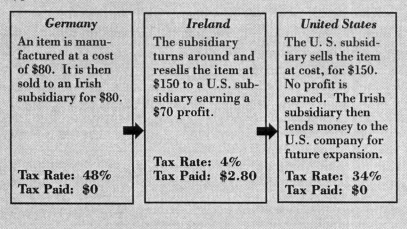

Germany	*Ireland*	*United States*
An item is manufactured at a cost of $80. It is then sold to an Irish subsidiary for $80.	The subsidiary turns around and resells the item at $150 to a U.S. subsidiary earning a $70 profit.	The U. S. subsidiary sells the item at cost, for $150. No profit is earned. The Irish subsidiary then lends money to the U.S. company for future expansion.
Tax Rate: 48% Tax Paid: $0	Tax Rate: 4% Tax Paid: $2.80	Tax Rate: 34% Tax Paid: $0

Source: Larry Martz and Rich Thomas, "The Corporate Shell Game: How Multinational Firms Use 'Transfer Pricing' to Evade at Least $20 Billion in U.S. Taxes," *Newsweek*, April 15, 1991, 48-49, ©1991, Newsweek, Inc. All rights reserved. Reprinted by permission.

Transfer prices are manipulated upward or downward depending on whether the parent company wishes to inject cash into or remove cash from a subsidiary. Prices placed by a subsidiary on imports from a related subsidiary are raised if the multinational company wishes to move funds from the receiver to the seller, but they are lowered if the objective is to keep funds in the importing subsidiary. Similarly, prices on exports from a subsidiary to a related subsidiary are raised if the multinational company wishes to move funds from the importer to the exporter.   Multinational companies have been known to use transfer pricing for moving excess cash from subsidiaries located in countries with weak currencies to countries with strong currencies in order to protect the value of their current assets.   Transfer prices are also manipulated in order to give a better credit rating to a foreign subsidiary. Showing that a subsidiary has a good record of earnings makes it easier for it to borrow money in local money markets.

These are some of the ways in which transfer prices are used advantageously by multinational companies. However, transfer prices can create serious internal management control problems because the manipulation of transfer prices forces the subsidiaries it affects to show profits that are allocated to them rather than actually earned by them. Hence, allocated profits reported by subsidiaries should not be used to measure their performance because they do not reflect the real performance of the subsidiaries being monitored.

It is possible that a foreign country could have severe inflation for months or years without any devaluation of its currency. This situation could help a subsidiary in that country to earn high profits, but they would rightly be attributable to the high inflation rate rather than good management. On the other hand, when devaluation of the local currency vis-a-vis the U.S. dollar occurs within a given accounting period, the subsidiary, although well managed and profitable in terms of the local currency, may show a loss when its income statement is translated into U.S. dollars. This situation could result in a faulty evaluation of the subsidiary's management. What further complicates this problem is that, although inflation and deflation generally tend to be approximately equal in magnitude in the long run, they are rarely exactly equal within a given period of time. More often than not, devaluations are inadequate to compensate for domestic inflation.

The profitability criterion may have to be modified for a subsidiary that is located in a country where the government lets it be known that it expects the subsidiary to make positive contributions to the nation's economy. This requirement may compel the subsidiary to engage in activities that may not contribute to its short-run profitability, such as a maximum use of expensive locally produced components (even though they may not meet quality requirements) and a no-layoff policy for the local labor force.

There are many company-wide logistical decisions that are actually made above the subsidiary level but that affect the subsidiary's profitability for better or worse. For example, executives at the parent company level might decide to serve third markets that were previously served by Subsidiary A, by exports from Subsidiary B. This turn of events would adversely affect the sales volume and consequently the profits of Subsidiary A. It would therefore be erroneous to assume that the reported profits of Subsidiary A and Subsidiary B reflect the performance of their respective managements without taking into consideration the impact on the subsidiaries' operations of the parent company's decision to shift exports to third markets from Subsidiary A to Subsidiary B.

DESIGNING AN EFFECTIVE INTERNATIONAL CONTROL SYSTEM

An effective control system cannot rely upon reported profits and ROI as the dominant measures of performance of a foreign subsidiary because the corporate headquarters of the company, rather than the subsidiary manager, makes most of the major decisions affecting the profitability of the subsidiary. To obtain a more accurate picture of a subsidiary's performance, one must be certain to eliminate extraneous factors such as results, positive or negative, caused by decisions made above the subsidiary level; or results due to environmental variables, such as unprecedented fluctuations in the price of raw materials (for example, the unexpected sharp increase in the price of petroleum in 1974); or results due to government actions over which subsidiary management could not exercise any control. Thus, a subsidiary manager should be held accountable for results that were caused by actions that he or she could initiate, without external interference, and by decisions that he or she could make unilaterally. The profit-and-loss statement or the ROI of a subsidiary should be adjusted to reflect its actual performance, taking into account the above-mentioned factors. It is quite conceivable, under such a system, for subsidiary managers to be rated quite favorably in spite of their having a poor profit-and-loss statement. The opposite is also possible; a manager who shows huge profits may still be judged a poor manager if his or her performance warrants such a judgment.

In addition to financial measures, an assessment should also use nonfinancial measures of performance, such as market share, productivity, relations with the host-country government, public image, employee morale, union relations, community involvement, and so on. Most companies do take into account some nonfinancial factors. However, it might be advisable to formalize the process, with scorecard ratings for all subsidiaries based on the same broad range of variables. Finally, the level of performance expected from a foreign subsidiary in the following year should consider the characteristics of its environment and how it is likely to change from the current year. Thus, an environment that was generally favorable one year might be expected

to change for the worse the following year, and the level of performance expected should be appropriately lowered as well. Not doing so
could lead to unhealthy pressure on the subsidiary manager, perhaps
inducing him or her to make decisions about maintenance expenditures or service to customers or the funding of process improvements
that are detrimental in the long run to both the subsidiary and the
company as a whole.

The control procedures and techniques to be used should be
understandable and acceptable to the subsidiary heads concerned, and
the subsidiary heads should actively participate in formulating them.
Each subsidiary should be given realistic objectives that take into
account its internal and external environment. The control system
should detect and report deviations from subsidiary plans as soon as,
or before, they occur. This information should then be made available
to higher management and to the subsidiary head. The control system
should not be allowed to stagnate, but should be revised and improved
as change in the subsidiary's environment require. Finally, top
management must tie compensation to results actually achieved, and
outstanding performance must be tangibly rewarded.

SUMMARY

In this chapter we looked at the managerial control process in an
international context. The focus was on the problems and characteristics of control systems adopted by multinational companies in order
to manage their foreign subsidiaries, with emphasis on ways to
improve the process.

Managerial control is the process of ensuring that actual performance is equal to planned performance. The purpose of control is to
facilitate the implementation of plans by continuously monitoring the
performance of the people responsible for carrying them out.

There are four principal elements in the control process: (1) the
establishment of standards against which performance is to be
measured, (2) the development of devices or techniques to monitor
individual or organizational performance, (3) the comparison of actual
performance with planned performance, (4) the initiation of corrective
action to eliminate significant deviations of performance from plans.

The process of control and the problems associated with it are far
more complex in a multinational company than in its purely domestic
counterpart because of the multiple cultural, economic, political, and
legal environments in which its subsidiaries operate. Several divisive
factors, such as geographic distance, language barriers, cultural

distance, and differing frames of reference between the parent company and foreign subsidiary managers are responsible for distortion in the information that is required for control purposes.

Multinational companies use several forms of monitoring devices to control their foreign subsidiaries. Among the so-called direct controls commonly used are: periodic meetings at headquarters between subsidiary and regional heads and corporate executives, visits by corporate executives to foreign affiliates, the staffing of subsidiaries with home-country nationals, and the organizational structure. Indirect controls include such devices as periodic reports from subsidiaries detailing their performance for a given period, a range of financial controls such as budgetary control and financial statements, and financial ratios that depict the financial health of an operating unit.

Most companies use profits and return-on-investment figures as the two dominant criteria to evaluate the performance of subsidiaries. However, these measures may not accurately reflect the real performance level of a subsidiary because corporate or regional managers, not the subsidiary manager, make many significant decisions that affect the subsidiary's performance. Besides, there are several forces in the subsidiary's environment that the subsidiary manager cannot control and that significantly affect, favorably or unfavorably, the subsidiary's performance. Therefore, the profit-and-loss statement or the ROI of a foreign subsidiary should be adjusted to reflect its actual performance by removing from consideration positive or negative results that were due to forces or factors beyond the control of the subsidiary manager.

Nonfinancial measures, such as market share and productivity, should be used in conjunction with the financial measures. The performance level expected from a subsidiary should change from year to year depending on the characteristics of the environment in which it will have to operate from one year to the next.

QUESTIONS

1. Why is the control process more difficult to implement in a multinational company as opposed to a purely domestic company? Discuss factors that influence the effectiveness of a multinational company's control system.
2. What are direct and indirect controls? Give examples.
3. Explain why the reported profits of a foreign affiliate may not be a good measure of its true performance.
4. What are the essential features of a sound international control system?

FURTHER READING

Clutterbuck, David. "Breaking Through the Cultural Barriers." *International Management* (December 1980).

Daniel, Shirley J., and Wolf D. Reitsperger. "Management Control Systems for J.I.T. : An Empirical Comparison of Japan and the U. S." *Journal of International Business Studies*, Vol. 22, no. 4 (Fourth Quarter, 1991): 603-617.

Denali, Jacquelyn, "Keeping Growth Under Control," *Nation's Business*, Vol. 81, no. 7 (July 1993): 31-32.

Drucker, Peter F. *An Introductory View of Management*. New York: Harper & Row, 1977.

Gannon, Martin J. *Management: An Organizational Perspective*. Boston: Little, Brown, 1977.

Geringer, Michael J. and Colette A. Frayne. "Human Resource Management and International Joint Venture Control: A Parent Company Perspective." *Management International Review*, Vol. 30 (1990): 103-120.

Phatak, Arvind V. *Managing Multinational Corporations*. New York: Praeger Publishers, 1974.

Robbins, Sydney M., and Robert B. Stobaugh. "The Bent Measuring Stick for Foreign Subsidiaries." *Harvard Business Review* (September/October, 1973).

Steiner, George. *Strategic Planning*. New York: The Free Press, 1979.

NOTES

[1] Martin J. Gannon, *Management: An Organizational Perspective* (Boston: Little, Brown, 1977), 140.

[2] Peter F. Drucker, *An Introductory View of Management* (New York: Harper & Row, 1977), 424.

[3] George A. Steiner, *Strategic Planning* (New York: The Free Press, 1979), 268.

[4] Gannon, *Management: An Organizational Perspective*, 143.

[5] Steiner, *Strategic Planning*, 220.

[6] Ibid., 221.

[7] Gannon, *Management: An Organizational Perspective*, 141.

[8] Ibid., 221.

[9] David Clutterback, "Breaking Through the Cultural Barriers," *International Management* (December 1980): 41.

[10] Ibid.

[11] Arvind V. Phatak, *Managing Multinational Corporations* (New York: Praeger Publishers, 1974), 225.

[12] Sydney M. Robbins and Robert B. Stobaugh, "The Bent Measuring Stick for Foreign Subsidiaries," *Harvard Business Review* 51, no. 5 (September-October 1973), 82.

[13] Larry Martz and Rich Thomas, "The Corporate Shell Game: How Multinational Firms Use 'Transfer Pricing' to Evade at Least $20 Billion in U. S. Taxes," *Newsweek*, April 15, 1991, 48-49.

Index